CLINICAL SOCIOLOGY REVIEW
Volume 5, 1987

Editorial Board

Acknowledgments: Every article submitted to *Clinical Sociology Review* is read by a combination of at least one member of the editorial board or an assistant or associate editor, and two other reviewers. These reviewers are chosen because of the relevance of their knowledge for evaluating the manuscript.

A number of authors have commented on both the thoughtfulness and helpfulness of the reviewers' comments. This is a real tribute to those colleagues who have served so well in this capacity. *Clinical Sociology Review* acknowledges with thanks the help of the following special reviewers:

Ruth Andes	C. Allen Haney	Marvin B. Scott
Nathan Church	William E. Hardy	Clovis R. Shepherd
Stephen Day	John Heapes	Jon Snodgrass
Estelle Disch	Fred Hoffman	Marijean Suelzle
Nancy diTomaso	Ann Johnson	Marvin Sussman
William Ewens	Marie Kargman	Alex Swan
Jonathan Freedman	Alfred McClung Lee	Barrie Thorne
Richard J. Gagan	Leonard Perlin	Adrian Tiemann
Judith Gordon	Phillip Robinette	Karen Van Beyer
		Joan L. Weston

CLINICAL
SOCIOLOGY
REVIEW
Volume 5, 1987

Clinical Sociology Review is published annually by Brunner/Mazel, Inc., in association with the Sociological Practice Association: A Professional Organization of Clinical and Applied Sociologists.

Clinical Sociology Review publishes articles, essays, and research reports concerned with the clinical uses of sociological theory, findings or methods, which demonstrate how clinical practice at the individual, small group, large organization or social system level contributes to the development of theory. Articles in the *Review* are generally expected to be relevant to intervention at some level. Articles may also be oriented toward the teaching of clinical sociology. Manuscripts will be reviewed both for merit and for relevance to the special interests of the *Review*.

Manuscript submissions should follow the American Sociological Association style guidelines, including reference citation style, and should include an abstract. There is a $10.00 processing fee which is waived for members of the Sociological Practice Association. Send four copies of the manuscript to: David J. Kallen, Editor, Clinical Sociology Review, Department of Pediatrics/ Human Development, East Lansing, MI 48824; (517) 353-0709.

Books for consideration for review in *Clinical Sociology Review* and unsolicited book reviews should be sent directly to the book review editor, Howard Rebach, 225 West College Avenue, Salisbury, MD 21801.

Subscription inquiries should be sent to the publisher, Brunner/Mazel, Inc., 19 Union Square West, New York, NY 10003. Single copies of Volume 5 are $20.00.

Membership and other inquiries about the Sociological Practice Association should be directed to: Dr. Elizabeth Clark, President, SPA, RD 2, Box 141A, Chester, NY 10918.

Library of Congress catalog card number 82-646082

ISSN: 0730-840X
ISBN:0-87630-483-8

Clinical Sociology Review
Volume 5, 1987

Contents

Editor's Preface 7

About the Authors 9

HISTORY OF CLINICAL SOCIOLOGY

The Whyte Line   *Jan Fritz*   13

Solving the Hotel's Human Problems   *William Foote Whyte*   17

The Parable of the Spindle   *Elias Porter*   33

Social Inventions for Solving Human Problems   *William Foote Whyte*   45

THEORIES AND METHODS OF CLINICAL SOCIOLOGY

The Theoretical Base of Clinical Sociology:
Root Metaphors and Key Principles   *Roger Straus*   65

Participatory Research: Methodology and Critique   *Richard Couto*   83

PRACTICE OF CLINICAL SOCIOLOGY

An Alcoholism Program for Hispanics   *Fred Hoffman*   91

Uses of Clinical Sociology in Crisis Intervention Practice
                                              Bryan D. Byers   102

Looking Closely at Quality Circles:
Implications for Intervention   *Martin L. Abbott*   119

Sociological Strategies for Developing Community Resources:
Services for Abused Wives as an Example   *Mary C. Sengstock*   132

The Sociological Practitioner as a Change Agent in a Hospital Setting:
Applications of Phenomenological Theory and Social Construction of
Reality Theory
        Clifford M. Black, Richard Enos and John A. Holman   145

Salvador Minuchin: A Sociological Analysis of
His Family Therapy Theory   *Mark Kassop*   158

The Clinical Sociologist as a Health Broker   *John G. Bruhn*   168

TEACHING OF CLINICAL SOCIOLOGY

Habermas' Sociological Theory as a Basis for
Clinical Practice with Small Groups   *Valerie Ann Malhotra*   181

BOOK REVIEWS

*Counseling in Marital and Sexual Problems: A Clinician's Handbook
(3rd ed.)*, edited by Robert F. Stahmann and William J. Hiebert
                                              Lance W. Roberts   193

Working with the Elderly: Group Process and Techniques (2nd ed.)
by Irene Burnside   *Rae B. Adams*   195

The Disabled State by Deborah A. Stone   *S. Randi Randolph*   197

Group Workers at Work: Theory and Practice in the 80's,
edited by Paul H. Glasser and Nazneen S. Mayadas   *Howard Rebach*   201

*Child Maltreatment and Paternal Deprivation:
A Manifesto for Research, Prevention and Treatment*
by Henry B. Biller and Richard S. Solomon   *Katherine Williams*   204

Editor's Preface

Volume 5 of *Clinical Sociology Review* continues the tradition of organizing contributions into five general areas: History of Clinical Sociology, Theories of Clinical Sociology, Practice of Clinical Sociology, Teaching of Clinical Sociology, and Book Reviews. As in years past, the division among these areas is somewhat arbitrary since there is overlap among the focus of the articles. Volume 5 has a higher proportion of contributions on practice, and less on teaching than in previous volumes. The reasons for this are not clear, but the distribution of articles published does reflect the distribution of articles received.

The publication of Volume 5 is an appropriate time to express appreciation to both authors and reviewers. Without the insightful comments of the reviewers the quality of the *Review* would not be assured. These colleagues have given generously of time and effort to evaluate contributions to the *Review*, and to suggest to authors ways in which the articles might be modified so that they would communicate important ideas and experiences to the readers of the *Review*. At the same time, contributed manuscripts are the lifeblood of any journal. Authors have maintained good humor in the face of sometimes extended delays in the review process, and have responded thoughtfully to the suggestions of the reviewers.

History of Clinical Sociology. In this section, **Fritz** introduces the work of **William Foote Whyte,** one of the pioneers in sociological intervention. The summary of his intervention interests is based in part on interviews with him, and in part on a review of his work. Two examples of Whyte's work are presented: his 1947 article on solving human problems in the hotel industry, and his 1981 presidential address to the American Sociological Association on using social inventions to solve human problems. An article by **Elias H. Porter** shows the value of Whyte's social system approach to solving human problems.

Theories and Methods of Clinical Sociology. This section contains two contributions which extend our understanding of sociologically based intervention. First, **Straus** extends clinical theory, showing how differing views of how the world functions affect our understanding of the mechanisms of change. **Couto** points out the differences between academic and participatory research, and how the latter can play an important role in bringing about change.

The Practice of Clinical Sociology. Clinical sociology is useful both in general intervention and in the design of programs for specific groups. **Hoffman** describes the development of an alcoholism treatment program for a specific group, Cuban refugees, whose cultural background requires modification in the traditionally Anglo-oriented treatment program. **Byers** shows how a knowledge of social theory is helpful in crisis intervention, ranging from the interpretation that the event is a crisis to the development of appropriate intervention strategies. **Abbott** discusses the ways in which a study of quality circles could be used to develop interventions that would increase the effectiveness of the circles in reaching their goals. **Sengstock** shows how sociological knowledge and methods can be used in development of a community program to help abused women. Continuing in the theme of the uses of theory in intervention, **Black, Enos and Holman** show how intervention based on phenomenological theory and the social construction of reality brought important change in a hospital, and **Bruhn** discusses how the clinical sociologist can serve as a broker in health affairs. Moving from large organizations to the family, **Kassop** shows the sociological base of the theories of the family therapist, Salvador Minuchin.

The Teaching of Clinical Sociology. Jurgen Habermas' theories of communication and interaction were used by **Malhotra** to analyze the interactions of women in a small group interaction oriented course on the psychology of women. Part of the emphasis of this course was to bring about change; the course appears to have succeeded in this.

Book Reviews. Robert's review of Stahmann and Hiebert's third edition of *Counseling in Marital and Sexual Problems: A Clinician's Handbook* indicates that despite unevenness and an underrepresentation of clinical sociological approaches, it should be useful to the practitioner. **Adams** finds the comprehensiveness of Burnside's *Working with the Elderly: Group Process and Techniques* appropriate. Stone's *The Disabled State* is primarily oriented toward political scientists, according to **Randolph,** but its perspectives are important to clinical sociologists. **Rebach** finds that the symposium, *Group Workers at Work: Theory and Practice in the 80's,* edited by Glasser and Mayadas, has some utility for clinical sociologists interested in working with small groups. **Williams** finds Biller and Solomon's *Child Maltreatment and Paternal Deprivation: A Manifesto for Research, Prevention and Treatment* disappointing in its definition of almost all consequences of father absence as maltreatment.

About the Authors

Martin L. Abbott, "Looking Closely at Quality Circles: Implications for Intervention," is Associate Professor of Sociology at Seattle Pacific University. Past director of the Criminal Justice Program at Pepperdine University, Dr. Abbott has current research interests in worker participation programs in business and industry.

Clifford M. Black, "The Sociological Practitioner as a Change Agent in a Hospital Setting," is the Associate Dean in the School of Community Service at North Texas State University in Denton, Texas. He is a Licensed Professional Counselor (LPC) in the State of Texas, and a Certified Clinical Sociologist (CCS). He was instrumental in developing the first State Affiliate of the Clinical Sociology Association and establishing the first Ph.D. program with opportunities for training and experience in Sociological Practice and Clinical Sociology.

John G. Bruhn, "The Clinical Sociologist as a Health Broker," is Dean of The School of Allied Health Sciences, Special Assistant to the President for Community Affairs, Professor of Preventive Medicine and Community Health, The University of Texas Medical Branch at Galveston, and Professor of Preventive Medicine and Community Health, The University of Texas School of Public Health in Houston.

Bryan D. Byers, "Uses of Clinical Sociology in Crisis Intervention Practice," is an investigator for Adult Protective Services in South Bend, Indiana. His professional activities have focused on training and practice in crisis intervention, suicidology, and thanatology. He is also a deputy coroner. He has published in *Brain and Cognition, Emotional First Aid: A Journal of Crisis Intervention, International Journal of World Peace,* and *Professional Psychology.*

Richard A. Couto, "Participating Research: Methodology and Critique," is the director of the Center for Health Services at Vanderbilt University, which conducts a series of programs to assist community leaders and residents in low income areas of the rural South. His previous publications and media projects deal with a range of issues related to poverty, regional development, and community organizing. His most recent book, *Streams of Idealism and Health Care Innovations,* is a study of student service-learning and community mobilization. He is a member of the Division of Medical Administration and the Peabody College, Department of Human Resources. He attained his Ph.D. in political science at the University of Kentucky.

Richard Enos, ''The Sociological Practitioner as a Change Agent in a Hospital Setting,'' is the chairperson of the Social Work Department at North Texas State University and a Certified Clinical Social Worker (CCSW), who has had experience in both clinical social work practice and administration. He has published extensively in both social work and sociology journals.

Jan M. Fritz, ''The History of Clinical Sociology: The Whyte Line,'' is a Science Associate at the National Cancer Institute. She is a past president of the Clinical Sociology Association (now the Sociological Practice Association) and chair-elect of the American Sociological Association Section on Sociological Practice. She is the author of *The Clinical Sociology Handbook* and co-author of *The Clinical Sociology Resource Book.*

Fred Hoffman, ''An Alcoholism Program for Hispanics,'' is an acculturation specialist with the Scientific Analysis Corporation, and with a resettlement program for mentally ill refugees in Los Angeles. He teaches sociology at Cerritos College and works as a culture broker for American Indians, undocumented immigrants, and refugees.

John E. Holman, ''The Sociological Practitioner as a Change Agent in a Hospital Setting,'' is the director of the Criminal Justice Institute at North Texas State University, and is a Certified Clinical Sociologist (CCS). He administers an Inmate Rehabilitation Program at the Denton County Jail in Denton, Texas. In addition, he is actively involved in alternative sentencing programs and research in the state. He has experience working with NIMH and the Public Health Service.

Mark Kassop, ''Salvador Minuchin: A Sociological Analysis of His Family Therapy Theory,'' is Associate Professor of Sociology at Bergen Community College in Paramus, New Jersey. He is currently a Family Therapy Extern at Bergen Pines County Hospital in New Jersey. His research activities are aimed at developing a bridge between sociological theory and psychotherapy theory and practice in respect to marriage and family issues.

Valerie Ann Malhotra, ''Habermas' Sociological Theory as a Basis for Clinical Practice with Small Groups,'' is Associate Professor in the Department of Sociology and Social Work at Texas Woman's University, Denton, Texas, where she has developed sociological practice courses in the graduate program in sociology. She is also in private practice in individual and family therapy in Denton. She is a Certified Clinical Sociologist. Her academic interests include the theory/research/practice nexus and sociological theory.

Mary C. Sengstock, "Sociological Strategies for Developing Community Resources: Services for Abused Wives as an Example," is Professor and Chair of the Department of Sociology at Wayne State University in Detroit, Michigan, and a Certified Clinical Sociologist. Her clinical experience has been primarily in the area of the identification and organization of service needs, such as those described in this article. She has also written extensively in the area of elder abuse, and has done research on spouse abuse, and on the Iraqi-Chaldean community of Metropolitan Detroit.

Roger A. Straus, "The Theoretical Base of Clinical Sociology: Root Metaphors and Key Principles," edited the first *Clinical Sociology Newsletter* in 1978 and subsequently helped found the Clinical Sociology Association (now the Sociological Practice Association). Since then, he has published over a dozen papers in clinical sociology, new religious movements, adult socialization and social psychological theory, written a "trade" book, *Strategic Self-Hypnosis* and edited the S.P.A.-sponsored textbook, *Using Sociology: An Introduction from the Clinical Perspective*. After teaching for several years at Alfred University, in 1986 he accepted a position in market research as a Study Director with National Analysts Division of Booz, Allen and Hamilton in Philadelphia.

History of Clinical Sociology

The Whyte Line

Jan M. Fritz
National Cancer Institute

William Foote Whyte, Professor Emeritus with the School of Industrial and Labor Relations at Cornell University, has been President of the American Sociological Association, the Society for Applied Anthropology, and the Industrial Relations Research Association. He currently is Research Director for Cornell University's Programs for Employment and Workplace Systems, an organization that undertakes participatory action research for labor-management groups in order to save jobs, cut costs, and help companies become competitive.

Whyte began his sociological and anthropological fieldwork long before he knew what those terms meant. As a high school student he wrote a weekly column about school activities for the community paper, the *Bronxville Press*. "The Whyte Line," as the column was called, gave the results of his first field interviews conducted in the local elementary schools.

Whyte has continued his work as a participant observer for 50 years and is well known for his studies of street corner society in Boston, oil companies in Oklahoma and Venezuela, restaurants and steel and plastics fabrication plants in Chicago, the Mondragon worker cooperative in Spain, factories in New York, and villages in Peru.

The three articles reprinted here—"Solving the Hotel's Human Problems," "The Parable of the Spindle," and "Social Inventions for Solving Human Problems"—allow us to focus on the clinical aspects of Whyte's work. After graduating from the University of Chicago in 1942, Whyte returned to Chicago to work with the Committee on Human Relations in Industry in 1944. Through the Committee, he began his work with the Hotel Radisson in Minneapolis, and in 1947 he published "Solving the Hotel's Human Problems" in *The Hotel Monthly*.

Correspondence to Jan M. Fritz, NIH National Cancer Institute, Blair Building, Room 4A01, Bethesda, MD 20205.

The article is an excellent introduction to Whyte's earliest clinical work. Whyte served as a consultant both to the staff members involved in human relations research at the hotel and to hotel executives to help them with change initiatives. The editor of *The Hotel Monthly* (1947:37) indicated at the time Whyte's article appeared that labor turnover at the Hotel Radisson was now down as low as 7% a month. He continued:

> It is reasonable to assume that the policies and practices instituted through the human relations activities headed by Professor Whyte is largely responsible for reducing labor turnover by 66% and is an impressive demonstration of the value of the work that was done at the Radisson.

This action research project in a large hotel was a direct outgrowth of the restaurant studies Whyte had recently completed. Those studies were done in the mid-1940s under the sponsorship of the National Restaurant Association and were discussed in *Human Relations in the Restaurant Industry* as well as in what Whyte (1984:258) has described as "one of the best articles I've ever written," "The Social Structure of the Restaurant."

The second article in this section, "The Parable of the Spindle,"[1] was not written by Whyte and, in fact, only mentions him in the author's note at the bottom of the first page. The writer, Elias Porter, a psychologist, wrote the piece for the *Harvard Business Review* in 1962. Porter (1987) used the parable to show the value of a social systems approach. He specifically developed the story to use with potential employees of the System Development Corporation who would be dealing with classified materials in air defense. He wanted a concrete example which would discuss the systems approach he used but would not deal in any way with defense matters.

Porter had heard of Whyte's work in the restaurant industry through a colleague and then talked with Whyte about the spindle when he came to speak at the System Development Corporation. Porter thought Whyte had invented the spindle, the spike on which food service personnel place order slips for the kitchen. This simple device helps eliminate arguments in restaurants about which order was placed first and eliminates some possible friction between cooks and servers who have status differences within a restaurant. The spindle already was in use in some restaurants when Whyte conducted his restaurant research in 1944 and 1945. Whyte did not invent the spindle, but it was his associate, Edith Lentz Hamilton, who pointed out the utility of the spindle in the restaurants that were studied. Whyte (1984:258) credits her with this discovery in his *Learning from the Field*,[2] a book which is largely autobiographical and provides a great deal of background information about Whyte's field research projects.

The last article included in this series, "Social Inventions for Solving Human Problems," is Whyte's 1981 presidential address to the American Sociological Association. Whyte (1982:1) said that this was "a time for rethinking sociology" and that we need to do a better job of showing the practical relevance of the field. Whyte thinks this can be done, in part, by giving special attention to the "discovery, description and analysis of social inventions for solving human problems."

Whyte was a consultant on research issues during the 1950s in Venezuela and then in the 1960s for Prudential Insurance Company. For six years, until 1984, he worked with an interdisciplinary group of professors at Cornell to extend the benefits of science and technology to limited resource farmers in developing countries and to design a new model for research and development in agricultural settings.

In the 1980s Whyte again moved beyond the roles of field researcher and research consultant. In 1982 he was one of the founders of Programs for Employment and Workplace Systems. As in 1947, he was a researcher as well as a consultant on change initiatives. Now, though, he was a participant-consultant on workplace democracy issues for Rath Packing Company and Hyatt Clark Industries. Whyte's recent work involves both participatory intervention and innovation.

When Whyte (1984:19-20) was a research fellow at Harvard from 1936–1940, he says he "was conditioned to believe that if research was to be truly scientific, researchers' values must be set aside." Throughout his career he gradually began to abandon the idea that there must be a strict separation between scientific research and action projects. He "began exploring how research can be integrated with action in ways that will advance science and enhance human progress at the same time."

A study of the development of William Foote Whyte's professional career demonstrates his early and recent activity in what has come to be known as clinical sociology. "The Whyte Line," shows how science and action can be combined to improve the human condition.

NOTES

1. I am indebted to John Glass for first calling this article to my attention.
2. I am indebted to Ray Kirshak for reminding me of the wealth of information in this book which would be useful in this project.

REFERENCES

Porter, Elias H.
    1962   "The parable of the spindle." Harvard Business Review 10, no. 3:58-66.
    1987   Interview. February 11.
The Hotel Monthly
    1947   "About the author." June:37.
Whyte, William Foote
    1947   "Solving the hotel's human problems." Hotel Monthly.
    1948   Human Relations in the Restaurant Industry. New York: McGraw-Hill.
    1949   "The social structure of the restaurant." American Journal of Sociology
                54(January):302-310.
    1977   "Potatoes, peasants and professors: A development strategy for Peru." Sociological
                Practice 2, no. 1:7-23.
    1981   Street Corner Society. Chicago: University of Chicago Press. Originally published
                1943.
    1982   "Social inventions for solving human problems." American Sociological Review
                47, no. 1:1-13.
    1984   Learning from the Field: A Guide from Experience. Beverly Hills, CA: Sage.
    1987   Interviews. February 2, 11 and 17.

Solving the Hotel's Human Problems

William Whyte
University of Chicago

The People Make the Organization

"Unless you can build up good, stable, and cooperative relations among them, you don't have an organization which will continue to function and make a profit."

That point of view is steadily gaining ground in American management. Forward looking executives are now casting about to develop better ways of handling the human problems of their organizations. This effort has led to a great expansion in personnel departments.

In general, the hotel industry has lagged behind other industries in the development of personnel work, and many hotels are now seeking to move ahead in this area. This is a healthy sign, but I suggest that the hotel industry would be making a grave mistake if it simply tried to catch up with what other people are doing.

There is valuable work being done in some of industry's personnel departments. There is also much time, effort, and money being expended in activities which are either useless or of very limited value because they fail to grapple with basic problems. Therefore the hotel which is now launching its own personnel program should not seek to imitate established practices but should rather try to develop a program tailor-made to its own needs.

No Magic Formulas in Personnel Work

What does the executive or department head need to know in order to manage his organization effectively? There are many answers to this question, but I suggest that if he can answer the following two questions, he can then get all the other answers he needs to have. Here are the questions:

Reprinted from The Hotel Monthly, June 1947, pp. 36–41,66.

1. How can I get accurate information on the functioning of my organization?
2. How can I act on such information so as to improve the functioning of my organization?

    The efficient hotel management today keeps elaborate records of the financial aspects of its business, and these serve as one sort of measure of the functioning of the organization, but behind the figures stand the people—workers, supervisors, and department heads. If their relations with each other are not organized effectively, costs go up. If there is friction among workers, between workers and supervisors, or between departments, it is impossible to give cheerful, thoughtful, and efficient service, and sooner or later the loss of guests will show up in the balance sheet.

    We have found in our research that a company may have good systems for employee selection and training, for merit rating and job evaluation; it may pay good wages and provide insurance and other benefits, and still it will suffer from low employee morale, from absenteeism and labor turnover, from internal friction and low efficiency—unless the human relations of workers, supervisors, and department heads are organized with skill and understanding. On the other hand, as an effective organization is built up, it becomes easy to develop whatever personnel systems are helpful in improving efficiency and job satisfaction.

    The moral is: there are no magic formulas in personnel work that produce a good organization. The first principle for effective action is:

Know your organization.

Hotel Radisson Scene of Experiment in Better Personnel Relations

It is one of the aims of the Committee on Human Relations in Industry to provide executives with the information they need for effective action. However, we feel that in the long run the business should not have to rely upon a university for such a vital function. It should be possible to develop the function within the organization itself. To learn how this might be done, it was necessary for us to experiment.

    I am happy to say that the first opportunity for such an experiment was offered us by the hotel industry by the Hotel Radisson in Minneapolis, owned by Thomas J. Moore and Byron E. Calhoun, the latter until recently in active charge of the Radisson. Mr. Calhoun was seriously concerned over labor turnover and other human relations problems. In his two years as vice-president and general manager, he had not been able to find a personnel manager who was effective in this field. We agreed to provide him with a man trained in our human relations research on condition that he set up the project on an experimental basis, making provision for research within the personnel department.

    In mid-July of 1945, the project got under way with the following personnel:

Meridith Wiley, who had a year's training in our field research and an M.A. degree in Business Administration, became personnel manager of the hotel.

Edith Lentz, who had a year of research on the human problems of the restaurant industry, went in as a research assistant. While the whole project was financed by the hotel, Miss Lentz was on the payroll of the university being directly responsible to the Committee on Human Relations in Industry. She worked closely with Mr. Wiley throughout the project, spending full time in the hotel. She had no administrative responsibilities so her time was entirely devoted to research.

So that we would have a full record of the experiment, we arranged to have the work supervised by the Committee on Human Relations in Industry. Copies of all interviews and other data typed out by Miss Lentz or Mr. Wiley came in to the university, and it was my job, representing the Committee, to keep fully informed on developments at the Radisson and help Mr. Wiley and Miss Lentz to interpret the research findings. I spent something more than one day each month at the Radisson for this purpose and to discuss strategies of action with Mr. Wiley and Miss Lentz. I also conferred regularly with Mr. Calhoun and other hotel executives to interpret to them the development of the personnel program and get their ideas upon problems that needed attention.

Cleared with Unions First

On our first day at the Radisson, we sat down with officials of unions having contracts with the hotel and explained our intentions to them at some length. They pledged their cooperation, and there has never been any difficulty in our relationships from the first day on.

We were also formally introduced to department heads and supervisors of the hotel in a first day meeting. Here our reception was, if not hostile, at least reserved. People wondered what changes we were to bring about and quite sensibly withheld judgment until they should have a chance to see how the new program would affect them.

The first three months served as an adjustment period. Mr. Wiley's first job was to fit himself into the organization. While he tried to become familiar with people and problems, he consciously avoided bringing in any changes. While some people concluded from this slowness that nothing at all was going to happen, the period did serve to allay anxieties and build relationships between personnel manager and executives which were essential to all future actions.

Miss Lentz began her research at once. She was free to move about the organization and interview workers, supervisors, and department heads upon the human problems they faced. In her approach, she avoided interruptions, argumentation, and moral judgments and made every effort to draw full expression of problems not limited to the answering of specific questions. The problem was to get people to talk out their thoughts and feelings about their work situation.

Miss Lentz also fitted herself in through helping out with the work of certain departments at rush times. Since she had served as a waitress for three months in our restaurant study, it was easy for her to take on this role.

Before the end of the first three months, we had, through the observations of Mr. Wiley, and through Miss Lentz' research, a general picture of the human problems of the hotel, with detailed information on two departments. It was time to begin to act.

The Problems of the Organization

The actions of Mr. Wiley must be seen against the background of the problems that became evident in the first three months. This is the picture as we saw it.

1. Interdependence of Departments—Pressure of Customers.   The hotel was functioning at capacity, with a tremendous demand for rooms and for food and drinks. Even so the customer demand was highly variable, running from the occasional slack day to the peak of activity of large banquets and the sustained pressures of market weeks. Within a single day, especially in the food departments, the tempo of activity was highly cyclical so that neither workers nor supervisors had the emotional security of a steady routine.

All organizations are made up of parts which are interdependent at least in the sense that one part cannot cease functioning without affecting other parts, but the interdependence of departments in a large hotel is much greater than this minimum. There the activities of many of the departments must be synchronized from hour to hour, from minute to minute, and, in some cases, even from second to second. To serve customers well in the dining rooms requires skillful timing of activities of employees in kitchen and dining rooms. To move guests in and out of rooms efficiently requires close cooperation between front office and housekeeping department and between housekeeping and laundry departments.

At some points, departments mesh so closely together that it is difficult to tell where one leaves off and the other begins. This gives rise to confusions in authority and responsibility. When this is added to the pressures of customers reacting through the highly interdependent parts of the organization, the human relations problems become acute.

2. Autocratic Supervision!   To meet the demands for quick action, the hotel tends to develop an autocratic structure in which orders are communicated rapidly from the top down but there is little effective communication from the bottom up.

3. Unclarified Personnel Policies.   The hotel had been under its present management for only two years, and that period had been one of great expansion of personnel and organizational change in order to meet the war boom volume of business. In such a situation, it was inevitable that there should be some confusion and uncertainty remaining on certain items of personnel policy.

4. Union Management Friction. While the hotel had signed union shop contracts, and the top executives wished to get along with the unions, no adequate grievance procedure had been developed. Cases were taken up outside of the hotel with a representative of the hotel association. Since he represented a large number of hotels, this often meant serious delays in handling grievances. And it meant also that he did not have an intimate knowledge of the internal problems of the Radisson.

Research and Action

We got into action first upon problems of communication in the organization. The discussion was opened in a meeting of department heads, which I was asked to address. Bringing in research materials from outside of the hotel, I pointed out the human relations difficulties which arose in organizations where communication was channeled predominantly in one direction, from the top down. I emphasized the importance of the interviewing approach and the holding of group meetings to build up two-way communication.

Department heads participated in the discussion with apparent interest, but the general reaction seemed to be that these were nice theories which would never be worked out at the Radisson in practice. At this point, Mr. Calhoun came into the discussion and gave his emphatic endorsement to our point of view. As he made it clear in this and in subsequent meetings that it was the policy of management to ease downward pressures and build upward communication, he made possible the important changes which were to follow.

Trouble Spots Uncovered in Coffee Shop

At about this time (three months from the beginning of the project), Miss Lentz had completed her study of the coffee shop, and Mr. Wiley was prepared to act on this. The study showed that waitresses and first line supervisors were working under heavy pressures from above and felt that they did not have sufficient opportunities to bring their problems to the attention of higher authorities. In addition to the pressures of customers, the waitresses were troubled by friction with kitchen personnel and food checkers. There were also several problems of physical conditions, the chief one involving the water spigot. At this time the waitresses had to walk the entire length of the large kitchen to fill their water pitchers. This added appreciably to their work load, but, more important than that, it seemed to symbolize management's lack of concern for the employees, as they had complained about the condition without getting any action.

For some months previous to the beginning of the study, this had been a major trouble spot in the organization. Turnover figures had been the highest of any department in the house, averaging close to 50% a month, which meant, of course, that no stable work group was being built up.

The easing of pressures from above, which followed the discussions described earlier, was particularly noticed in this department. The waitresses were soon heard to comment upon the relaxing of emotional tensions. Miss Belliveau, the department head, also reacted favorably to this change and was able to handle her supervision with the quiet confidence so important for stabilizing the department.

After conferring with Mr. Wiley, Miss Belliveau began holding meetings of all members of her department to discuss dining room service problems. The waitresses spoke freely in these discussions and afterwards spoke enthusiastically about the meetings.

The meeting approach was also used to handle problems of dining room kitchen relations. Miss Belliveau suggested to Mr. Wiley that it might be a good idea to ask chef Bernatsky (now food and beverage manager) to sit in on one of the discussions. Mr. Wiley agreed and went to the chef to explain the developments and issue the invitation.

Thanks to skillful handling by Mr. Bernatsky and Miss Belliveau, the meeting brought about a remarkable change in the kitchen-dining room relations. The waitresses began by expressing their complaints against kitchen employees and the organization of work in the kitchen. Mr. Bernatsky encouraged them to speak freely, and it was evident that they were getting many long-standing complaints off their chests. Mr. Bernatsky was able to meet some of the complaints by promising to make specific changes in the kitchen. Where he was not able to make changes, he explained his problems thoroughly to the waitresses, and they seemed satisfied to let these complaints drop. When all the waitress complaints had found expression, the direction of the meeting underwent a striking change, and the waitresses began asking Mr. Bernatsky for his advice on how they should handle certain problems they faced in getting service from the kitchen. Under these circumstances, Mr. Bernatsky was able to get across advice and direction which would never have been acted upon had he presented them in lecture form.

Removing the Trouble Spots

The meeting led to action by the chef on a number of counts. The waitresses complained that Sunday morning was the worst time for kitchen-dining room relations, and Mr. Bernatsky agreed to give particular attention to this problem. They suggested a more convenient arrangement of fruit juices so that they could be served without delay. This was worked out. They complained particularly against one cook whose station seemed to be a major friction point. This man was transferred to another station, so that he would not be in direct contact with the waitresses.

Other examples of action growing out of the meeting could be cited, but the list itself is not the important thing. As Mr. Bernatsky himself pointed out to us, once before he had tried to improve the arrangement of work for waitresses by changing the position of cups and saucers at one station. The waitresses had greeted the change with indignant protests. On the other hand, the changes growing out of the meeting were greeted with enthusiasm. As one waitress said,

> Honest, it's like a miracle. That kitchen's a different place. It's almost a pleasure to go out there, no fooling!

The moral here is simple. When changes are made without the consultation of people affected by them, the people generally oppose the changes. Only when changes grow out of such consultation do they make a contribution to employee morale as well as to efficiency.

The spigot problem was taken to Mr. Calhoun by Mr. Wiley. We found that the same plea had come up a year earlier and had been turned down on the grounds that a completely new set of dining rooms and kitchen were to be built as soon as materials and labor were available. But in the course of that year the volume of restaurant business had doubled and it was still impossible to say when the new construction could begin. Under these circumstances, minor physical adjustments were certainly in order, Mr. Calhoun felt, and he ordered the change made. Placing the spigot inside the dining room meant a great saving of work for the waitresses, but, more important than that, it served to demonstrate to the girls that they could make their needs felt and that management was genuinely concerned with their problems.

In Four Months Labor Turnover Dropped to 7.7%

By the end of the year, the departmental labor turnover which had been running between 35% and 50% a month up to July had dropped steadily and was down to 8.0% in November and 7.7% in December. There had been no similar trend in figures for the whole hotel where the figures ran steadily close to 20% a month. From having the highest turnover record, the department dropped to where it had become one of the most stable in the organization.

To add to these statistics, we can cite the judgment of Mr. Calhoun, Mr. Bernatsky, and Miss Belliveau that the work was running much more smoothly. And Mr. Calhoun emphasized that this meant the dining room was meeting a much higher standard of service to the customers than had been the case some months before. He added the impression that the whole "atmosphere" of the dining room had changed for the better.

Housekeeping Department Tackled Next

The next efforts were made in the housekeeping department where Mr. Wiley worked closely with Mr. Hale, the department executive, and Mrs. Grogan, the assistant department head. Here, as in the following case, I will not attempt to describe all developments but will limit myself to points which illustrate new possibilities in this approach to personnel work.

The group meetings which had proven so successful in the dining room were instituted here also, under the leadership of Mr. Hale and Mrs. Grogan. Miss Lentz was invited to sit in on all meetings and keep a detailed record of their progress. She had already done considerable interviewing in the department, so she was by that time well known to the employees. Following the third weekly meeting, she made a quick canvass of employee sentiment, asking more than 25 of the maids (more than half of the total in the department) how they felt about the meetings. In general, she found that the maids welcomed the meetings and felt they were exceedingly helpful, but a few of the women expressed certain criticisms and reservations. Some mentioned points in the conduct of the meetings which made them uneasy and hesitant about expressing their thoughts and feelings.

Miss Lentz turned over these data to Mr. Wiley and discussed them with him. Mr. Wiley then laid out before Mr. Hale and Mrs. Grogan both the favorable and unfavorable reactions. On the basis of this discussion, Mr. Hale and Mrs. Grogan agreed as to how the future meetings should be conducted so as to improve their effectiveness. Miss Lentz's subsequent observations showed that they were following through on the revised plan of procedure with skill and understanding. And when she later checked employee sentiment again, she found that the former criticisms were no longer being expressed.

In this case, the personnel department provided not only advice and consultation but also a testing of results so that the department heads were able to increase their effectiveness on the basis of analyzed experience.

Food Checkers Have Problems, Too

Miss Lentz next took up a study of the problems of the food checkers, who are stationed in the kitchen to total the checks of waiters and waitresses and to see that the food is served according to specifications. She found here serious problems in supervision and interdepartmental relations, which were worked on by Mr. Wiley. Since these problems did not involve any new applications of our personnel approach, they will not be discussed here.

In her work with the checkers, Miss Lentz developed an interesting combination of efficiency engineering with human relations research. She found that the women complained that the work load was too heavy, that too many things had to be done at the same time. Specifically, they had difficulty in handling the room service phone at the same time as they were checking the trays of waiters and waitresses serving three different dining rooms through the single food checking stand.

On the basis of her observations and interviews, Miss Lentz made up a work flow chart which clearly illustrated the existing difficulties. Mr. Wiley set this before the executives of the restaurant section and also presented Miss Lentz's other data. After a lengthy discussion, they worked out two major changes.

Redistribute the Work Load

The room service phone was taken away from the checker stand, thus relieving the checkers of considerable work pressure. The work flow was then rechanneled. To serve two of the dining rooms, waiters and waitresses walked in the same direction. No change was made here. But waitresses serving the third dining room had to cut across the traffic. That dining room had its own checker's stand which, up to that point, had been used only to check beverages. Food checking was combined with beverage checking at this stand so that the food checking facilities were doubled. This redistribution of the work load was accomplished with the addition of just one employee.

The checkers reacted to the changes enthusiastically. One of them expressed the common view in this way:

> Honestly you have no idea how different it is. It's just a new job altogether, that's all. It isn't only that the work is cut almost in half, either, but the confusion is so much less.
>
> You see, when all the dining rooms were busy at once, before this new stand opened, half the waitresses would go in one direction when they left the stand, and the others would want to go the other way. They were forever getting into each other's way, and we were always afraid of trays upsetting or food splashing over the dishes. Not only that, but we didn't have time to be polite to people.
>
> The room service phone would ring all the time, and we were just too busy to be courteous. I admit it, I know myself. I just *had* to be short with people. We tried to cut out every unnecessary work to save time. Now—oh, I feel swell today. It is like heaven, really it is.

The waitresses and waiters noted the difference and were particularly appreciative of the new checker stand. As one of them said,

> Say, that new checker's stand is swell, isn't it? That certainly made a big difference in our service. Gee, we used to have to stand around and all the food would get cold while we waited. Then the customers would gripe. It wasn't our fault, it was just that we had to wait out at that checker's desk. I'm sure glad this new desk is in operation.

In the course of the year, Miss Lentz also did research in the front office, the laundry, the service department (bellmen), and one of the other dining rooms, and, of course, her contacts through the organization brought in scattered data on departments not specifically studied. Since my emphasis here is on outlining a new role for the personnel man, it is not necessary to go into details on this research.

Develop Way to Get Quick Action on Grievances

In the course of developing his work with management, Mr. Wiley worked out a new relationship between management and the unions. This was not done according to a prearranged plan. We would have preferred to have line supervisors and executives act for management on grievances, but at the time our work began grievances were not being handled inside the hotel at all. Recognizing the well-established principles that grievances should be handled quickly and in well-defined organizational terms, Mr. Wiley became increasingly active in this field. Union stewards and business agents would come to him with grievances. He would then go to the appropriate department head to discuss ways of handling the problem. As Mr. Wiley had more experience in handling grievances than the department heads, this naturally resulted sometimes in the personnel manager steering the executive toward the solution which he felt was required by the union contract and by good industrial relations practices.

In many cases there was ready agreement on the disposition of the grievance. In some cases, the department heads accepted Mr. Wiley's opinion with reluctance. They were, of course, free to stand on their own opinion and appeal to Mr. Calhoun for support, but in all cases so far grievances have been settled without appeal to the top.

According to all our evidence, the personnel manager's handling of grievances has not given rise to any serious problems in his relations with supervisors and executives. On the other hand, we find the union leaders very pleased with the new arrangement. They can get quick action on grievances, and they are now dealing with a coherent management policy in this area, so they know much better what to expect. Nor does this mean that all of the cases are settled in favor of the unions. On a number of occasions Mr. Wiley has told them that, on the basis of his investigations, he feels the grievance is not justified. So far they have accepted his judgment in these cases. They seem to be convinced that he will bring in a favorable decision for the union, when the facts warrant it, and therefore they are willing to trust his honesty and his judgment when the decision goes the other way.

We do not look upon this present arrangement as the ideal way of handling grievances. However, in working out human relations problems, we always have to start from where we are and measure progress from that point. The present system is clearly a great improvement over the former situation in which grievances were not handled within the hotel at all. In this field, as in others, it is Mr. Wiley's aim to build up a situation in which department heads make the decisions upon problems arising in their own departments. In the future it is likely that the department heads will play an increasingly active part in the settlement of grievances.

Defining the Personnel Man's Role

As we worked on the problems of the Radisson, we clarified our ideas on the personnel man's new role. We present here what seem to us the principles of effective action that can be applied in developing this work in other organizations.

1. Keep People's Confidences.   In the course of time, if they do their jobs skillfully, the personnel man and especially his research assistant will be entrusted with much highly confidential information: how the individual feels about his superiors, his anxieties about his own job performance, his reactions to management rules, the personal problems he faces outside of the organization, and so on. Such data are essential for the understanding of human relations, and yet, if allowed to leak out, they can be highly damaging to the informants. Personnel men and research assistants must set for themselves a high standard of professional ethics on this point. They must promise to keep confidences, and they must keep their promises. People will naturally be suspicious in the beginning, but when they find that the things they have allowed to slip out when under emotional pressures do not come back at them from other sources, they learn to trust the personnel man and the research assistant.

2. Don't Ask Who Is to Blame for the Problems You Find. Try Instead to Explain Why People Act as They Do.   In industry, as in other social structures, it is customary for those in positions of responsibility to try to determine who is to blame for the problems discovered and then to fix upon an appropriate form of punishment. At its worst, this approach leads to the punishment of innocent scapegoats. At best, the approach may fix responsibility for mistakes in a manner which will generally be thought fair, *but* it does not tell us why the individual made the mistake or what actions should be taken to help him function better in the future. We often find people handling their problems badly because they are under heavy pressure from superiors, they are facing conflicting demands, or they are otherwise bound by conditions beyond their control. In such cases, criticisms from superiors or from other people only accentuate the problems. On the other hand, an analysis of human relations will often point to changes that will relieve pressures and solve problems.

Furthermore, if the personnel man seeks to lay the blame, he gets involved in the politics of the organization. He is known to be *for* some people and *against* others, and all his actions are discounted on this basis. Only if he casts aside moral judgments and analyzes behavior in terms of human relations can he gain a reputation as a disinterested technician of organization.

3. Work with the Man Most Directly Concerned with the Problem.   For example, if a study of a department brings out certain problems involving the relations of the department head with his subordinates, every effort should be made to work these out through consultation between personnel man and department head. The department head will naturally fear that all his failings will be reported over his head and that he will then be subjected to increased pressure from his boss. Such fears will further disturb his performance and make him hostile toward the personnel man. On the other hand, if the department head gets help in the analysis of his problems and in the improvement of his performance, he can add to his sense of confidence and security.

We should not give the impression that this result is easily obtained. The problems of changing the behavior of supervisors are exceedingly complex and difficult, and we still have much to learn on this score. In some cases it may prove impossible to change behavior through working only with the man most directly concerned, and we have found it necessary to take problems up at higher levels (which involves us in problems to be discussed below). However, Mr. Wiley has always made every effort to solve each problem at the lowest possible level and thus to avoid suspicion that his job is to carry tales to the boss. We feel that this has been an important factor in building confidence in the program.

4. Work with the Man at the Top to Help Him Understand His Impact upon the Organization.   I have already noted the key importance of the top executive in setting the pattern in human relations for his organization. This means that, unless the boss is willing and able to examine his own behavior, the personnel program will be seriously handicapped. It takes a big man to be able to do this. At the Radisson, we were extremely fortunate in this respect. In making arrangements for the project, Mr. Calhoun told us that he was chiefly interested in getting help for himself. He recognized that he sometimes failed to gain his ends through mistakes in the field of human relations. He hoped to improve his own social skills and understanding. Mr. Wiley and I found in the course of our work that we were indeed able to make suggestions to Mr. Calhoun involving his own activities and have them acted upon with skill and understanding. At the same time, we learned a great deal about problems at the executive level through our discussions with Mr. Calhoun.

At first we were reluctant to take up lower level problems with the top executive even when they could not be worked out below him because we were not sure how Mr. Calhoun would handle these situations. However, we found that this was not as serious a problem as we had first anticipated. In the first place, the personnel man does not present the only channel through which the executive can become aware of human relations problems. He may learn that "something is wrong somewhere" through checking figures for labor turnover, through receiving union complaints, through a drop in production figures, or in still other ways. The personnel man then does not become involved in bringing an unsuspected problem to the attention of the executive and thereby perhaps exposing one of his subordinates to criticism. In all cases so far in our experience, it has been possible to start with discussion of problems whose existence is already recognized by the executive and, on the basis of research, to clarify the nature of the problem and to outline possibilities for effective action.

As time went on, we were able to present Mr. Calhoun with an increasingly full picture of the human relations problems of his organization. We could do this without jeopardizing the positions of his subordinates because discussions were not pitched on the level of laying the blame and "reading the riot act." Mr. Calhoun asked two general questions: What is the nature of the problem? And what can I do to help solve the problem? Discussions in this area led to greater social understanding and the development of more effective executive leadership.

5. Present Facts and Interpretations, But, as Much as Possible Let the Man Who Must Act Decide for Himself upon His Course of Action. We do not believe that the personnel man should take it upon himself to solve all human relations problems for supervisors and executives. If he proceeds in that way, they will either rebel against his "interference" or else become so dependent upon his judgment that their own capacities are seriously weakened. Instead, it should be the function of the personnel man to build a *problem solving organization*. That means that he should present supervisors and executives with the facts and interpretations which he feels are necessary in reaching sound decisions, but the actual decision-making process should be left to those in positions of line responsibility. While this may lead to mistakes in judgment which could be avoided by following the personnel man, the procedure seems to us essential in building up the long-run effectiveness of the organization. The supervisor or executive cannot learn to handle his human problems with skill and understanding unless he works out his own decisions.

6. Develop Personal Influence, But Avoid the Use of Authority.   We feel that the personnel man should function in a strictly advisory capacity. As he learns to help the line officials toward the solution of their human problems, he will gain a constructive influence in the organization. But if he tries to exert authority—to tell line officials what they must and must not do within their departments—then he only confuses the structure of the organization and creates friction.

We have heard some personnel men say they could do a better job if they only had more *authority*. This is, we feel, an illusion. In general, we find that people cannot effectively serve two bosses. The only person who is in a position to lead and direct them is the line official who has the full-time responsibility for this job. The personnel man can be much more effective if he serves as advisor and aide to the line than if he tries to direct activities himself.

7. Leave Rewards and Punishments in the Hands of the Line.   This means that promotions and salary increases, demotions and firings should all be handled by the executives. It means that reprimands for poor performance should be given by line officials and not by the personnel man, and the personnel man should avoid giving the impression that he is putting people "on the spot" with the boss. While he may compliment people for doing a good job, the really important recognition must come from line executives. While not handling rewards and punishments himself, the personnel man can work with supervisors and executives to improve their performance so that they may win top management's approval and avoid adverse criticism. The administration of these incentives should remain with the executives.

Conclusions

Our new approach to personnel work may be summed up in this way:

1. The personnel man, in this project, had command over a body of scientific knowledge. While we fully recognize the relatively undeveloped state of the science of human relations, the personnel man had been trained in this field through course work, and, more importantly, through a year of field research. On human problems, therefore, he based his judgment on this background of knowledge and was less likely to be led astray by his personal reactions to the individuals involved.

2. The personnel man had access to human relations research dealing directly with the problems of his own organization. When problems came to his attention,

he did not need to guess at their origin or solution. His judgment was based upon past studies made by his research assistant or upon studies specifically designed to bring in data upon the problem in hand.

There are certain other aspects of human relations research that deserve special mention here. When the research interviewing program is skillfully carried out, that in itself tends to relieve tensions and have a generally favorable effect upon human relations. However, the interviewing approach alone cannot be counted on to solve many human relations problems. For example, in one department the first month of interviewing was accompanied by a striking drop in labor turnover. We hoped that this favorable result could be capitalized upon by prompt action upon the problems the interviews brought to light. Unfortunately, due to problems which need not be discussed here, the necessary changes did not take place until six months later. In the meantime, turnover figures had jumped back to their former high level. According to our interpretation, the drop in turnover was due only in part to the feeling of relief on the part of the employees who had a chance to get their problems off their chests. They also felt, though no promises had been made to them, that the interviews would bring favorable changes in human relations. When these changes did not follow, the morale profit from the interviewing was dissipated. Therefore, if the employees are given to understand that there is a relationship between interviewing and action, the benefits from the interviewing program can only be preserved if there is a follow through.

In the course of our research, we tied in certain aspects of management engineering (studies of the flow and organization of work) with our human relations approach. I feel that this is a necessary development. Too many managements look upon efficiency and human relations as two sharply separated subjects. To build up efficiency, they call upon their best engineering talent to conduct time and motion studies, to set up incentive pay systems, and so on. In all too many cases, these elaborately worked out programs fail to achieve management's objectives because they meet resistance from informal groups of workers or from unions themselves. This resistance is clearly a problem in human relations. We feel that the long run efficiency of industry can be served best by a skillful integration of engineering and human relations programs so that any engineering changes are carried through on the basis of the best human relations knowledge available.

A personnel research program, we feel, should not end with recommendations for action. Just as the chemist and the engineer must test their plans in the laboratory, so the personnel department should be so organized that it is able to follow very carefully any action which takes place as a result of its recommendations. At the Radisson Hotel, we were able to make such follow-up studies.

My emphasis upon interviewing for relieving tensions, upon efficiency engineering and human relations, and upon the importance of testing results should not obscure the main stream of our personnel research program, which involves the detailed study and analysis of the total social system—of the relations of workers to workers, workers to supervisors, supervisors to supervisors, supervisors to department heads, union business agents to department heads, and so on. It is this study of the structure of the organization of human relations which provides the framework for all our thinking and action in this field.

3. The personnel man was not limited to bottom-level problems. He was free to operate upon problems at all levels in the organization. The results obtained were made possible only by the changes in human relations which were brought about at high levels in the organization. Had Mr. Wiley been confined to bottom-level programs, the whole program would have broken down.

4. The personnel man was given high status in the organization. He reported directly to Mr. Calhoun, the operating executive of the hotel. In the beginning, the university connection no doubt served to give status to the personnel program, but, as Mr. Wiley developed his relationships with the hotel personnel and began to bring about favorable changes, his high position became more secure, and he was listened to with increasing respect.

This report should not give the impression that the changes in human relations were entirely due to the efforts of University of Chicago trained people. It is the essence of such a personnel program that it rests ultimately upon the social skill and understanding of the line executives and supervisors. The personnel man can serve to provide a sounder basis for executive action, but unless key people in the organization take an interest in working out human problems, nothing will be accomplished. We were fortunate that the executives came to take a keen interest in the development of the program. And here, of course, the key man was Mr. Calhoun. His intelligent interest and solid support set the tone for the entire organization. It would have been impossible for us to move forward in this experimental direction had he been hostile or even indifferent to the program. That emphasizes once more the point that a personnel program designed to meet the needs of this critical age can only be developed if it has the support and lively interest of top management.

We still have much to learn in this field, but even now we feel that the initial experiment has shown such possibilities as to give us hope that the personnel man may at last come into his own as a scientist of organization so equipped and placed that he will be able to meet the pressing human relations problems of our industrial society.

The Parable of the Spindle

Elias H. Porter

More and more we hear the word "systems" used in discussions of business problems. Research people are studying systems, experts are looking at organizations as systems, and a growing number of departments and companies have the word "systems" in their names.

Just what is a system in the business sense? What does it do? What good is it to management? To answer these questions I shall first use a parable from the restaurant industry. What, you may ask, can executives in manufacturing, retailing, or service systems learn from restaurant systems? I readily admit that if you envisage only menus, customers, waitresses, and cooks in a restaurant, you will find no transferable knowledge. But if you see (as I hope you will) inputs, rate variations, displays, feedback loops, memory devices, queuing, omissions, errors, chunking, approximating, channeling, and filtering in a restaurant system—then you should indeed find some practical value in my parable.

The implications of the parable will be discussed specifically in the second part of the article, after we have reduced it to a paradigm.

THE PARABLE

Once upon a time the president of a large chain of short-order restaurants attended a lecture on "Human Relations in Business and Industry." He attended the lecture in the hope he would learn something useful. His years of experience had led him to believe that if human relations problems ever plagued any business, then they certainly plagued the restaurant business.

The speaker discussed the many pressures which create human relations

Reprinted by permission from the Harvard Business Review, May/June, 1962, copyright © 1962 by the President and Fellows of Harvard College, all rights reserved.

Author's note: I am indebted to William Foote Whyte of Cornell University for having developed the spindle in real life.

problems. He spoke of psychological pressures, sociological pressures, conflicts in values, conflicts in power structure, and so on. The president did not understand all that was said, but he did go home with one idea. If there were so many different sources of pressure, maybe it was expecting too much of his managers to think they would see them all, let alone cope with them all. The thought occurred to him that maybe he should bring in a team of consultants from several different academic disciplines and have each contribute his part to the solution of the human relations problems.

And so it came to pass that the president of the restaurant chain and his top-management staff met one morning with a sociologist, a psychologist, and an anthropologist. The president outlined the problem to the men of science and spoke of his hope that they might come up with an interdisciplinary answer to the human relations problems. The personnel manager presented exit-interview findings which he interpreted as indicating that most people quit their restaurant jobs because of too much sense of pressure caused by the inefficiencies and ill tempers of co-workers.

This was the mission which the scientists were assigned: find out why the waitresses break down in tears; find out why the cooks walk off the job; find out why the managers get so upset that they summarily fire employees on the spot. Find out the cause of the problems, and find out what to do about them.

Later, in one of the plush conference rooms, the scientists sat down to plan their attack. It soon became clear that they might just as well be three blind men, and the problem might just as well be the proverbial elephant. Their training and experience had taught them to look at events in different ways. And so they decided that inasmuch as they couldn't speak each others' languages, they might as well pursue their tasks separately. Each went to a different city and began his observations in his own way.

The Sociologist

First to return was the sociologist. In his report to top management he said:

> I think I have discovered something that is pretty fundamental. In one sense it is so obvious that it has probably been completely overlooked before. It is during the *rush hours* that your human relations problems arise. That is when the waitresses break out in tears. That is when the cooks grow temperamental and walk off the job. That is when your managers lose their tempers and dismiss employees summarily.

After elaborating on this theme and showing several charts with sloping lines and bar graphs to back up his assertions, he came to his diagnosis of the situation. "In brief, gentlemen," he stated, "you have a sociological problem on your hands." He walked to the blackboard and began to write. As he wrote, he spoke:

> You have a stress pattern during the rush hours. There is stress between the customer and the waitress. . . .
> There is stress between the waitress and the cook. . . .
> And up here is the manager. There is stress between the waitress and the manager. . . .
> And between the manager and the cook. . . .
> And the manager is buffeted by complaints from the customer.
> We can see one thing which, sociologically speaking, doesn't seem right. The manager has the highest status in the restaurant. The cook has the next highest status. The waitresses, however, are always "local hire" and have the lowest status. Of course, they have higher status than bus boys and dish washers but certainly lower status than the cook, and yet they give orders to the cook.
> It doesn't seem right for a lower status person to give orders to a higher status person. We've got to find a way to break up the face-to-face relationship between the waitresses and the cook. We've got to fix it so that they don't have to talk with one another. Now my idea is to put a "spindle" on the order counter. The "spindle," as I choose to call it, is a wheel on a shaft. The wheel has clips on it so the girls can simply put their orders on the wheel rather than calling out orders to the cook.

When the sociologist left the meeting, the president and his staff talked of what had been said. It made some sense. However, they decided to wait to hear from the other scientists before taking any action.

The Psychologist

Next to return from his studies was the psychologist. He reported to top management:

> I think I have discovered something that is pretty fundamental. In one sense it is so obvious that it has probably been completely overlooked before. It is during the *rush hours* that your human relations problems arise. That is when the waitresses break out in tears. That is when the cooks grow temperamental and walk off the job. That is when your managers lose their tempers and dismiss employees summarily.

Then the psychologist sketched on the blackboard the identical pattern of stress between customer, waitress, cook, and management. But his interpretation was somewhat different:

> Psychologically speaking, he said, we can see that the manager is the father figure, the cook is the son, and the waitress is the daughter. Now we know that in our culture you can't have daughters giving orders to the sons. It louses up their ego structure.
>
> What we've got to do is to find a way to break up the face-to-face relationship between them. Now one idea I've thought up is to put what I call a "spindle" on the order counter. It's kind of a wheel on a shaft with little clips on it so that the waitresses can put their orders on it rather than calling out orders to the cook.

What the psychologist said made sense, too, in a way. Some of the staff favored the status-conflict interpretation while others thought the sex-conflict interpretation to be the right one; the president kept his own counsel.

The Anthropologist

The next scientist to report was the anthropologist. He reported to top management:

> I think I have discovered something that is pretty fundamental. In one sense it is so obvious that is has probably been completely overlooked before. It is during the *rush hours* that your human relations problems arise. That is when the waitresses break out in tears. That is when the cooks grow temperamental and walk off the job. That is when your managers lose their tempers and dismiss employees summarily.

After elaborating for a few moments he came to his diagnosis of the situation. "In brief, gentlemen," he stated, "you have an anthropological problem on your hands." He walked to the blackboard and began to sketch. Once again there appeared the stress pattern between customer, waitress, cook, and management:

> We anthropologists know that man behaves according to his value systems. Now, the manager holds as a central value the continued growth and development of the restaurant organization. The cooks tend to share this central value system, for as the organization prospers, so do they. But the waitresses are a different story. The

only reason most of them are working is to help supplement the family income. They couldn't care less whether the organization thrives or not as long as it's a decent place to work. Now, you can't have a noncentral value system giving orders to a central value system.

What we've got to do is to find some way of breaking up the face-to-face contact between the waitresses and the cook. One way that has occurred to me is to place on the order counter an adaptation of the old-fashioned spindle. By having a wheel at the top of the shaft and putting clips every few inches apart, the waitresses can put their orders on the wheel and not have to call out orders to the cook. Here is a model of what I mean.

Triumph of the Spindle

When the anthropologist had left, there was much discussion of which scientist was right. The president finally spoke. "Gentlemen, it's clear that these men don't agree on the reason for conflict, but all have come up with the same basic idea about the spindle. Let's take a chance and try it out."

And it came to pass that the spindle was introduced throughout the chain of restaurants. It did more to reduce the human relations problems in the restaurant industry than any other innovation of which the restaurant people knew. Soon it was copied. Like wild fire the spindle spread from coast to coast and from border to border.

So much for the parable. Let us now proceed to the paradigm.

THE PARADIGM

Each of the three scientists had seen a different problem: status conflict, sex rivalry, and value conflict. Maybe it was none of these but simply a problem in the division of work between men and machines and how they are related one to the other: a problem of system design. Let us explore this possibility by observing the functions which the spindle fulfills.

Functions Served

First of all, the spindle acts as a memory device for the cook. He no longer needs to remember all the orders given him by the waitresses. This makes his job easier and less "stressful"—especially during the rush hours.

Secondly, the spindle acts as a buffering device. It buffers the cook against a sudden, overwhelming load of orders. Ten waitresses can place their orders on the spindle almost simultaneously. The cook takes them off the spindle according to his work rate—not the input rate. This makes his job easier, more within reach of human capacity—especially during the rush hours.

Thirdly, the spindle acts as a queuing device—in two ways. It holds the orders in a proper waiting line until the cook can get to them. When dependent on his memory only, the cook can get orders mixed up. It also does all the "standing in line" for the waitresses. They need never again stand in line to pass an order to the cook. This makes their jobs easier—especially during the rush hours.

Fourthly, the spindle permits a visual display of all the orders waiting to be filled. The cook can often see that several of the orders call for the same item. He can prepare four hamburgers in about the same time as he can prepare one. By reason of having "random access" to all the orders in the system at that point he is able to organize his work around several orders simultaneously with greater efficiency. This makes his job easier—especially during the rush hours.

To appreciate the fifth function which the spindle serves, we must go back to the procedures used before the advent of the spindle. In looking at these procedures we are going to examine them in "general system behavior theory" terms:

On the menu certain "information" exists in the physical form of printed words. The customer "transforms" this information into the physical form of spoken words. The information is once again transformed by the waitress. Now it exists in the physical form of written notes made by the waitress. Once again the information is transformed as the waitress converts her notes into spoken words directed to the cook. The cook transforms the information from the physical form of spoken words to the physical form of prepared food. We have an "information flow" which looks like this:

$$\text{Menu} \xrightarrow{\text{Printed Words}} \text{Customer} \xrightarrow{\text{Spoken Words}} \text{Waitress} \xrightarrow{\text{Written Notes}} \xrightarrow{\text{Spoken Words}} \text{Cook} \xrightarrow{\text{Prepared Food}}$$

Now every so often it happened that an error was made, and the customer didn't get what he ordered. Of course, you and I would have been the first to admit that we had made an error, but not all cooks and waitresses have this admirable character trait. This is rather understandable since the waitress was trying to do things correctly and rapidly (she wanted all the tips she could get!), and when she was suddenly confronted with the fact that an error had been made, her first reaction was that the cook had goofed. The cook, on the other hand, was trying to do his best. He knew in his own heart that he had prepared just what she had told him to prepare. "It's the waitress' fault," was his thought.

So what did the cook and waitress learn? Did they learn to prevent a recurrence of the error? Indeed not! The waitress learned that the cook was a stupid so-and-so, and the cook learned that the waitress was a scatterbrained so-and-so. This kind of emotionalized learning situation and strainer-of-the-interpersonal-relations any organization can do without—especially during the rush hours.

Changes Effected

Consider now how the spindle changes all this. The waitress prepares the order slip and the cook works directly from it. If the waitress records the order incorrectly, it is obvious to her upon examining the order slip. Similarly, if the cook misreads the slip, an examination of the order slip makes it obvious to him. The fifth function of the spindle, then, is to provide "feedback" to both waitress and cook regarding errors. The spindle markedly alters the emotional relationship and redirects the learning process.

As errors are examined under conditions of feedback, new responses are engendered. The cook and waitress may find the present order slip to be hard to read, and they may request the manager to try out a different style of order slip. Now they are working together to solve the system's problems rather than working against each other and disregarding the system's problems. Maybe they find that abbreviations cause some random errors. For example, it might be that HB (Hamburger) and BB (Beefburger) get mixed up just a little too often, so the cook and waitress get together with the manager and change the name of Beefburger to Caravan Special on the menu because the new symbol (CS) will transmit itself through the system with much less ambiguity—especially during the rush hours.

HANDLING OVERLOAD

Had I been asked a few years ago to advise on human relations problems in the restaurant industry as a professional psychologist, my approach would have been limited to what I now call a "component" approach. My thinking would have been directed at the components in the system—in this case, the people involved. I would have explored such answers as incentive schemes, human relations training, selection procedures, and possibly some time-and-motion studies. My efforts would have been limited to attempts to *change the components to fit in with the system as designed no matter how poor the design might be*.

But now I would first concern myself with the "information" which must be "processed" by the system. My concern would be centered on the functions which would have to be performed by the system and how they might best be performed. I would concern myself especially with how the system is designed to handle conditions of information overload.

It is significant that in our parable the three scientists each discovered that the human relations problems arose mostly during the rush hours, in the period of "information overload." How a system responds to conditions of overload depends on how the system is designed. Let us look at how various design features permit the handling of conditions of overload in a number of different kinds of system.

Increase in Channels

One of the most common adjustments that a system makes to an excess input load is to increase the number of "channels" for handling the information. Restaurants put more waitresses and cooks on the job to handle rush-hour loads. The Post Office hires extra help before Christmas. The telephone system has recently introduced automatic-switching equipment to handle heavy communication loads; when the load gets to a certain point, additional lines are automatically "cut in" to handle the additional calls. Even our fire departments increase "channels." If there is not enough equipment at the scene, more is called in. Department stores put on additional clerks to handle holiday crowds. Military commanders augment crews in anticipation of overload conditions. Extra communication lines may be called up. More troops are deployed.

Almost everywhere we look we see that systems are very commonly designed to increase or decrease the number of channels according to the load.

Waiting Lines

But there comes a time when just increasing the number of channels is not enough. Then we see another common adjustment process, that of "queuing" or forming a waiting line. There are few readers who have not had the experience of waiting in a restaurant to be seated. Other examples are common. Raw materials are stored awaiting production processes. Orders wait in queue until filled. Manufactured goods are stored on docks awaiting shipment. The stock market ticker tape falls behind.

We have already seen how the spindle makes it unnecessary for the waitresses to queue to give orders. And we are all familiar with the modern custom in most restaurants of having a hostess take our names and the size of our party. What happens when the hostess takes our names down on paper? For one, we do not have to go through the exasperating business of jostling to hold our position in line. Also, the "holding of proper position" is done by machine; that is, it is done by the list rather than by our elbows.

Use of Filtering

The hostess' list also illustrates the way in which a system can make still a third type of adjustment, that of "filtering." Because she jots down the size of the group, she can now selectively pull groups out of the queue according to the size of the table last vacated. Some readers will recall that many restaurants used to have all tables or booths of the same size and that everyone was seated in turn according to how long he had waited. It used to be infuriating for a party of four to see a single person being seated at a table for four while they continued to wait. The modern notion of accommodations of varying sizes, combined with the means for filtering, makes the use of floor space much more efficient and the waiting less lengthy. We can see filtering in other systems as well:

• The Post Office handles registered mail before it handles other mail, delivers special delivery letters before other letters.

• In the case of our other most important communication system, the telephone system, there is no way for dial equipment to recognize an important call from an unimportant call; it cannot tell whether a doctor is dialing or the baby is playing. However, where long-distance calls must go through operators, there is a chance for filtering. For instance, in trying to place a call to a disaster area the operator may accept only those calls which are of an emergency nature.

• Military systems assign priorities to messages so as to assure differential handling.

• Orders may be sent to production facilities in bunches that make up a full workday rather than in a first-in-first-out pattern. Special orders may be marked for priority attention.

Variations of Omission

A system can be so designed as to permit "omissions," a simple rejection or nonacceptance of an input. The long-distance operator may refuse to accept a call as a means of preventing the lines from becoming overloaded. The dial system gives a busy signal and rejects the call. A manufacturing organization may reject an order it cannot fill within a certain time. A company may discontinue manufacture of one line temporarily in order to catch up on a more profitable line that is back ordered.

As another example of how the design determines what adjustments the system can make, consider the way the short-order restaurant system design utilizes the omission process:

If waiting lines get too long, customers will turn away. That is not good for business, so restaurants often practice another kind of omission. On the menu you may find the words, "No substitutions." Instead of rejecting customers, the restaurants restrict the range of inputs they will accept in the way of orders. Thus time is saved in preparing the food, which in turn cuts down the waiting time in the queue.

The goal of most restaurants is to process as many customers per unit time as is possible. With a fixed profit margin per meal served, the more meals served, the more profit. But when people are in the queue, they are not spending money.

One solution to this is the installation of a bar. This permits the customers to spend while waiting. It is a solution enjoyed by many customers as well as by management.

Chunking and Approximating

Another big timesaver in the restaurant system is the use of a fifth adjustment process, that of "chunking." Big chunks of information can be passed by predetermined arrangements. You may find a menu so printed that it asks you to order by number. The order may be presented to the cook as "4D" (No. 4 Dinner), for example. The cook already knows what makes up the dinner and does not need to be told each item with each order. Preplanning permits chunking, and chunking frees communication channels.

Somewhat akin to the chunking process is a sixth adjustment process, "approximating." To illustrate:

• A business forecaster may not be able to make an exact count of future sales, but he may predict confidently that the sales will be small, moderate, or large.

• An overburdened Post Office crew may do an initial sorting of mail as "local" or "out of town."

• An airborne radar crew may report a "large formation" headed toward the coast.

• An intelligence agency may get a report of "heightened" air activity in a given area.

•An investment house may predict "increased" activity in a certain line of stocks.

• Stock market reports state that industrials are "up" and utilities are "down."

Approximating thus means making a gross discrimination of the input rather than making a fine discrimination.

Trading Errors

A rather unusual adjustment process that a system can adopt to cope with overload is to accept an increase in the number of errors made. It is almost as if systems said to themselves, "It's better to make mistakes than not to deal with the input." For example, the sorting of mail is not checked during rush periods. Mail which is missent must be returned, but in a rush that risk is worth the cost; more mail gets sent where it is supposed to go even though there are more errors. Thus, quality control is given up for the sake of speed. On the other hand, some systems are so designed as to be insensitive to errors. The telephone system will permit you to dial as many wrong numbers are you are capable of dialing.

It is interesting to see in the restaurant system design a deliberate making of errors of one sort in order to prevent the making of errors of another sort during rush hours:

Picture yourself and a couple of friends dropping into a restaurant during the middle of an afternoon. You are the only customers there. The waitress takes your order. You ask for a hamburger with "everything on it." The next person asks for a hamburger but wants only lettuce and a slice of tomato on it. The third person asks for a hamburger but specifies relish and mayonnaise. The work load is low. There is time to individualize orders.

But during rush hours it would be too easy to make errors. Then the cook prepares only the meat and bun. The waitress goes to a table where there are bowls with lettuce leaves and tomato slices and little paper cups of relish and mayonnaise. On each plate she places a lettuce leaf, a tomato slice, a cup of relish, and a cup of mayonnaise. In most instances she will have brought something that the customer did not order, and in this sense she would have made an "error"; but she would have avoided the error of not bringing the customer something he *did* want.

Other examples of the same type are common. For instance, a sales department sends out brochures to everyone who inquires about a product so as not to miss someone who is really interested. Again, the Strategic Air Command, as a central policy, uses this deliberate making of one type of "error" to avoid a possible error of more severe consequences. The commander may order the force launched under "positive control." It is better to have launched in error than to be caught on the ground and destroyed.

CONCLUSION

And so we see that there is a new frame of reference, a new point of view coming into use in approaching the problems of organizations. This new frame of reference looks at organizations as systems which 1) process information, transforming the information from one form into another, and 2) are or are not designed to cope with the conditions of overload that may be imposed on them. This new frame of reference is expressed as an interest in how the structure or design of an organization dynamically influences the operating characteristics and the capacities of the system to handle various conditions of information overload.

At the University of Michigan there are some 50 scientists whose primary interests lie in looking for similarities and differences in system behavior at all levels. They examine single cells, whole organs, individuals, groups, and societies for the manners in which these systems cope with their environments in common and in unique ways. They search the work of other scientists for clues to system behavior at one level that is followed at higher or lower orders of organization. As for the application of this "system frame of reference," one finds such organizations as System Development Corporation, the RAND Corporation, and the MITRE Corporation using it in approaching the complex problems of advanced military systems. Here is just a sampling of specific developments that bear close watching:

• Because it is possible to view organizations as systems which process data in a continuous sequence of "information transformations" and which may make numerous types of adjustments at the points of transformation, a wholly new concept of training has arisen. In the past, training in business and industry as well as in the military was largely limited to training a man or men to do a given task in a certain way. Now training can be provided that teaches a man or men to adopt adjustment processes suited to the design of the system and the condition of overload. In other words, training for flexibility rather than rigidity is now possible. It should not be long before internal competition is replaced by internal cooperation as the main means of enhancing production.

• Because it is possible to view a business or industry as an information processing system, it is possible to stimulate the information flow on digital computers and, by controlling the adjustment processes at each point where the data are transformed, to learn what effects and costs would be involved in change. The manager will then be able to test his policies realistically on the computer before committing himself in action. A computer program called SIMPAC (Simulation Package) has already been developed at System Development Corporation for this purpose.

• A digital computer program capable of "learning" has been developed. By analyzing how data can be sensed, compared with other data, and stored in the computer's "memory," scientists have been able to "teach" a prototype computer program to recognize letters of the alphabet, cartoon characters, and spoken words. One can look forward to the day when, opening a bank account, he will be asked to sign his name in a variety of situations—e.g., standing, sitting, bending over, and maybe even after a couple of martinis. The computer will learn to recognize his signature from these samples, and at the clearinghouse, after that, his account will be automatically debited and the payee's account automatically credited.

Ludwig von Bertalanffy, the father of general system theory, predicted that general system theory would unify the sciences, thus making it possible for a scientist trained in one area to talk in common terms with another scientist trained in another area.[1] It also seems certain that business and industry will soon profit from the application of the theory of how systems behave.

---

[1]"General System Theory," *General Systems* (Ann Arbor, Society for General Systems Research, 1956), Volume I, pp. 1-10.

Social Inventions for Solving Human Problems

William Foote Whyte

This is a time for rethinking sociology. In President Reagan's initial budget proposal for 1982, we were told, in effect, that what we (and other social scientists) do in research is of little relevance in solving national problems. On past performance, we do not warrant that judgment, but let us not expend our energies in defending past accomplishments. We must do better in the future to demonstate the practical relevance of sociology.

We can meet that challenge if we reorient the way we do sociology. I suggest that we conceptualize this focus in terms of the discovery, description, and analysis of *social inventions for solving human problems*.

Let me start with a definition. A social invention can be

—a new element in organizational structure or interorganizational relations,
—new sets of procedures for shaping human interactions and activities and the relations of humans to the natural and social environment,
—a new policy in action (that is, not just on paper), or
—a new role or a new set of roles.

We can leave it to the historians to determine whether the social invention we study is *new* in the sense that nothing quite like it has ever been done before in the history of mankind. For sociologists, the important point is that the ideas underlying the invention are new to the people involved in developing and applying them. Even if they have consciously copied from elsewhere, at least they had to adapt the copy to their own social, economic, and cultural environment.

American Sociological Association, 1981 Presidential Address. Reprinted from the American Sociological Review 1982, 47:1–13, by permission of the American Sociological Association. Copyright by the American Sociological Association.

Before going farther, let me distinguish between *invention* and *intervention,* two words that sound similar but have different meanings.[1]

Whatever else it may be, an *intervention* is something brought into an organization or community from the outside. An *invention* is a new creation which may and often does emerge in a community or organization, without any direct outside influence. While an *intervention* may indeed involve the introduction from outside of what I would call a *social invention,* I am here primarily focusing on inventions more or less autonomously created within the organization or community in which they are utilized. Quite apart from concerns over terminological exactitude, I emphasize the autonomous creation of social invention to suggest that human beings have enormous resources of creativity that permit them to devise their own social inventions, without waiting for an outsider to intervene and invent what the community or organization needs.

To illustrate the potential utility of this line of research, let me focus in some detail on the study of social inventions in two fields of human affairs quite separate from each other: worker industrial production cooperatives in Spain and agricultural research and development organizations in Latin America. In both of these studies I have done field work myself, but the more systematic studies have been carried out by younger colleagues (Ana Gutiérrez-Johnson and Lynn Gostyla) who have also made major contributions to the analysis.

THE STIMULUS OF MONDRAGÓN

I first began to focus my ideas in this direction when I presented a paper (Johnson and Whyte, 1977) on the Mondragón system of worker production cooperatives at the 1976 meeting of the American Sociological Association.[2] I was excited by what we were learning regarding a system of worker production cooperatives in the Basque country of Spain that had been started by five men in 1956 and two decades later had expanded to 65 cooperative production firms with 14,665 worker-members. By the end of 1980, in spite of a serious slowdown in the Spanish economy, the system had grown to include 87 worker cooperatives with over 18,000 members.

Since the conventional wisdom held that worker cooperatives were a form of industrial organization that had little promise of success (Blumberg, 1968:3-4), it seemed important to let my colleagues know about Mondragón.

When later published, this article did indeed attract a good deal of attention, but I was taken aback by the reception the paper received from one of the discussants. The critic denied that the case had any general significance. In the first place, he attributed the success of the Mondragón system to the Basque culture, whose peculiar features could not be duplicated anywhere else in the world. In the second place, he cited the contribution of an extraordinary individual, José María Arizmendi, who was indeed the founder of the system and the principal person who guided its development until his death in 1977.

Let me deal first with the cultural determinism argument. To be sure, there is a cultural base to the Mondragón system, but that base accounts only for the Basque inclination toward cooperative forms of organization. Culture explains neither the structural form of the Mondragón system nor its extraordinary growth.

Basques themselves are conscious of this cultural base; they speak of "our associative tendencies." Indeed, one author (Johnson, 1982) claims that there are in the Basque provinces many more worker production cooperatives outside of the Mondragón system than within. Therein lies the clue to the limitations of the cultural explanation, for we find that these other cooperatives have not joined together to constitute integrated and expanding organizational systems. Rather, they conform to the traditional Basque pattern: small, closed social systems with strong in-group solidarity. Mondragón departs markedly from this traditional culture pattern. It is an open system, constantly expanding in individual members and in the number of firms it links together. In Mondragón internal cohesion is balanced by strong linkages of the firms with the communities out of which they have arisen. No cultural explanation can account for the basic differences between the Mondragón system and the traditional Basque cooperatives.

Let us now consider the limitations of the great man theory of the history of Mondragón. Father José María Arizmendi was indeed an extraordinary human being, and I counted it a great privilege to have several conversations with him. However, let us shift our focus away from the personality and character of the founder and concentrate upon the design of the organizational structure, on interorganizational relations, and on sets of procedures for shaping interactions, activities, and relations of humans to the natural and social environment. If we look for innovations in social policy and in the creation of new roles, we can visualize Don José María and his associates as the creators of a series of social inventions. While it may take an extraordinary individual to create an important social invention, it should be possible for mere mortals to identify that social invention, describe it, and analyze it in ways that will permit others to adapt it to their own interests and needs.

I shall illustrate by describing two sets of social inventions contributing to the growth of individual units and the development of the total system.

1. The legal and financial structure of the Mondragón firm solves problems which have led to the disintegration of many worker cooperatives all around the world. When a worker cooperative is built on the basis of member stock ownership, it can go out of existence either because the firm goes bankrupt or because it is highly successful. In the latter case, as the firm becomes more prosperous and expands, what we call "collective selfishness" takes over. The original members realize it is to their financial advantage not to dilute their equity by sharing ownership with newly hired labor. When worker-owners retire and want to sell, their stock has so increased in value as to be beyond the reach of nonowning workers, and so inevitably that stock shifts into the hands of private investors.

In Mondragón, the financial instrument is *debt* rather than *equity*. Each member's initial contribution is conceived of as a loan, to be deposited in the worker's account with the firm. Furthermore, members' shares in the annual profits or surplus of the firm are not distributed in cash but are deposited to member accounts, where they are used by the firm to finance its future growth. Each member account (initial contribution plus profit sharing plus interest) constitutes a fund available in full to the worker upon retirement and which can be withdrawn, with certain deductions, if the member leaves before retirement age.

Many worker cooperatives have failed because, in good times, they have distributed profits in cash to members and have not retained in the firm enough money for reinvestment and as a reserve fund against future losses. The Mondragón legal and financial inventions provide strong protection against such disasters.

We estimated in 1976 that roughly half of the extraordinary growth of the Mondragón system was accounted for by the reinvestment of 70% of the profits each year in the member accounts—beyond the 15–20% always retained in a reserve fund.

2. The other half of the system's growth was provided by loans from **Caja Laboral Popular,** a cooperative bank founded in 1959, three years after the launching of the first worker production cooperative. A cooperative bank or credit union was certainly not a Mondragón invention. However, up to that time in Spain as well as elsewhere, credit unions had been utilized for individual savings and for loans to finance the purchase of consumer goods. While the Caja does have individual savers who deposit money and take out personal loans, its primary purpose has been to finance the creation and expansion of industrial cooperatives, consumer cooperatives, housing cooperatives, construction cooperatives, and education cooperatives.

The Caja has experienced extraordinary growth. By the end of 1980 it had 300,000 individual depositor-members and capital close to one billion dollars. The Caja has also invented programs not ordinarily associated with banking institutions. It has an entrepreneurial department with a staff of over 100 to provide organizational skills and general technical assistance in working with cooperative organizations in the process of formation or expansion.

The Caja has also proven to be a key factor in linking together into a single system so many industrial production cooperatives. Besides providing technical assistance to the group seeking to create a cooperative firm, the Caja lends 60% of the initial capital needed and supplies additional credit to cover the losses of the new firm for the first two years of its existence. As a condition for receiving this assistance, the initial members of the firm establish a constitution and bylaws compatible with the framework established by José María Arizmendi and the cofounders of the first firm. Thus, while each firm is completely autonomous in its internal operations, the common organizational framework and financing mechanisms make the difference between isolated firms and an organizational system. Furthermore, besides providing management consulting services, the Caja helps individual firms to band together to share costs of services such as personnel, legal, purchasing, and marketing.

INVENTIONS IN AGRICULTURAL RESEARCH AND DEVELOPMENT[3]

In recent years I have been working closely at Cornell with an interdisciplinary group of professors ranging across the plant, animal, and soil sciences and including economists, political scientists, and anthropologists. What brought us together was the common recognition that, except where they have access to irrigation, small farmers in developing countries have so far received little benefit from the great scientific advances of the "green revolution." In working together, we were moving toward a common diagnosis of the problem of extending the benefits of science and technology to these limited resource farmers and were also designing a new model for agricultural research and development. While I have profited greatly by information and ideas brought to me by colleagues with experience in Asia and Africa, I shall illustrate this process of diagnosis and reformulation in terms of my own field experience in Latin America.

Before we can identify a particular social invention in agricultural research and development we have to visualize the traditional system for carrying out these activities. According to the research literature and my own field work in Latin America, the traditional R & D system had the following characteristics:

1. Agricultural research was concentrated in experiment stations.

2. The links between agricultural research and extension have been weak. Researchers tend to look down on extension agents, and the agents often complain that researchers are too interested in scientific purity to give attention to practical applications. This is part of a broader problem of lack of coordination among government and private agencies. Small farmers have often found that the recommended inputs to improve their farms are not available in local markets. If they can get the credit they need to follow extension recommendations, the money generally arrives much later than the optimal time for its use.

3. The activities of extension agents and the flow of credit have tended to be concentrated especially upon the more affluent farmers.

4. Extension agents have generally followed a communications strategy, disregarding the social organizations of rural communities. That is, they have

customarily dealt with farmers on a one-on-one basis or through public announcements and demonstration projects.

5. Social scientists, studying the diffusion of innovation, have defined the problem as *resistance to change*. That is, they have viewed peasants or small farmers as being locked into their traditional culture and therefore inclined to reject improvements that would raise their standard of living. In this framework, the problem is how to overcome resistance to change by these irrational or nonrational small farmers.

If that is the general pattern you perceive, what does it suggest for the next steps in research? I see my own exploration and analysis proceeding through the following four stages.

1. Discovery of the Fallibility of Agricultural Professionals.   Some years ago in Peru I began to hear of cases in which small farmers had followed the recommendations of agricultural professionals and had suffered disastrous results. This stirred my interest, and I was then able to document similar events in Africa, Asia, and elsewhere in Latin America. Now I asked myself, why was it that such blunders of agricultural professionals had been news to me?

The conventional research strategy assumed that the recommendation offered had been practically and economically sound—which is the same thing as assuming the infallibility of the professional. Therefore, if the small farmer rejected the innovation, he could not do so on rational economic grounds. This led naturally to what I have been calling "the myth of the passive peasant." The causes for "resistance to change" cannot be located in the impracticality of the innovations recommended but must rather be found in the culturally determined psychological makeup of the small farmer.

Now I was also learning what factors could lead the agricultural professional into serious errors. In the first place, years ago professionals seriously underestimated the effects of the enormous variability in soil, water, and general climatic conditions that affected farmers from one region to another and even in different parts of a small geographical area. If the professional had not tested his recommendation in the same area where it was to be applied, the chances of being wrong were very high indeed.

2. On the Value of Peasant Ideas and Information.   Now I asked whether small farmers might have valuable information and ideas that the professional lacked. I found the value of peasant information and ideas demonstrated most dramatically in the famed Puebla project in Mexico, the International Maize and Wheat Center (CIMMYT: 1975). Located in one state of Mexico, the project's purpose was to demonstrate how small farmers could increase their yields of corn.

Puebla was primarily a demonstration project rather than a research project. The designers of the project thought they already knew how to help the small farmers grow more corn, and the research was designed primarily to measure the effectiveness of this *technology transfer* project. The project involved methods of growing corn but also assistance in securing credit for the farmers, who would need additional funds to buy the inputs necessary.

Over a period of several years, the project enrolled increasing numbers of farmers and demonstrated approximately a 30% increase in corn yields—significant but hardly impressive compared with results then being achieved with high yielding varieties of rice and wheat. Furthermore, the number of adopters of the Puebla project technology, as measured by the number of farmers receiving credit through the program, leveled off at a point where only a quarter of the corn farmers in the program were participating. This led the Mexican professionals implementing the program to wonder why adoption was not continuing to grow. Rather than falling back on the traditional explanations of peasant traditionalism and resistance to change, they went out into the field to observe and study the nonadopters.

The revelation that was key to my reformulation was put to me in this way by Mauro Gomez, Puebla Project General Coordinator (1970–1973):

> In Mexico we have been mentally deformed by our professional education. Without realizing what was happening to us, in the classroom and in the laboratories we were learning that scientists knew all that had so far been learned about agriculture and that the small farmers did not know anything. Finally we had to realize that there was much we could learn from the small farmers.

To oversimplify a complex set of results, the Mexican field workers discovered that the basic reason some of these farmers were not adopting the Puebla recommendations was because they were making twice as much money following their own methods. The Puebla program was geared to the monocultural production of corn—that is, planting corn in rows with no other crops between the rows. The most successful nonadopters planted beans between the rows of corn. They were making much more intensive use of their small plots of land and also making more efficient utilization of fertilizer, which now served two crops instead of one.

When the Mexicans made this discovery, they naturally asked themselves, "Why is it that we have been telling them they should not plant anything between the rows?" Not finding any rational explanation, they recognized the force of tradition: "That is not the way they raise corn in Iowa." In other words, their recommendations had been based implicitly upon the model of farming in the

Midwest corn belt. The monocultural strategy made sense in Iowa where affluent farmers plant large acreages of corn and use tractors, which require space between the corn rows for most operations.

Promoters of the Puebla program realized that, where land and capital were in short supply and labor was relatively cheap and abundant, tractors were not practical. However, instead of recognizing that the rationale for leaving empty space between rows of corn depended upon the use of the tractor, they simply proceeded on the implicit assumption that, since the Iowa corn farmers were highly efficient, their methods must be applied in Puebla. In this case, we must ask, who is tradition bound, the agricultural professional or the peasant farmer?

The traditionalism of the agriculture professionals is strikingly illustrated in the basic Puebla report of CIMMYT, the International Center for Maize and Wheat Improvement, which was responsible for the project. The report has a schizophrenic character. The authors faithfully describe the slowing down of the adoption process and the discovery that farmers intercropping beans and corn were making up to twice as much money off of their crops as those who faithfully followed the Puebla recommendations. Furthermore, they describe how, three years after the project's beginning, project officials endorsed intercropping and stimulated the growth of organizations of corn and bean farmers. At the end of their report, however, they arrive at this extraordinary conclusion:

> Clearly, the job of adjusting and delivering adequate technology, as well as that of inducing farmers to use the recommended technology is very difficult and it is far from being accomplished in the Puebla area. (CIMMYT, 1975)

Of course, it is difficult to persuade small farmers to adopt a new agricultural technology when it promises to cut their crop income in half. How could a group of highly competent agricultural professionals come to a conclusion that bore no relation to the facts they themselves had documented? To answer that question, we must distinguish between accidental and systemic errors. An accidental error is one which may be committed by anyone at any time; a systemic error is caused by the *conceptual scheme* the researchers bring to bear upon the problem. The designers of the Puebla Project began with a conceptual scheme that visualized the development process as a problem in the *transfer of technology* in ways designed to overcome the *resistance to change* on the part of *passive peasants*. Their own findings were clearly incompatible with such a scheme, but, as historians and sociologists of science have noted, the discovery of discrepant facts may not be sufficient to overthrow an established theory—or, I would add, a more modest construct such as a conceptual scheme. Especially in the early stages of the development of a science, those attached to the established paradigm tend to ignore the facts that don't fit or to make patchwork adjustments in the theory. A popular theory is discarded only after it is confronted with over-whelming contrary evidence *and* the emergence of a new theory which fits both the old facts and the new facts that have now become available. The writers of the Puebla Project report stayed with their defective conceptual scheme because they had nothing better to put in its place. It remained for those who followed their pioneering work to move toward the new paradigm.

These reflections prompted me to abandon any thought of further studies of peasant resistance to change. I did not go to the other extreme to assume that small farmers are always eager to embrace change but simply assumed that, in general, they are no more resistant to change than are the professionals in their own field of activity. Therefore, when small farmers decline to adopt a proposed innovation, we can generally assume that either (a) they have enough sense to know it would not work, or (b) they lack the money to buy the necessary inputs or cannot get those inputs in local markets.

3. The Active Participation of Farmers in Agricultural R & D.   Such analyses led me to the conclusion that effective R & D systems in developing countries must involve the active participation of small farmers in the R & D process. Cases along this line are beginning to appear all over the world, but here I shall concentrate on my own studies, first in Guatemala and then in Honduras (Gostyla and Whyte, 1980; Whyte, 1981).

The new program began in Guatemala with the creation of ICTA, the Institute of Agricultural Science and Technology, out of what had been a sprawl-ing agricultural bureaucracy. ICTA was designed not only to do more and better research but especially to do research in ways that would benefit small farmers.

The designers of ICTA recognized that, if their program was to meet its new responsibilities, more of its research must be done on the fields of small farmers. While abandoning total reliance on the artificial setting of the experiment station was a necessary condition for aiding small farmers, a mere change in location of research was not sufficient to reach the new objectives.

As various observers have noted, the conventionally minded plant scientist, when ordered to do his experiments on the fields of small farmers, will try insofar as possible to approximate the control over the experimental process which he enjoyed on the experiment station. If the new location was to provide information beyond the response of crops to different soil and climate conditions, then ICTA needed to devise a set of social inventions through which small farmers could play active roles. Furthermore, in order to provide a realistic base for these field experiments, Peter Hildebrand and his Guatemalan associates had to develop social inventions to provide them with baseline information on the nature of the indigenous farming system practiced in the area studied.

The Socio-Economic unit, organized by Hildebrand, began field work by delimiting an area of study within which the small farmers were practicing basically similar farming systems—that is, planting the same crops, using roughly the same inputs and systems of cultivation. In such an area, any improvement developed on one farm would have wide applicability throughout the area. Note that such studies are based upon the assumption that the baseline for introducing changes is *not zero;* the baseline must be a *systematic knowledge of the indigenous farming system.*

The invention of the methodology for discovering and analyzing an indigenous farming system went through three stages of development. The first stage involved intensive field studies in which the social scientists interviewed many farmers, observed their farming practices, and also worked with 25 farm families to develop daily records of labor utilization, activities carried on, inputs used, and money expended. This methodology produced for the first time in Guatemala a systematic description of an indigenous farming system. Though important for research purposes, this methodology was too costly for general utilization throughout large areas of Guatemala. It required the services of eight to ten professionals working in the field and in their offices throughout an agricultural year and then going back to the same area a second year to check on the yields the farmers had achieved and the quantities and prices of the crops they marketed.

On the basis of what they had learned in the first stage, the Socio-Economic unit devised a shortcut field survey methodology. In this stage the social scientists spent about two weeks in the field interviewing a sample of small farmers. When they found that the data produced by the shortcut methodology were close enough to those yielded by the more intensive first stage studies to be used for planning purposes, the researchers had solved the cost-effectiveness problem.

The second stage left a major problem still unresolved: data gathered by anthropologists, economists, and sociologists had low credibility with plant scientists, who dominated ICTA. In the third stage, the Socio-Economic unit overcame this problem by working out an arrangement with the plant scientists to carry out the area surveys jointly.

For each day in the field, the members of this joint team went out in pairs, a social scientist with a plant scientist, and each evening the team got together to discuss results and to raise questions for further checking. Each day also the composition of the pairs was changed so that each social scientist gained experience with each plant scientist, and vice versa. This strategy gave each team member a broad range of interdisciplinary and interpersonal experience. As the new methodology came into widespread use, we found plant scientists increasingly basing their experimental strategies upon information provided by the field farming system surveys.

On the basis of solid information regarding the indigenous farming system practiced in the area of intervention, the Socio-Economic unit now devised another set of social inventions designed to involve small farmers as active participants in the experimental process. The design of the program was based on the assumption that the innovations to be tested out needed to be fitted into the indigenous farming system and must at first involve only minor modifications of that system, which would be within the financial capacity of the small farmers.

The experimental process was carried out in two stages. In the first stage, professionals of ICTA were in control, but they planned the experiments in active consultation with small farmers and rejected any change which the farmers considered impractical. In the second stage, the farmers themselves assumed control, with ICTA professionals standing by as observers and consultants.

ICTA had solved the problem of involving small farmers actively in the experimental process, but this was done at first only on a very small scale at a few locations. For the methodology to be applied widely within ICTA itself, leaders of the organization had to invent solutions to a number of problems involving administrative decentralization and interdisciplinary collaboration. Let me pass over these now to point to a major area of still unresolved organizational problems in Guatemalan agricultural R & D.

We found there a striking contrast between ICTA, an innovative research organization, and DIGESA (General Agricultural Services Administration), an extension organization still following the conventional pattern of organization and practice imported from the United States years earlier. The emphasis was upon supervised credit. The extension agent worked out for the small farmer the production plan to be used as a basis for securing credit from the agricultural bank and then closely monitored his farming activities. With this strategy, the agent could not work with more than 40 to 50 farmers in any given year. Reaching any large percentage of small farmers through such a model would be prohibitively expensive.

This was much more than simply a problem of numbers. The DIGESA model was still based implicitly on the myth of the passive peasant: the notion that he could not change unless guided and controlled by professionals. The ICTA model was based on an assumption of reciprocity and mutuality: professionals and small farmers had much to learn from each other. When we finished our field work, Guatemala was still struggling to overcome the structural and social theory problems blocking the effective integration of research with extension.

In neighboring Honduras we discovered social inventions which appeared to be enabling the Ministry of Natural Resources to overcome the organizational problems we had observed in Guatemala. In the first place, the directors of research and of extension occupied offices across the hall from each other and worked closely in planning joint programs. Extension agents were beginning to participate actively in farming system surveys. Some of them acknowledged that they were embarrassed initially with this new approach because they had been telling the farmers what to do for several years, and now they were asked to make a new beginning by finding out first what the farmers were actually doing and why. Still, this interview and observation approach was providing the foundation for a new and more collaborative relationship between extension and small farmers.

Increasingly, extension agents were getting away from a one-on-one strategy, encouraging the formation of groups of farmers so that extension could work with the group and through its informal leaders. This group-based strategy was facilitated enormously in Honduras by the existence of large and powerful peasant movements. In each village the peasant organization aims to establish a cooperative for buying inputs, selling crops, and planning and financing production. As these base-level cooperatives have gained strength, they have been joined together to form regional cooperatives, including eight to ten local units.

At this point, a creative official of the Food and Agricultural Organization, Rolando Vellani, began working with the cooperative movement. After extensive interviews with farmer leaders, he helped each regional cooperative work out a program of weekly meetings with the regional heads of all of the government agencies related to agriculture. Vellani's group helped the regional leaders plan the crops to be planted and determine the inputs and equipment they would need to carry out the plan. Then, as the officers of the regional cooperative met with regional government officials, they presented a production plan complete with a collective loan application to the agricultural bank.

These organizational innovations involved in the building of local and regional cooperatives and in linking them with government agricultural agencies have made possible the achievement of extraordinary economies of scale, especially in the provision of agricultural credit. For example, in Mexico agricultural scientist Antonio Turrent told me in 1977, "Even ten years after the beginning of the Puebla Project, it is impossible to get credit to the Puebla farmers less than a month after they can most efficiently utilize it for buying fertilizer and other inputs."

When a government credit agency has to deal with hundreds of small farmers or even with small groups of farmers, such bureaucratic delays are commonly observed all over the developing world. In Honduras, the head of the regional office of the agricultural bank meets weekly with leaders of the regional cooperative and is thoroughly familiar with the process of production planning and the estimation of financial needs. With this background of knowledge, he needs little additional time to study the loan application and, with a single stroke of the pen, can release funds for hundreds of farm families. The leaders of the regional cooperative then assume responsibility for distribution of the funds to the base organizations. The costs of administering these loans from regional cooperative to farm families are carried by the regional cooperative itself, as the loan includes 1 or 2% for travel and office expenses for cooperative officials.

When we were visiting Honduras in February of 1980, Vellani described the recent emergence of a third level of the peasant cooperative organization:

a national federation of regional cooperatives. The national federation already included six regional cooperatives, and others were in the process of formation. Again Vellani and his group had facilitated the establishment of linkages with government, this time at the national level. There is now in practice in the capital city a monthly meeting at which the operating heads of all agriculture-related government agencies sit down for a day-long meeting with the leaders of the national federation to discuss and plan agricultural programs and policies. This national meeting provides a linkage at the top level between farmers and government while building on the local and regional cooperatives.

IMPLICATIONS FOR FUTURE RESEARCH AND PRACTICE

The analysis of social inventions in these cases raises as many questions as it answers, but that in itself is an indication of a fruitful research strategy. For example, I find it striking to discover important social inventions developing under such inhospitable environments as those imposed by the repressive dictatorships of Franco in Spain and the military juntas which have governed Guatemala since the CIA engineered the overthrow of a democratically elected government in 1954. These cases suggest that the resourcefulness and creativity needed to produce significant social inventions may be found even under governments that impose severe limitations on human freedom. This is not to suggest, however, that social inventions at the local level or in one part of a government agency will be sufficient to transform a repressive dictatorship into a progressive democracy. This analysis simply points to the need for further study and reflection regarding the relations between small-scale changes, built on participatory strategies, and the issues of reform or revolution at the national level.

IMPLICATIONS FOR RESEARCH METHODS AND SOCIOLOGICAL THEORY

The study of social inventions involves more than a shift away from more traditional topics. It also involves major changes in research methods and theory development. Let us explore these implications, starting by contrast with what I take to be the standard model of social research taught to our graduate students.

According to that standard model, the researcher goes through the following steps.[4] He reviews the literature and consults with his colleagues regarding the problem he would like to study. Then he selects hypotheses that he wants to test, arming himself with a combination of reasonably well-supported hypotheses that he can reinforce, hypotheses that involve conflicting evidence from past research, and perhaps a novel hypothesis or two that he can think up himself. With this theoretical armament in place, he picks out a target population for study—and with this research style, the ''target population'' is well named. He then moves in to persuade the gatekeepers controlling access to this target population that, if they let him do the study, somehow the information he gathers will be useful to them as well as to him. Having done the study, if he isn't too busy writing his scientific papers and proposals for new research, he may return to the gatekeepers with what he has learned.

Where did this research style come from? I suspect that sociologists have been unconsciously following a physics model. In physics, the phenomena under study are fixed, at least in the sense that, though they are in constant movement, they follow a reasonably standard orbit. The physicist is experimenting on the basis of a highly developed and coherent body of theory. And finally, since the phenomena are under the control of the investigator, he does not require their active participation in the experiment.

This model is much less appropriate in sociology or organizational behavior. The phenomena we study are in movement, and new combinations are constantly emerging. Our theory base is much less firm, and our links from data to theory are often exceedingly shaky. Furthermore, we are dealing with active human beings, who can contribute to our study if we allow them to participate. Under these conditions, before adopting the standard model, we should at least ask ourselves: Do we really know the territory we are investigating? Or are we just mechanically applying a given research instrument?

In the research strategy required for the study of social inventions, you do not start out with a preestablished research design. Of course, you don't start out with a blank mind either. You consult the research literature, but you refuse to be bound by it. In the first place you assume that the published literature is likely to be a decade behind the most interesting things happening in the field. Furthermore, while the literature may illuminate a problem, it may also impose intellectual blinders that guide you along traditional pathways. In many cases it is less important to gather new data than to develop a new way of organizing and interpreting data. For example, few problems in sociology have received more research attention than the *diffusion of innovation,* yet, as I have pointed out, researchers on changes in agriculture in developing countries have generally followed a conceptual scheme based on a misdiagnosis of the problem and have therefore provided findings that are worse than useless.

Before preparing your research design, you go out into the field. Through interviewing and observation, you develop a rough map of the social, economic, and technological territory. You gain a preliminary idea of social processes—of the interactions and activities in which people are engaged—in order to diagnose and solve their problems.

After some period of immersion in the field, fortified by reading about it, you discover a general pattern along the following lines. The people you are studying have their own conventional definitions of the problems they are facing.

Conventional solutions are proposed and sometimes tried out. More often than not, the conventional solutions don't work, and the problems remain—or else the conventional solution solves one problem but creates other equally intractable problems.

You also discover that people have characteristic ways of adjusting to the recognition that their standard model is not working well. They lapse into *normative* thinking. They do not question the model itself but instead assume that it would work well if only they could recruit better people for leadership positions, provide better training for supervisors, and develop better means of monitoring activities, and punishing people who are not doing what they are supposed to do. Over the years, from field studies of piece rate systems in industry (Whyte, 1955) to studies of agricultural research organizations, I have found this a common reaction to the perceived deficiencies in the workings of the standard model.

Assuming that, in order to arrive at scientific generalizations, sociologists must gather systematic data on a number of cases having important characteristics in common, we have too often been trapped into studying the *standard model* in all our various fields of research. Thus we can demonstrate ad nauseam how the standard models are not working the way their proponents claim they should. If we confine our studies to cases where the principal actors are defining their problems in similar ways and attempting similar solutions, with similar results, we can only speculate as to what would happen if the actors defined the problems differently and took different lines of action.

Instead, let us assume that our preliminary diagnosis is accurate and then look for situations where actors are defining the situation differently and devising different solutions—in other words, where they are trying out social inventions.

Having discovered a social invention, you then move in to observe, interview, and gather documentary material so that you will eventually be able to provide a systematic description of that invention. You then seek to evaluate the invention or set of inventions.[5] This is not simply a matter of judging the degree of success or failure. If the invention appears to work, this judgment does not tell us *why* or *how* it works. If we are to be able to describe a social invention in a way that makes it potentially useful in other situations, we must grasp the social principles underlying its effectiveness in the case under study.

As I have argued in the Mondragón case, evaluation necessarily involves abstracting social inventions from the social and cultural context in which we find them. Unless we do this, we are vulnerable to two types of errors: We attribute success to an invention, whereas in fact the favorable outcome depended primarily on the cultural context; or we abandon as a failure a potentially sound invention which was implemented in an incompatible context. The first error is less serious for, in that case, as the social invention is tried out in a new context, the invention-context relations will become more evident and the invention can then be reevaluated. On the other hand, if a potentially sound social invention is undermined by an unfavorable context, that invention may be discredited and lost forever.

An example of the second type of potential error is a social invention of AID sociologist James Greene, designed to serve two purposes: to help rural communities in Peru to provide public works for themselves without undue burdens on the national government and to strengthen local governments through their involvement in building, financing, administering and maintaining such projects. An important and novel feature of FOROCO (the Revolving Community Loan Fund) was a procedure designed to prevent the diversion of public funds to private purposes, a practice which had discredited many of such cash-aided self-help projects in other parts of the world. The branch bank could make disbursements to suppliers of materials only when they presented duplicate copies of disbursement certificates the bank had received from its regional office. Furthermore, the local mayor had to accompany the supplier to the bank, certify to the receipt of the materials, and present the authorizing ordinance passed by the local government, together with a repayment plan based on receipts from a special tax levied by the local government. The duplicate copy of the disbursement certificate came to the local government and then to the suppliers through Cooperación Popular, the government agency which provided technical assistance to the community in drafting the plan and to the local government in drafting the necessary ordinances and tax levies.

FOROCO got under way impressively with villagers volunteering their labor and committing themselves to repay loans for materials and equipment through the local government, which thereby gained significant taxing power for the first time in Peruvian history. But then the program bogged down, with increasing defaults on the loans, and AID subsequently wrote off the Revolving Community Loan Fund as a failure.

What happened? At this time, for one of the very few times in Peruvian history (1963–1968) the President was faced with an opposition majority in Congress. Viewing with alarm the popularity of the new program, the opposition leaders pushed through a *grants* program, promising to give villagers the same public works without any payment obligation. Faced with the choice between a gift and a loan, villagers naturally opted for the gift, and those who were already committed to loans did not see why they should have to pay for what other villagers elsewhere were getting for nothing.

In such a case, the sociologist can perform an important service by showing that a social invention, abandoned as a failure, may actually be successful if planted in a different political context.

This research strategy has important implications for the choice and timing of research methods. The questionnaire or survey has long been the favorite method of sociologists, but you do not go out looking for social inventions by doing a survey. When it comes to evaluating success or failure, however, it is important to know the opinions and attitudes of the people who are affected by a social invention, and here the survey can be an indispensible instrument.

This research strategy also has important implications for the relations between the researcher and the people he/she studies. It is folly to treat those who have created an important social invention as passive subjects of research. We need to learn from them the personal experiences and thought processes that led them to create the social invention as well as their theories of why the invention works or why it fails to work as well as they think it should. That is not to say that we function simply as reporters, passing on the wisdom of the social inventors. We must look for the underlying principles of social dynamics, whose discovery will enable us to describe and analyze a social invention in such a way that other human beings in other situations may be able to adapt and utilize it.

In seeking to apply the results of our research, we should think in terms of social inventions rather than in terms of attitudes, beliefs, and values. For example, when I was beginning a study of a remarkable shift from conflict to cooperation in the Inland Steel Container Company (Whyte, 1951), one day I confessed over the telephone to a vice-president of the parent corporation that I was having difficulty in figuring out the change. He commented, "Yes, that did puzzle me for a long time, but I have finally figured it out."

In eager anticipation, I asked for the answer. His reply: "They learned to trust each other."

For a moment I sat there speechless, waiting for something else to come out of the receiver, but that was all there was. I drew a deep breath and said, "Well, I guess you're right, but *how* did they learn to trust each other?"

The vice-president laughed and said, "You're the sociologist. It is up to you to figure that out." That is the challenge to sociologists.

I am not denying the importance of subjective mental phenomena, but, we are rarely able to change behavior simply by telling people that they should change their attitudes. Attitudes, beliefs, and values do indeed change as people, in grappling with persistent social problems, devise creative ways of restructuring their activities and interactions and their relations to the physical and social environment. In studying the social inventions that enable people to bring about such changes, we can build a more useful applied sociology. And, as we study the implementation of social inventions in new socioeconomic and technological contexts we will also contribute to the building of sociological theory.

Sociologists and other social scientists have begun to realize the significance of social inventions developed in Mondragón and in innovative agricultural research and development programs. Practitioners and professors are beginning to use such inventions in project planning and in rethinking social theory. I do not claim to be the discoverer of any of these social inventions. My aim has been to conceptualize them in such a way as to stimulate new strategies for research and action.

May I suggest that the research strategy presented here is itself a social invention?[6] Lest this seem too grandiose a claim, let me qualify it in two ways.

In the first place, I do not claim to be the originator of the concept of social invention. It appeared in the sociological literature of the 1920s and 1930s, and, in all probability, its origin could be traced back further decades or centuries.[7] Until now, however, the concept has been peripheral to sociology, having no recognized place in the mainstream of sociological theory and research methods. I am suggesting that we bring the concept into the mainstream as a key organizing principle both for theory and practice.

In the second place, to state that something is an invention tells us nothing at all about its potential value. Very few of the mechanical inventions receiving patents ever get developed to the point of widespread utilization. The value of this social invention will not be determined by what I say about it. You, my colleagues, will make that judgment. If you don't use the invention, this address will rest quietly in the files of the *American Sociological Review*. If you do use it—and improve upon it—then this Presidential Address will prove to have more than ceremonial value.

NOTES

1. In fact, several colleagues wrote to congratulate me for selecting "Social *Intervention*" as the theme of the 1981 ASA meeting.
2. The Mondragón study was part of a research program supported by the Center for Work and Mental Health (NIMH–R01 29259).
3. Much of the research reported here was supported by a Cooperative Agreement between AID and the Rural Development Committee of Cornell University.
4. In describing this model, I use the masculine pronoun because I assume that men have been primarily responsible for creating the model.
5. In this paper, I have not dealt with the problem of evaluation of Mondragón or of the Guatemalan or Honduran programs. Evaluation research has become a well-established field of sociology on which I have nothing to add beyond noting that it is a good idea first to make sure that you have focused on something worth evaluating.
6. I am indebted to Renee Fox for this point.
7. I am indebted to Warren Dunham for reminding me that William F. Ogburn used the concept in the 1920s. I am also indebted to Sheldon Stryker for pointing out that Stuart Chapin also used the concept (see References).

REFERENCES

Chapin, F. Stuart
    1928   Cultural Change. New York: The Century Co. (see particularly pp. 357–58).
CIMMYT (Centro Internacional de Mejoramiento de Maíz y Trigo. In English: International Center for Maize and Wheat Improvement)
    1975   The Puebla Project: Seven Years of Experience, 1967–1973. El Batán, Mexico.
Blumberg, Paul
    1968   Industrial Democracy: The Sociology of Participation. New York: Schocken.
Gostyla, Lynn and William F. Whyte
    1980   ICTA in Guatemala: The Evolution of a New Model for Agricultural Research and Development. Ithaca, NY: Rural Development Committee, Center for International Studies, Cornell University.
Johnson, Ana Gutiérrez
    1982   The Evolution of the Mondragón System of Worker Cooperatives. Unpublished Cornell University Ph.D. thesis.
Johnson, Ana Gutiérrez and William F. Whyte
    1977   "The Mondragón system of worker production cooperatives," Industrial and Labor Relations Review 31:18–30.
Ogburn, William F.
    1922   Social Change. New York: B. W. Huebsch.
    1956   "Inventions, population, and history." Pp. 62–77 in Otis Dudley Duncan (ed.), William F. Ogburn on Culture and Social Change: Selected Papers. Chicago: University of Chicago Press. The paper was originally published in 1942 (see especially p. 66).
Whyte, William Foote
    1951   Pattern for Industrial Peace. New York: Harper & Bros.
    1955   Money and Motivation. New York: Harper & Bros.
    1981   Participatory Approaches to Agricultural Research and Development: A State of the Art Paper, Ithaca, NY: Rural Development Committee, Center for International Studies, Cornell University.

Theories and Methods of Clinical Sociology

The Theoretical Base of Clinical Sociology: Root Metaphors and Key Principles

Roger A. Straus
Alfred University

ABSTRACT

The theoretical base of clinical sociology is analyzed through Pepper's root metaphor method. Practice is found to be framed by the analogy between society and a complex ecosystem. The resulting world hypothesis is identified as Ecologism, within which the four relatively adequate world hypotheses identified by Pepper (Formism, Mechanism, Contextualism and Organicism) take their place as complementary alternatives differentially informing or guiding practice with respect to the analysis of categories, evaluation of linkages, intervention at the microsocial level of social actors and mesosocial level of organizations and other integrated social systems, respectively. Examples are drawn from the literature, and key analytical and methodological principles are identified for practice at each level.

"Clinical sociology . . . is identified as the application of the sociological perspective to interventions or social change. . . . The field of clinical sociology . . . might be distinguished . . . by its systematic theoretical base" (Gondolf, 1985:144). As the subdiscipline moves into an increasingly formal state of institutionalization, we need to specify that theoretical base as a guide to both thinking about and practicing clinical sociology.

Glassner and Freedman (1979), Cohen (1981) and Straus (1985) have demonstrated the clinical implications of social theory. The next step is to identify the theoretical frame and basic premises of sociological practice as it has been conceived in its period of rebirth, 1977–1986. Following Pepper's (1942) "root metaphor" method, we begin with an analysis of world theories in social science,

---

Correspondence to: Roger A. Straus, Ph.D., National Analysts, 400 Market Street, Philadelphia, PA 19106.

articulate the specific world hypothesis of Ecologism, which frames clinical practice, then show how this model of the human world informs, structures and guides formulation and practice of sociological interventions at every level of social organization.

Root Metaphors in Social Science

Philosopher Stephen C. Pepper (1942) argues that humans make sense out of the world by analogy with some aspect of common experience: "all the world's a stage," for example. Around this "root metaphor" philosophers and scientists proceed to build up theories about the world—world hypotheses—from and within which we develop paradigms (Kuhn, 1970) and the very understandings guiding our notions of truth, evidence and reality. Pepper identifies four relatively adequate, autonomous and nonreducible world hypotheses in scientific thought: Formism, Mechanism, Contextualism, and Organicism (to which we will add a fifth, Ecologism).

Western science and philosophy until the Industrial Revolution were dominated by *Formism*, a world theory revolving around the observation that, while every object of experience is unique, we nevertheless perceive types of things—blades of grass, stars in the night, eagles on the wing. It is as if each kind of thing were a more or less perfect copy of an ideal Form. Around this root metaphor of *similarity*, Formism analyzes the world in terms of underlying patterns or templates giving structure to experience (Pepper, 1942). Exemplified by Plato's parable of the cave, Formism views the world from the exalted heights of pure mathematics. It reenters modern science and scholarship as symbolic logic and the concept of "norms." Both interpret observed phenomena with reference to an ideal type and proceed to describe observed relationships in terms of abstract categories.

With the triumph of classical mechanics and subsequent emergence of industrial society, *Mechanism*, another world theory with Hellenic roots, supplanted Formism as the dominant world view in Western civilization. Based on the root metaphor of *a machine*, Mechanism depicts an orderly universe maintained by underlying cause-and-effect relationships involving material forces following the determinate laws of Newtonian science. If only we can figure out the "blueprint," humankind can predict and control the world. It was this root metaphor which inspired Comte's positivism and which has been more recently championed by proponents of "empirical sociology" (Straus, 1985). In both the lay and scientific cultures, "science" is generally equated with Mechanism. Similarly, the sociologist, by virtue of professional training, is steeped in mechanist categories, logic and methods.

Rejecting the static determinism of that world view, James, Dewey and Mead made the analogy between the world and a series of *acts* (e.g., Mead,

1938). Chicago School social psychology is premised upon their world hypothesis of *Contextualism*. Exemplified by symbolic interactionism (Blumer, 1969), it replaces the mechanist "universe" with a "multiverse" characterized by ever-emergent patterns of order shaped by the contexts within which they form and into which they are integrated as the context for subsequent action. Humans are seen as relatively autonomous subjects weaving the fabric of "society" out of their individual and joint lines of conduct, so that the separation between the "individual," "group," and "society" becomes largely arbitrary, depending on how much of the context one wishes to consider (Straus, 1981). Social reality is seen as a matter of consensus, social facts are always negotiable, the concept of a fixed, external reality irrelevant. Thus, Contextualism falters when it comes to dealing with social structures and orderly processes, generally. The concept of structure is essentially alien to this perspective. As Pepper put it, "The cosmos for these theories is not in the end highly systematic. . . . They regard system as something imposed upon parts of the world by other parts, so that there is an inherent cosmic resistance to determinate order in the world as well as a cosmic trend to impose it" (1942, p. 143).

Von Bertalanffy (1968) recognized that an entirely different logic and method from those of Mechanism or Contextualism is required to deal satisfactorily with integrated systems of interdependent elements or parts. This is the province of *Organicism*, a world hypothesis which initially likened the world to *an organism*. As we will see, the dominant metaphor in contemporary Organicism has shifted to that of *a system*. We are immediately drawn to the classical sociologies of Spencer and Durkheim and Parsons' (1951) structure-functionalism as examples of how "the organicist believes that every actual event in the world is a more or less concealed organic process" (Pepper, 1942:281). In his exegesis of Organicism, however, Pepper identifies this organic process with the dialectical working out of contradictions. In other words, both Durkheim's sociology and that of Marx are rooted in the same biological metaphor!

A Fifth Metaphor: Ecologism

When taken to the extremes of their logical development, however, Contextualism and Organicism prove only partially adequate to the task of dealing with social reality. To understand routinized patterns of joint action, the Contextualist must come to grips with the observation that people act as if there were social structure and as if human phenomena were commonly organized as described by the term "systems." Organicist systems theorists, on the other hand, must recognize the relatively autonomous, situated action of social actors and grapple with the problem of whether or to what degree observed phenomena can be profitably analyzed as "a(n integrated) system."

When we examine what sociologists working in either vein actually do, it seems that they overcome these limitations by organizing their practice theory as if they were likening the social world to *an ecosystem* displaying elements of both integration and dispersiveness, interdependence and autonomy. In fact, when Chicago School pioneers turned their attention to problems of the industrial city, this was precisely the root metaphor around which urban sociology was organized. They made the analogy between the human community and the natural ecology, i.e., the more or less systematic relationships between plant and animal populations within a specific environment (Park et al., 1925).

Flowing from this root metaphor emerges a new world hypothesis, *Ecologism*, differing from Pepper's four world theories in two basic ways. First, it seems to be restricted to a narrower universe of discourse, that of *creatura* (Bateson, 1979), the living world. Secondly, within its framing assumptions, Ecologism more or less systematically integrates discrete elements drawn from Organicism, Contextualism, Mechanism, and Formism. Just as ecology draws upon the fullest range of the natural sciences, Ecologist social science organizes a syncretic, nonlinear, multicentric picture of reality by putting together information generated by strategies and concepts from seemingly contradictory orientations. This is, in fact, the method known as complementarity, which seems necessary to obtain a clear picture of intersubjective reality (Bohr, 1958). Following this logic, the other world hypotheses take their place as complementary perspectives, each applicable to a different level or aspect of the whole, while Ecologism, itself, supplies the "big picture."[1]

Ecologism, then, provides our most complete analysis of the multifaceted *contexts* within which social life takes place. The basic premise of Ecologist sociology is that situations, communities, and whole societies can be analyzed in terms of differentiated groups interacting with one another and with their social and material environments in pursuit of optimal survival in a world of limited resources. In considering each of these elements and their interactions one must take into account the factors of autonomy, purposiveness, time, and contingency as suggested by Contextualism. As groups emerge and interact within their historical and material contexts, various relatively stable patterns of social relations are created. These tend toward the formation of multicentric human systems (Duhl, 1983) of increasingly wider scope, which are best understood and dealt with as suggested by Organicist systems theory.[2] Emergent social structures, however, are not necessarily "functional." Rather, they frequently represent instrumental arrangements by which powerful groups maintain and further their own interests at the expense of others, as even Sumner (1906) recognized.

The emergence of an ecological world view integrating the new American social psychology with the Organicism of classical European sociology seems to have triggered the development of clinical sociology as practiced by members of the Chicago School and described by Wirth (1931). The clinical implications of urban structure upon its inhabitants were directly explored by Faris and Dunham (1965) among others. For Wirth (1931) behavior problems could only be understood in terms of a multicentric and many-leveled social ecology, from the microenvironment of the individual classroom to the person's location within the total community.

An Ecologist concern with the socially structured environment and with the biological organism also underlies the contribution of W. I. Thomas (1923). Far less phenomenological or relativistic than is commonly accepted, his approach differs from Mead's Contextualism in stressing the primacy of the definitions imposed upon the individual by the structure of his or her social situation. For example, in their manifestly clinical work on child behavior problems, W.I. and D.S. Thomas (1938:571) champion a "situational approach" in which statistics and life study methods are combined to examine the shaping of individuals' conduct "partly by institutions, taken as situation, and partly by behavior of others, taken as situation." The oft-quoted statement "If men define situations as real, they are real in their consequences" is to be found as a generalization at the end of a paragraph describing a specific case in the methodological discussion at the end of this volume (p. 572). Merton (1968) holds the Thomas Theorem to be one of the central premises of sociology; it might therefore be said that Ecologism has yielded the paramount contribution of clinical sociology to the social sciences at large!

Another ecologist paradigm, conflict theory, even more strongly influences clinical macrosociology. While influenced by Marx, this paradigm is more directly related to Veblen (1899) and Simmel (1950), among others. Society is viewed in terms of a social order maintained in large part by the structural power exercised by elites controlling vital resources. On the one hand, conflict is seen to be a basic driving force behind social change, as suggested by the dialectical model in Organicism. On the other hand, the social order is seen in terms of more or less ad hoc arrangements created and maintained to support and further the interests of powerful groups. Lee's (1983) study of the origins and dynamics of terrorism in Northern Ireland, for example, attempts to clarify the realities of the situation by demonstrating that beneath all the rhetoric and violence lies the problem of a status quo enforcing historically rooted class differences.

As Mills (especially 1959) and Lee have made clear, this mode of analysis leads directly to a humanist concern with social justice and the relationship between specific social arrangements, social problems, human suffering, and/or well being:

> To be an effective clinical sociologist, even on the micro level, one has to be able to perceive as accurately as possible the social controls, manipulations, exploitations, and opportunities in a given

social situation, and has to be willing to intervene in a constructive manner on behalf of one's client. (Lee, 1984:45)

As I point out elsewhere . . . (1978:14–15), "sociological scientists who wish to continue to function as creative contributors to their discipline do not sell or knowingly give their services to those whose activities they diagnose as antisocial". . . . What these points suggest is that a long-term professional career in clinical sociology can only be an ethical one, ethical in the sense of serving humane goals. (Lee, 1979:508–509)

Thus, conflict theory can be said to supply the ethical basis for clinical sociology.[3]

ECOLOGISM, COMPLEMENTARITY, AND PRACTICE THEORY

The Ecologist paradigm provides our most comprehensive perspective on the social order. It contributes three overarching principles of practice theory. One is that sociological interventions create social change by operationally redefining the situation (Straus, 1984), that is, changing the pattern of social relationships and, consequently, of action and interaction between and within acting units. Second, clinical sociology employs the "cultural approach" (Wirth, 1931): the conduct and perspective of the individual can only be understood in terms of the culture and social structures of the concatenation of social groups in which that person holds statuses. Third, clinical sociologists rely on the sociological imagination (Mills, 1959), analyzing the specific problem or predicament (Brenner, 1985) in social and historical context, with particular attention to the consequences of clients' location within the social order (Glassner and Freedman, 1979). Ecologism also supplies the methodological frame of sociological practice, described by Freedman and Rosenfeld (1983) as "integrated levels of focus." The clinical sociologist approaches the specific case, taking into account the total social ecology, viewing the context of problem and resolution in terms of the manifold social groups, layers, and levels of social organization in which the client individual or system participates.

Ecologism, then, does not dismiss but subsumes the four relatively adequate alternatives described by Pepper (1942). Sarbin (1977) implies that each may "fit" a specific part or aspect of the whole; for example, he suggests that Mechanism is valid for limited parts of the human context, such as muscular reflexes or the firing of nerves. Extending his adaptation of Pepper, we find that each world hypothesis provides the categories, logic and method for dealing with a specific aspect or level of social reality as indicated in Table 1.

Table 1

WORLD HYPOTHESES AND CLINICAL SOCIOLOGY PRACTICE

Hypothesis	Root Metaphor	Function	Domain
Formism	Similarity	Informs	Patterns
Mechanism	A Machine	Informs	Linkages
Contextualism	An Act	Guides	Actors
Organicism	An Organism	Guides	Systems
Ecologism	An Ecosystem	Frames	Contexts

Formism

Too abstract to serve as a guide for clinical practice in and of itself, Formism provides a framework for clear thinking while enabling us to analyze process and relationship in terms of pattern. Its domain is that of *categories*. Weber's "ideal type" method (Gerth and Mills, 1947) is framed within this world hypothesis as is cybernetics (Wiener, 1948), from which we derive the concept of feedback. Formism also supplies a less well-known conceptual tool useful at any level of analysis: Bateson's integration of symbolic logic (Whitehead and Russell, 1910–1913) with communications theory (Shannon and Weaver, 1949). Bateson's (1972) "theory of logical types" provides a method of differential analysis based on the proposition that a set, class, or category exists in its own right, but at a "higher" (more abstract) level than the elements constituting that set. In other words, an organization as "social system" exists at a higher level of logical type than the "actors" and "interactions" constituting that system. Difference in "logical type" has practical relevance; phenomena at different levels exhibit different properties and operate according to different principles. "Strategic Brief Therapy" and other methods developed by the Mental Research Institute in Palo Alto (Fisch et al., 1982) are based upon an integration of Bateson's analysis with cybernetics and an abstract (hence, compatible) form of General Systems Theory.

Defining primary group members as participants in an interactional system created by the pattern of their communications, the Palo Alto group focus on bringing about change at the "higher," system level to resolve even "personal" problems. For example, get group members to change whatever they have been doing about a problem and that problem will tend to go away because their attempts at solving it have only served to maintain the problem by directing effort at the wrong level of logical type, since the substantive problem is a lower order manifestation of the pattern of interpersonal exchanges. Symptoms are best eliminated by changing that pattern at its own level of logical type (Watzlawick et al., 1967). While its application to sociological intervention remains to be more systematically developed (Tiemann, 1985), this approach has already influenced contemporary practice on the part of many clinical sociologists, creating a modern role for an ancient perspective.

Voelkl and Coburn (1984), for example, attribute their "strategic communication approach to family therapy" to the Palo Alto group, although they seem more strongly influenced by Haley (1981), who has come to stress coalitions and structures of power within families over structures of communication. Formism structures their definition of the situation and overall strategy, but ecologically tinged Organicism seems to guide their substantive analysis of family dynamics. Thus, they view substantive complaints as metaphors for systems problems and seek to alleviate those problems by directing members to act in ways that will indirectly resolve underlying issues of power within the family. Their example is paradigmatic in showing that, whatever the central theoretical orientation brought to bear upon the problem, the clinical sociologist ends up following Pepper's (1942) dictum of "purity in theory but reasonable eclecticism in practice."

Mechanism

While a truly Mechanist approach to intervention might be derived from the "empiricist" tradition within behavioral psychology, socially oriented researchers and clinicians have long argued that people cannot be reduced to stimulus-response machines (Wirth, 1931; Sarbin, 1977; Straus, 1977). Therefore, while not providing an adequate basis for sociological practice, Mechanism takes its place in elucidating the *linkages* between elements of situations—in determining the objective facts of the case and whether correlations between observed phenomena can be ascribed to mere chance. Mechanism contributes the "hard science" component to sociological thought and practice. Quantitative methods and, more generally, commitment to precision and rigor in defining, operationalizing, measuring, and evaluating phenomena and relationships are essential to clinical sociology, although the mechanistic interpretation of social dynamics is generally treated with some scepticism.

Practitioners such as Brian Sherman (1985) specialize in the clinical application of methodology without adopting a Mechanist world view or its associated instrumental values. In any case, it is not necessary to follow Comte and Marx to the point of a deterministic materialism while accepting the premise that we cannot ignore biology, demographics, economics, the physical environment, or other material "facts of life." One must, in other words, take into account the material elements of social situations.

Another Mechanist concept, functional analysis, strongly informs sociological thinking at every level. Originally derived from an interpretation of the organism as a system of material parts—note, for example, Durkheim's (1964) use of "mechanical" to describe the form of solidarity marked by a high division of labor—functional analysis influences clinical sociology in two major ways. One is to provide the strategy of generating the operational definition of social phenomena by inquiring as to their functions, "What do they do?" In the classic sociological tradition this is usually specified further as "What is its function in terms of the whole?" Clinical sociologists, however, are also likely to draw upon Malinowski's (1944) variant, in which we ask "What basic human need does this serve?" Functional analysis, however, is not identical to "functionalism" as an explanatory paradigm wherein its essential Mechanism is subordinated to an Organicist systems logic, implying a recognition on the part of the vast majority of social scientists that Mechanism as such is inadequate to the task of explaining social phenomena.[4]

Functional analysis also informs practice in that we tend to make the assumption that form follows function or at least that some arrangements are better suited to carrying out specific functions than others. In this regard, Merton's (1968) concepts of functional alternatives and latent versus manifest functions have strongly influenced clinical sociological analysis. For example, Warren analyzes the problem of maintaining a professional division of labor between sociological researcher and therapist when interviewing mental patients:

> The clinical and research functions of interviewing tend to overlap, despite the interest of sociological researchers in avoiding clinical interpretations or interventions. These interviews indicate that being therapeutic is often as much a matter of function as intention, as much an issue of being cast into a role as taking one on. (1985:83)

While Warren leaves unasked and unanswered the question of what, if anything, could or should be done about such functional crossover, this is just one example—cautionary, in her particular case—of how functionalist analysis can inform sociological practice.

Contextualism

Contextualism provides the sociological clinician's basic logic and approach when dealing with discrete *social actors*, substantive interactions between actors, or the construction of joint conduct and consensus reality. Its strength lies in generating understandings concerning how things work (albeit not "why" they do so—a mechanistic question in which the strict contextualist has no interest). From the beginning contextualism has been associated with qualitative methods including case studies and other observational strategies (Lofland, 1976). There is a close fit, then, between contextualist social science and the need of the sociological clinician for tools facilitating the process of analyzing the emergence of the specific situation or problem, in asking how it has come about, in sensitizing us to process, contingency, and possibility at the substantive level.

Qualitative methods are used at every level of practice to construct a substantive model of the client's situation used to develop and guide intervention. Kleymeyer, for example, describes how he trained interviewers hired for a quantitative evaluation of a South American medical center's ambulatory care unit to do qualitative observation and interviews in their spare time, producing some 2,000 descriptions of problematic staff-client interactions, which he then coded and grouped into "emergent analytical categories relevant to patient's use and disuse of the health services being studied" (1979:594). When these findings were presented to them, medical school administrators encouraged Kleymeyer to implement an actual intervention project described in his paper; the original evaluation project, on the other hand, was never completed.

Contextualism supplies the concept of conduct, which is central to clinical sociology at the microsocial level (Wirth, 1931). The sociologist examines the client's conduct both in terms of how the person constructs actions and in terms of the social context of action. Contemporary practitioners often describe their approach as applying symbolic interactionism, since both analysis and intervention tend to focus on meanings, motivations, attitudes, personal culture, and taking the role of the other.

Depending on the particular contextualist paradigm being drawn upon, more or less attention may be placed on the structure of the situation, on the negotiation of intersubjective realities, or upon the strategies actors employ to accomplish their purposes. Hurvitz (1979) describes a symbolic interactionist approach to marital counseling focusing on discrepancies in how partners perceive their role and the role of the other, with the goal of working out joint meanings and lines of action. Church's (1985) sociotherapy with couples employs dramaturgical analysis and the "social construction of reality" perspective. In the author's own "social behavioral" approach, explicit attention is placed on the situated nature of conduct and the ecological structure of its context, while the focus of intervention remains getting the client to change his or her act from the inside, so to speak, utilizing a cooperative form of hypnosis to reconstruct self-interaction (Straus, 1977, 1982).

Organicism

When focus shifts to organized collectivities—conventionally regarded as the sociologist's proper domain—Organicism supplies the most useful, hence prevalent, categories and analytical strategies. Had *World Hypotheses* been written subsequent to the development of general systems theory (von Bertalanffy, 1968), Pepper might well have described the root metaphor of Organicism as *systems*.

Many of the weaknesses he finds in this hypothesis seem to have been corrected or at least shored up by contemporary systems theory. In any case, an Organicist paradigm based upon the modern conceptualization of "open systems" operating according to the principles of general systems theory (Katz and Kahn, 1966) has become the guiding perspective for clinical sociologists working with collectivities from the level of secondary groups through the most complex formal organizations.

Those sociologists, however, who work within two earlier paradigms emerging out of 19th Century Organicism, structure-functionalism and Marxism, generally do not engage in clinical sociology. Practitioners adopting some variant of Parsons' (1951) analysis are more comfortable with the "applied research and policy consultation" role employing a paradigm of the adaptive upgrading of a generally benign status quo (e.g., Freeman et al., 1983). On the other hand, Marxists of the Old or New Left, tend to favor an "activist" role (Glassner and Freedman, 1979). For them, anything less than social revolution is unacceptable due to the inherent contradictions of capitalist society. Clinical sociologists tend to steer a middle course between these positions, seeking to resolve contradictions while conducting interventions designed to change or upgrade the structure and function of the client system. While some are more grounded in functionalism, adopting a "technical" discourse or approach and others are more "politicized" in orientation, their focus is upon changing the patterns of action and reaction forming the operational definition of the situation (Straus, 1984).

By defining relatively stable patterns of interpersonal conduct as social systems, Organicism enables us to deal with the situation at a higher level of logic type—as an integrated whole rather than an emergent aggregate of joint action. This concept of an integrated system as a unit of social life is one of Organicism's major contributions to practice. At the same time, Organicism contributes the principle of dialectical analysis, in which the sociologist studies contradictions within or between systems and how they are integrated into the organic whole. Dialectical analysis, we should note, may be conceptualized either in conventionally Marxian terms of contradictions between groups within the formal organization or in the mixed metaphor favored by contemporary "systems theorists" where these matters are described in terms of feedback, homeostasis, and negative entropy.

Exemplifying this latter type, Capelle's (1979) "systems analysis" treats client systems at any level of complexity in terms of boundaries, inputs, internal process and structure (including both developmental stages and subsystems), outputs, feedback, and articulation with other systems. On the other hand, Benello's (1982) description of his experiences in attempting to develop democratic, self-managed business organizations reveals an underlying systems model seeking to grapple with problems of contradictions self-consciously defined in politicized terms (as opposed to the technical discourse employed by more conventional systems theorists such as Capelle). Gutknecht even more explicitly integrates Ecologist concerns with culture, power and authority into an expanded "systems theory perspective [which] allows the clinical sociologist to operate at a variety of levels, drawing connections among them" and offers a unique, sociological base for effective organizational development practice (1984:103).

In many other cases, clinical sociologists working at this "meso" level incorporate these Organicist concepts, but apply them more generally as a method for systematically tracking dynamic relationships between structure and function, between elements of the whole, between acting unit and environment, and between units of social organization, regardless of whether or not they are considered to be "systems" in the technical sense of the word. Rice (1985) describes a rational planning model for public policy along these lines. Once again, while such practitioners draw heavily on concepts and strategies appropriate to the level of social organization being dealt with, there is explicit attention to integration of levels of focus and the ecological context of the problematic situation.

Ecologism

While many of the interventions we have described exhibit an overtly ecological awareness, when the sociologist turns attention to the broadest social canvas, entire *contexts* such as the great institutional structures of a society or of our planet as a whole, the assumption of systemic integration falters and microsocial contextualism clearly does not apply. Consequently, the clinical macrosociologist tends to fall back onto some form of critical analysis focusing on the arrangements between interest groups (Lee, 1979, 1983). Ecologism is also the model of preference in certain other types of clinical sociological endeavor.

Jones (1984) describes the role of "environmental sociologists" working as consultants to architects and community planners in terms of the Ecologist principles that (a) there is a reciprocal, interactive relationship between conduct and physical settings, and its corollary that (b) all physical designs emerge from social processes. Going beyond the role of sociological consultant, Preister and Kent describe an "issue-centered" approach to social impact management focusing on working with extant social networks in a way that "emphasizes the ecological process working with rhythms and multilevels of interaction. The ecological focus replaces the mechanistic and hierarchical focus of past sociological concentration . . . [and] offers a model for intervention at the community and organizational levels" (1984:121).

Ecologism, however, transcends both direct concern with environment issues and the macrosocial, policy oriented research exemplified by Lee. As we have seen, ecologically informed practice at any level relies heavily on strategies and concepts derived from this world hypothesis. Where problems of intergroup relations are central, however, an Ecologist perspective is utilized directly. This can take the "technical" orientation, as in conflict intervention (Laue, 1981). For example, Laue successfully piloted a "Negotiated Investment Strategy" in Gary, Indiana wherein the mayor, governor, and representatives from the city's major industry, U.S. Steel, were brought together to work out a framework for cooperation in dealing with major issues of joint concern (described in Fritz, 1985). In other cases, due to the nature of the problem and/or the practitioner's orientation, a more politicized discourse drawn from conflict theory will be employed. An exemplary paper by Hoffman, for example, describes working as an "acculturation specialist" with Cuban refugees in Los Angeles utilizing a model of "empowerment . . . the provision of information which is useful to help reach the goals and objectives desired by the client" as opposed to the model of behavior modification adopted by social workers dealing with the same population (1985:55). Other clinical sociologists engaging in cross-cultural interventions similarly tend to directly rely on the Ecologist perspective.

DISCUSSION

Practice is the ultimate test and corrective for theory; sociological practice has the effect of forcing one to recognize the contrived and partial nature of our theories about the world: there are no pigeonholes in reality, only in our schemata for reality. Analysis of the author's own career development and others' published and unpublished remarks suggest that clinical sociologists, if not initially (being trained within the theoretically Balkanized context of academic sociology), increasingly come to recognize that all theories are incomplete maps of overwhelmingly complex territories. While they might work from one or the other perspective with regard to any specific case or type of case, mature clinical sociologists do so in full cognizance of the overarching ecological frame of social life. Whatever their formal theoretical stance or discourse, in practice they come to, at least implicitly, incorporate Ecologist principles and operate in terms of integrated levels of focus.

We need to be realistic both in practice and in speaking about practice. Different hypotheses inspire different strategies, but in the end they boil down to accomplishing the same task of changing the operational definition of the situation (Straus, 1984). For example, while most sociologists working with individual social actors tend to employ a Contextualist analysis, a minority (e.g., Capelle, 1979; Lippitt, 1985) prefer to define individuals as systems and employ an Organicist discourse. How does this affect their practice?

The Contextualist, for whom order and stability are problematic, would focus on the divergent sequences leading up to the fixated line of action adopted by the subject, while the Organicist would assume that problematic conduct flows from the client's orderly systems of relationship. In either case, the sociologist would form a strategy to get the subject to act differently and to establish an appropriate support structure within the person's context. The Contextualist would be more likely to focus on redefining the operational situation through the subject's own action, the Organicist on restructuring the context. However, unless invited to intervene at the level of the interpersonal context (as in family therapy or doing stress management with organizations) one generally must begin with the subject's own act; even when one is in a position to intervene directly in the interpersonal system, implementation requires working with the individual participants (Goldman, 1984; Gutknecht, 1984). The difference, in other words, would mainly be in how one defines the change process, interprets, understands and talks about situation and intervention. Contextualist and Organicist might disagree in theory but they would end up doing much the same thing, as can be seen from the literature.

Why? Because, in practice, theory is merely a tool for making sense of the empirical situation; the test of practice theory lies in results and results depend on changing that situation as it happens to be, however we define it. The sociologist must take into account the ecological structure of the situation and deal with both the relatively autonomous conduct of the social actor and the definitions of the situation imposed by the socially organized context.

Our point, then, is not that radically different strategies are utilized depending on the analytic perspective employed, but rather that Ecologism best describes the whole, while the four relatively adequate alternatives represent divergent lines of theoretical development systematically explicating and defining points of leverage and appropriate strategies for dealing with specific aspects of that whole. Problems centering around the relatively autonomous conduct of individual actors dealing with their contexts are most profitably dealt with through the Contextualist metaphor, while complex phenomena characterized by relatively stable patterns of relationship between acting units tend to exhibit integrated, systems properties and are most suitably treated in terms of Organicism. In the first case we are dealing with the emergence of orderly relationships through situated action, in the second we are dealing with the emergence of situated action as a consequence of ongoing, orderly relationships. These views are complementary not contradictory; each selects out, highlights or downplays certain aspects of the whole according to the logical structure of their perspective. However, where the sociologist is dealing with interpersonal or intergroup problems of conflict over power or cultural difference—that is, when joint action becomes problematic or relationships themselves are central issues of concern—both perspectives falter and must be supplemented with Ecologist concepts. As a "second order" world hypothesis, Ecologism fills in gaps between these complementary alternatives and provides an expanded frame of reference subsuming the others.[5]

Granted that eclecticism is confusing; practice, as Pepper (1942) remarks, involves other than cognitive considerations, so that pragmatism (as well as the background and predilection of the individual practitioner) often overrides both theoretical purity and any neat categorizations the analyst will make. Generalization of an Ecologist frame represents a strategy for minimizing self-contradictions stemming from the eclecticism of practice while providing our best approximation to the true complexity of social life. Elucidation of this theoretical framework, it is hoped, will both enhance the subdiscipline's claims to professional validity and provide a more solid base for training within and the future development of the field.

NOTES

1. This discussion of Ecologism does not seek to develop the world hypothesis in as systematic a matter as Pepper's analysis of the other four. It remains uncertain as to whether Ecologism can meet all of Pepper's (1942) criteria for adequacy; however, our purpose here is to identify the practice theory of clinical sociology as opposed to formal philosophical discourse.

2. Evolution toward a single, tightly coupled system encompassing the total biosphere is complicated or neutralized by various anabolic and self-limiting processes as well as the tendency of open systems to "break" and reform into new systems as internal and external conditions change (Prigogine and Stengers, 1984).

3. Two other major theoretical paradigms, exchange theory (Blau, 1967; Homans, 1973) and "human ecology" (Hawley, 1950) are framed within an Ecologist perspective. Both are drawn upon by sociological clinicians, exchange theory in particular (Cohen, 1981). However, as their application is generally subordinated to the overarching Chicago School and Conflict perspectives and space is limited, we shall not elaborate on their contribution at this time.

4. As a humanist, von Bertalanffy (1968) recognized and decried the Mechanist interpretation of systems. While evolution toward a more thoroughgoingly Organicist systems theory can be seen in writings of structural-functionalist exemplars, theirs remains a mixed paradigm. Mechanism's continuing influence on systems thinking is critiqued by Glassner and Freedman (1979) in terms of the computer as root metaphor.

5. Previously, the author (Straus, 1984) identified four levels of sociological intervention: persons, groups, organizations, and social worlds. Persons represent the ideal type of an acting unit dealing with its environment; conduct, or social action is the primary focus of Contextualist social theory. Organizations, on the other hand, represent an ideal type of integrated, multicentric human system and are the focus of Organicist social theory. Primary groups may be considered either as structures of joint action or as relatively integrated systems and treated in terms of either perspective according to the needs or interests of the sociologist. Communities or whole societies as ecological contexts comprised of both integrated and nonintegrated acting units are directly handled through Ecologist paradigms, while social worlds might be treated either in terms of integration or joint action of emergent collectivities and may be conceptualized in either Organicist or Ecologist terms.

REFERENCES

Bateson, Gregory
    1972   Steps to an Ecology of Mind. New York: Ballantine.
    1979   Mind and Nature. New York: Dutton.
Benello, C. George
    1982   "The experience of developing worker management," Clinical Sociology Review 2:93–114.
Blau, Peter M.
    1967   Exchange and Power in Social Life. New York: Wiley.

Blumer, Herbert N.
    1969   Symbolic Interactionism. Englewood Cliffs, NJ: Prentice-Hall.
Bohr, Niels.
    1958   Atomic Physics and Human Knowledge. New York: Wiley.
Brenner, Berthold
    1985   "Social problems as affliction and social problems as hazard," Clinical Sociology
              Review 3:109–115.
Capelle, Ronald G.
    1979   Changing Human Systems. Toronto: International Human Systems Institute.
Church, Nathan
    1985   "Sociotherapy with marital couples," Clinical Sociology Review 3:116–128.
Cohen, Harry
    1981   Connections. Ames: Iowa State University Press.
Duhl, Bunny
    1983   From the Inside Out and Other Metaphors. New York: Brunner/Mazel.
Durkheim, Emile
    1964   The Division of Labor in Society. New York: Free Press.
Faris, Robert and H. Warren Dunham
    1965   Mental Disorders in Urban Areas. Chicago: University of Chicago Press.
Freedman, Jonathan A. and Pincus Rosenfeld
    1983   "Clinical sociology: the system as client." Paper presented at the joint meetings
              of the Eastern Sociological Society and Clinical Sociology Association, Baltimore.
Freeman, H. E., R. Dynes, P. H. Rossi and W. F. Whyte, eds.
    1983   Applied Sociology. San Francisco: Jossey-Bass.
Fisch, Richard, John H. Weakland and Lynn Segal
    1982   The Tactics of Change: Doing Therapy Briefly. San Francisco: Jossey-Bass.
Fritz, Jan.
    1985   "Communities: making them work." Pp. 136–152 in R. Straus, Using Sociology.
              Bayside, NY: General-Hall.
Gerth, Hans and C. W. Mills
    1947   From Max Weber. New York: Free Press.
Glassner, Barry and Jonathan A. Freedman
    1979   Clinical Sociology. New York: Longman.
Goldman, Kathryn L.
    1984   "Stress management: the importance of organizational context," Clinical Sociology
              Review 2:133–136.
Gondolf, Edward W.
    1985   "Teaching clinical sociology: the introductory course," Clinical Sociology Review
              3:143–149.
Gutknecht, Douglas B.
    1984   "Organizational development," Clinical Sociology Review 2:94–108.
Haley, Jay
    1981   Reflections on Therapy. Chevy Chase, MD: Family Therapy Institute of Washing-
              ton, DC.
Hawley, A. H.
    1950   Human Ecology. New York: Ronald Press.
Hoffman, Fred
    1985   "Clinical sociology and the acculturation specialty," Clinical Sociology Review
              3:50–58.
Homans, G. C.
    1973   "Fundamental social processes," in N.J. Smelser, ed., Sociology: An Introduction,
              2nd ed. New York: Wiley.

Hurvitz, Nathan
    1979   "The sociologist as a marital and family therapist," American Behavioral Scientist 22:557–576.
Jones, Bernie
    1984   "Doing sociology with the design professions," Clinical Sociology Review 2:109–119.
Katz, Daniel and Robert L. Kahn
    1966   The Social Psychology of Organizations. New York: Wiley.
Kleymeyer, Charles A.
    1979   "Putting field methods to work," American Behavioral Scientist 22:589–608.
Kuhn, Thomas
    1970   The Structure of Scientific Revolutions, 2nd ed. Cambridge, MA: MIT Press.
Laue, James H.
    1981   "Conflict intervention." Pp. 67–90 in Olsen and Micklin, eds., Handbook of Applied Sociology. New York: Praeger.
Lee, Alfred McClung
    1978   Sociology for Whom? New York: Oxford University Press.
    1979   "The services of clinical sociology," American Behavioral Scientist 22:487–511.
    1983   Terrorism in Northern Ireland. Bayside, NY: General-Hall.
    1984   "Overcoming barriers to clinical sociology," Clinical Sociology Review 2:42–50.
Lippitt, Ronald
    1985   "Six problem-solving contexts for intervention decision making," Clinical Sociology Review 3:39–49.
Lofland, John
    1976   Doing Social Life. New York: Wiley-Interscience.
Malinowski, Bronislaw
    1944   A Scientific Theory of Culture and Other Essays. Chapel Hill: University of North Carolina Press.
Mead, George Herbert
    1938   The Philosophy of the Act. Chicago: University of Chicago Press.
Merton, Robert K.
    1968   Social Theory and Social Structure, enlarged ed. New York: Free Press.
Mills, C.W.
    1959   The Sociological Imagination. New York: Oxford.
Park, R. E., E. W. Burgess and R. D. Mackenzie, eds.
    1925   The City. Chicago: University of Chicago Press.
Parsons, Talcott
    1951   The Social System. Glencoe, IL: Free Press.
Pepper, Stephen
    1942   World Hypotheses. Berkeley: University of California Press.
Priester, Kevin and James A. Kent
    1984   "Clinical sociological perspectives on social impacts," Clinical Sociology Review 2:120–132.
Prigogine, Ilya and Isabelle Stengers
    1984   Order Out of Chaos. New York: Bantam.
Rice, Thomas
    1985   "American public policy formation and implementation." Pp. 153–171 in R. Straus, Using Sociology: An Introduction from the Clinical Perspective. Bayside, NY: General-Hall.
Sarbin, Theodore
    1977   "Contextualism." Pp. 1–41 in A. Landfield, ed., Nebraska Symposium on Motivation, Vol. 25. Lincoln: University of Nebraska Press.

Scott, Robert
    1971   The Making of Blind Men. Princeton, NJ: Transaction Books.
Shannon, C. E. and W. Weaver
    1949   The Mathematical Theory of Communications. Urbana: University of Illinois Press.
Sherman, Brian
    1985   "Doing sociological research that counts." Pp. 23–43 in R. Straus, ed., Using
            Sociology: An Introduction from the Clinical Perspective. Bayside, NY: General-
            Hall.
Simmel, Georg
    1950   The Sociology of Georg Simmel. Kurt Wolff, ed. and trans. New York: Free Press.
Smith, Walter Robinson
    1917   An Introduction to Educational Sociology. New York: Houghton Mifflin.
Straus, Roger A.
    1977   "The life-change process: weight loss and other enterprises of personal transfor-
            mation, including hypnosis, behavior modification and scientology." Ph.D. Dis-
            sertation. Ann Arbor, MI: University Microfilms.
    1981   "The theoretical frame of symbolic interactionism: a contextualist social science,"
            Symbolic Interaction 4, no.2:61–72.
    1982   "Clinical sociology on the one-to-one level: a social behavioral approach to coun-
            seling," Clinical Sociology Review 1:59–74.
    1984   "Changing the definition of the situation: toward a theory of sociological interven-
            tions," Clinical Sociology Review 2:51–63.
    1985   "Using social theory to make sense out of life." Pp. 4–22 in R. Straus, Using
            Sociology: An Introduction from the Clinical Perspective. Bayside, NY: General-
            Hall.
Sumner, William Graham
    1906   Folkways, reprint ed. 1980. New York: New American Library.
Thomas, William I.
    1923   The Unadjusted Girl. Boston: Little, Brown.
Thomas, William I. and Dorothy S. Thomas
    1938   The Child in America: Behavior Problems and Programs. New York: Knopf.
Tiemann, Adrian
    1985   "Discursions and excursions," Clinical Sociology Newsletter 7, no. 3:1–2.
Veblen, Thorstein
    1899   The Theory of the Leisure Class. New York: Macmillan.
von Bertalanffy, L.
    1968   General Systems Theory. New York: George Braziller.
Voelkl, Gary M. and Kenneth Colburn, Jr.
    1984   "The clinical sociologist as family therapist," Clinical Sociology Review 2:64–77.
Warren, Carol A. B.
    1985   "Clinical and research interviewing in sociology," Clinical Sociology Review
            3:72–84.
Watzlawick, Paul, J. H. Beavin and D. D. Jackson
    1967   Pragmatics of Human Communication. New York: Norton.
Whitehead, A. N. and B. Russell
    1910–
    1913   Principia Mathematica, 2nd ed. Cambridge: Cambridge University Press.
Wiener, Norbert
    1948   Cybernetics or Control and Communication in the Animal and the Machine. New
            York: Wiley.
Wirth, Louis
    1931   "Clinical sociology," American Journal of Sociology 37:49–66.

Participatory Research: Methodology and Critique

Richard A. Couto
Vanderbilt University

ABSTRACT

The epistemology of participatory research relates knowledge to action, especially the production of knowledge and political action to redress inequality. This paper identifies characteristics of participatory research and describes three research efforts which exemplify them in varying degrees. The tenets of participatory research suggest guidelines for degrees, the conduct of inquiry for social scientists interested in the relation of research to increased political participation and improved human services.

The relation of knowledge and action, along with other epistemological considerations of various research methodologies, has occupied the attention of social scientists. Much of the training of social scientists is in fact socialization to the canons of a discipline which require their intelligent use and knowledge of their comparative merits and limits. The distinction of fact and value is generally as far as most graduate students go in plumbing the philosophical depths of their discipline. Often the "value free" research these graduate students produce later as practitioners of a discipline is understood as innocent of politics and objective in any implications for action.

The disciplines of social science, in general, preserve a place for dissent from their dominant paradigms and their practice. Thus, one finds discussion of the relation of fact and value, of the value-ladened assumptions of "value free" research, and of the ontology beneath every epistemology. Equally problematic for a few researchers is the relation of knowledge to action.

Correspondence to: Richard A. Couto, Center for Health Services, Vanderbilt University, Nashville, TN 37232.

Participatory research is a methodology that deals explicitly with the relation of knowledge and action. The exponents of this methodology are critical of the political correlates of the standard methodologies of the social sciences, especially survey research, and espouse a different set of political correlates for research (Fals Borda, 1979; Hall, 1981, 1984; ICAE, 1980; LeBoterf, 1983). The tenets of participatory research are important for all social scientists who understand the production and dissemination of information as an intervention in a social and political process. In addition, these tenets are important for social scientists who value political interventions to reduce inequalities in society and to increase the ability of relatively powerless groups to improve their situation. As an introduction to participatory research, this paper suggests some of the characteristics of this methodology and discusses three hybrid examples of participatory research.

PARTICIPATORY RESEARCH

Participatory research assumes knowledge is related to power and power is related to change or to maintenance of the status quo. It borrows heavily from Marx and contemporary social theorists such as Paulo Freire and incorporates class analysis. Its central concerns are research, knowledge production, and empowerment related to the position of oppressed people, poor people, people with political or economic disadvantage.

One of the key assumptions of participatory research is that it will lead to change *by* the people who do research. Advocates thus distinguish participatory research from other research which assumes that change will come, if it comes about at all, by the action of people who read the work of others. The participatory research adherents eschew that hope for the intention of mobilizing people, especially those affected by the problem under study, in the process of doing the research. Research and action thus form a continuum and are part of a single process of political change.

There are several clear and distinguishing characteristics of participatory research:

(a) The problem under study and the decision to study it have origins in the community affected by the problem;
(b) The goal of the research is political or social change derived from the information gathered;
(c) Local people control the process of problem definition, information gathering and decisions about action following from the information; and
(d) Local people and professional researchers are equals in the research process. They are both researchers and learners.

These characteristics distinguish participatory research from survey research and other methodologies in several ways. First, there is more emphasis on researchers as learners. The participatory research process is a learning process for all involved, not a process whereby some people accumulate information about other people. Thus, the subject-object dichotomy is bridged and the reflexive nature of human interaction, whereby I am affected by those I intend to affect, is acknowledged and applied to research professionals as well. Participatory research is a dialogue over time and a mobilization of human resources for information gathering that may lead to action.

Second, the action focus differentiates participatory research from other forms of research. Participatory research is intended to be of direct and immediate benefit to a community and the research process is under local control. People learn in the process of doing. They are not merely applying what they know already. What information do we need? How do we go about getting this information? Who is going to get the information? What does the information mean? Is it enough information? How do we interpret the information? What action seems reasonable in the light of what we have learned? These are questions of process decided in open discussion among everyone involved.

Qualifying the Model

There are several anamolies, if not contradictions, about participatory research. For example, one of the functions of participatory research is to unmask the myth of science and to validate people's knowledge (Hall, 1975). But in practice this is very difficult to do without some person outside the community, with professional credentials, lending assistance or credence to local knowledge and claims about its validity.

The role of the outside expert is important despite the emphasis on local people in research. This role is not easy to integrate in local research efforts. There is the taint on the professional credentials of a person who lends assistance and credence to research efforts which stretch or violate the canons of a discipline and which relate to an apparent political position. Participatory research requires researchers to do precisely this to the dismay or horror of some colleagues. A professional researcher may deal with this difficulty by fashioning local residents into neophyte researchers to imitate the canons of a discipline and thus compromise the validity of local knowlege. Or a researcher may risk his or her professional credentials by participating in unorthodox research methods which then compromise the authority and ability of that person to lend credence to the information local people produce.

In addition, there is almost an inherent contradiction in writing a methodology of participatory research and emphasizing the origin of this research in the community. In the main, professionals read and write such material and provide "models" which may seriously compromise the character of participatory research and its origin in the community. In specifying a methodology of participatory research, we also create a new field of expertise with canons and strictures. This only enhances the role of the professional and creates new grounds for dichotomies which participatory research seeks to bridge.

Given the importance of the professional and the researcher from outside the community in participatory research, it is incumbent on us to recognize that role. Papers such as this are read primarily by professional researchers and we need to take cognizance that our role may make participatory research possible even as it compromises it. Professionals and researchers have an important role in the assistance of the production of information that may lead to change. We will be better prepared to fulfill that role if we focus on the characteristics of participatory research that we can preserve despite our participation rather than on its community character which we jeopardize by our support.

It may be useful to speak of participatory research as a hybrid research effort which combines survey research and methodological tenets from participatory observation. Three examples will suggest hybrids of survey research and participatory observation that exemplify the role of an outside researcher assisting another group to undertake change. This, in turn, offers guidelines for the role of professional researchers in participatory research.

Applying the Model

The Yellow Creek Concerned Citizens (YCCC) is a community organization in Bell County in Eastern Kentucky started in response to the pollution of Yellow Creek from a municipal sewerage plant inadequate to treat the waste material from a tannery in Middlesboro, Kentucky. After a long process of political conflict on the local and state level, the YCCC decided to conduct a household survey of people along the creek to determine illnesses that might be related to the contamination of the creek. Many good features came from this survey. Local residents acting as surveyors received 98% cooperation, which is a much higher rate of response than is ordinarily expected. The survey provided YCCC members new anecdotal information on the pollution problem and the opportunity to share their views and efforts with their neighbors. The survey was on many counts a large success.

However, the survey also demonstrates important limits to the methodology and its place in a political conflict. First, community residents, with outside assistance, constructed a survey that was too long to code and analyze adequately. Subsamples of the total number of people interviewed when controlled for such factors as smoking or age proved too small for adequate analysis. Most responses were not included in the final analysis and responses to questions related to the appearance and smells of the creek proved to be as important in demonstrating a nuisance as the effort to establish a causal link of exposure and illness. Second, the use of many different volunteers meant incorrect coding and a host of errors that required enormous amounts of time to rectify. The point is that the relation of information to action needs to be kept in mind in devising the survey instrument which must be as simple as possible in light of its purpose. Participatory research is not a scientific study even though sound principles of survey research and sampling can and should be observed.

Undertaking this form of study was a risk to the political goal of YCCC, which was the cessation of dumping untreated sewerage and industrial waste into Yellow Creek. Such a study shifts the grounds for cessation from nuisance and quality of life questions to the health and illness of people. In addition, such a study may open up another fight for a community group which generally has barely enough resources to deal with one conflict at a time. Often the community group is forced to defend their findings before a professional audience, such as epidemiologists (Gibbs, no date). In such a case, the conservative bias of epidemiology as a science becomes the grounds on which the argument turns even though it is precisely this bias which makes some alternative research necessary to establish reasonable grounds, short of death and illness, on which to halt pollution.

In retrospect, this survey was only one part of a political conflict and served many useful purposes. The survey was almost forced upon YCCC by their critics who denied a problem and challenged YCCC to prove a problem. YCCC demonstrated integrity in the conduct of the survey and a good-faith effort to document the problem and this helped win greater public approval. The survey established reasonable, if not scientific grounds, for improving conditions on Yellow Creek. YCCC has gained much as a result of their efforts, of which the survey was part, including a new water utility system and electoral victories in city government. The resolution of the central issue awaits long-delayed court action (Couto, 1986a).

A second example of hybrid participatory research involves survey research undertaken in six rural, low-income communities to establish a baseline from which to measure the effectiveness of a community-based intervention in maternal and infant health and development. University students worked with local women and trained them in interviewing techniques and sampling methods. In addition, they supervised the completion and coding of questionnaires to guarantee uniform responses and to minimize mistakes. The questionnaire was shortened, in light of the Yellow Creek survey experience, to include items of central importance to the community-based interventions, but again proved too long.

The results proved important in several ways. The survey provided the six programs criteria with which to judge if they were serving the most important needs of the community and the families with the greatest need. It provided each of the programs information with which to judge differences in the behavior and outcomes among their clients compared with a community average or profile. It also provided information to document the hunger, poverty, and inadequate health insurance of women and children in each community.

The consequences of the process are as important as the results of the survey. Local women were employed to conduct the survey. These women were identified according to their ability, including leadership potential, and concern with local issues. This survey was an orientation for them to the issues of maternal and infant health in their communities. Subsequently, when funds became available, many of the women who conducted the survey took employment in the program to extend its services to low-income pregnant women and mothers with infants (Couto, 1985a, 1986b).

A third hybrid example of participatory research is a study of the homeless in Nashville, which became part of the formation of a proposal to establish a health care clinic for homeless people there. Social service agency heads, responsible for the conduct of programs and services on behalf of the homeless, conducted several enumeration studies of the homeless. This involved waking at 4:00 a.m. and visiting shelters, single room occupancy hotels, jails, alleys, abandoned cars, the underpart of bridges and the other sleeping places of homeless people to count them.

Eventually, this enumeration provided information on the numbers and demographics of the city's homeless people to advocacy groups and the city and social service agencies' directors. This, of course, is very important. But, equally important, the process of enumeration organized a set of agency directors around the issue of homelessness, informed them about the homeless, and prepared them to cooperate and to take advantage of opportunities to introduce new services for the homeless. Such an opportunity came with a request from the Pew and Johnson Foundations for proposals to conduct health services for the homeless. Several agency staff members collaborated in the successful proposal and implemented new and integrated services for the homeless. These achievements flowed from the cooperation and information entailed in the enumeration (Couto, 1985b).

CONCLUSION

Obviously, the three examples are very different. The Yellow Creek comes closest to the model of participatory research; the Nashville homeless study is least similar to that methodology. In the first, people directly affected by the problem designed and implemented the information gathering. In the latter, the people directly affected by homelessness were studied by others who designed and implemented the information gathering. On the other hand, in the first, community people attempted to replicate a scientific study. In the latter, the study was simple and descriptive, with little effort at analysis or correlation.

Because of this, the study of the homeless in Nashville was the least expensive; computer time and staff time required to compile and code large amounts of data increased the cost of the other two research efforts. The three examples also differ according to who initiated the information gathering and why it was important to them.

Mindful of these differences, we may still make some generalizations from these examples. First, elements of survey research and participatory observation can combine in various manners to form hybrids of participatory research. Second, professionals can play a role in participatory research as they did in these cases, but this almost guarantees a hybrid methodology. To prevent the boundaries of participatory research from becoming too fluid and ill defined, these cases suggest questions to ask of research that relate it to the model of participatory research.

Does the research focus on a particular problem rather than on characteristics of the people studied?

Does a problem of the community or a hypothesis of the researcher drive the study?

Is there education, training, and involvement of people besides the outside researcher and staff?

Does the research include dialogue over time about the problem, information gathering, the findings and appropriate action to take?

Does this dialogue include, as equal partners, the people affected by the problem and the professionals and researchers?

Is the research replicable and ordinarily affordable by a group with few resources?

These questions may help us to stay focused on the promise of participatory research, even as its expression varies. That promise entails the link between knowledge and action and concentrates on information gathering that is accountable to the people under study, if not under their control. Finally, that promise entails new roles for researchers and those researched as equal partners, dependent on each other, to see that we act on what we come to know.

REFERENCES

Couto, Richard A.
  1985a   Fair Starts for Children: An Assessment of Rural Poverty and Maternal and Infant Health. Nashville: Center for Health Services, Vanderbilt University.
  1985b   "Health care and the homeless of Nashville: dealing with a problem without a definition." Urban Resources 2, no. 2:17–23.
  1986a   "Failing health and new prescriptions: community-based approaches to environmental health risks." in Carole E. Hill (ed.), Contemporary Health Policy Issues and Alternatives: An Applied Social Science Perspective. Athens: University of Georgia Press.

1986b   "Appalachian explanations for America's new poverty." Forum for Applied Re-
           search and Public Policy 1, no. 2:101–110.
Fals Borda, Orlando.
1979   "The problem of investigating reality in order to transform it." Dialectical An-
           thropology 4, (Spring):33–35.
Gibbs, Lois Marie
no date   Health Surveys: Think Before You Count. Arlington, VA: Citizen's Clearinghouse
           for Hazardous Wastes.
Hall, Bud L.
1975   "Participatory research, an approach for change." Convergence 8, no. 2:24–32.
1981   "Participatory research, popular knowledge and power: a personal reflection."
           Convergence 14, no. 3:6–19.
1984   "Research, commitment and action: the role of participatory research." International
           Review of Education 30, no. 3:289–300.
International Council for Adult Education.
1980   Report on the International Forum on Participatory Research. Toronto: International
           Council for Adult Education.
LeBoterf, Guy
1983   "Reformulating participatory research." Assignment Children 63/64:168–194.

Practice of Clinical Sociology

An Alcoholism Program for Hispanics

Fred Hoffman
Scientific Analysis Corporation

ABSTRACT

An alcoholism recovery home was established for Mariel Cuban refugees, but client selection procedures and program were inappropriate. A viable alternative was found with Hispanic Alcoholics Anonymous, and the program was converted to this approach. Problems of professionalism and the clinical relationship to AA emerged. Clinical interventions are inappropriate in the AA context, but sociologists may adopt the ethnographer's role. Exploration of the transcultural adaptation of AA ideas for an Hispanic population proved therapeutic when clients were placed in roles such as collaborator and cultural informant. Sociologists involved with groups in which clinical roles are inappropriate may find subjective refuge in the role of ethnographic researcher.

Cross-cultural prevention and treatment of alcoholism are not new, but the development of viable programs for most unacculturated populations has been delayed due to funding agencies' lack of commitment and the absence of an effective, practical approach. Appropriate programs had to wait until the ethnic enclaves having alcoholism problems could evolve means for helping their own members overcome drinking. After that it became possible for clinical sociologists, using the "culture broker" approach (Hoffman, 1985; Weidman, 1975, 1983), to assist in the creation of cross-cultural programs to serve individuals who are not included in the ethnic enclaves.

Although alcoholism prevention and treatment exist for Hispanics in the United States, most such programs are designed to serve English-speaking or bilingual "Chicanos" and Puerto Ricans. The new Hispanic immigrants largely constitute an unserved population, ineligible for services due to their illegal status and undocumented residence. When 125,000 Hispanic immigrants sud-

---

Correspondence to: Fred Hoffman, Scientific Analysis Corporation, P.O. Box 26642, Los Angeles, CA 90026.

denly arrived in South Florida from the Cuban port of Mariel in Spring 1980, the need emerged for new forms of human services programs, among them alcoholism treatment.

Alcocer (1982) reported that Cuban immigrants seemed to have lower rates of problem drinking than other Hispanic populations, but this was based on study of immigrants who arrived prior to the Mariel influx. Page et al. (1985: 324) found an unusually strong pattern of denial of intoxication and habitual abuse among Cuban males, particularly among older Cuban males. Alcoholism among Cuban immigrants is a much greater problem than had been supposed.

As soon as the Mariel wave of Cuban immigration began, the Miami Mental Health Center's Substance Abuse Unit felt the impact. Amaya (1983:37) described the new arrivals:

> Some alcoholics arrived in Miami misdiagnosed, labeled as psychotic and brought straight from hospital beds to the dock involuntarily, and completely separated from their families. Others came to the boatlift straight from the prisons where they had been imprisoned for some crime committed while under the influence of alcohol or other drugs. The saddest cases were those who were manipulated to join the boatlift by their own families because the family was tired of their addictive behavior and wanted to get rid of them. There were also a few who managed to join the boatlift in a chemical blackout only to become aware of their situation when the alcohol or other drugs wore off and they found themselves in the middle of the ocean suffering from the effects of withdrawal.

These refugees' drinking problems progressed after they arrived in the host country. Sudden freedom was accompanied by loneliness, unfamiliarity with the language and customs, and unemployment. Thousands of refugees whose prospects for resettlement were poor remained in refugee camps and many, alcoholics and others, were turned out by their sponsors and compelled to live on the streets or returned to federal custody. According to Amaya, during the first year of the Marielitos' presence in Miami there occurred "at least 27 murders involving Mariels . . . in or around bars. Some of them were addicts who were so despondent over the condition they found themselves in that they set up circumstances to get themselves killed because of the pain they could no longer bear" (p. 38).

The Treatment Program: Beginnings and Problems

Southern California is another center of Hispanic immigration, but the Cuban ethnic enclave is much smaller and less important than the one in South Florida.

Mental health treatment is available for Hispanic Americans, but local government agencies are reluctant to provide social services for undocumented Hispanics who are in this country illegally. A few hundred Mariel Cubans have been sent to Southern California under federal programs for refugees whose prospects for sponsorship and success in the United States seemed poor due to physical or mental illness, old age or substance abuse. In the Fall of 1983, an alcoholism treatment program was established for institutionalized Mariel Cuban refugees in a psychiatric halfway house in East Los Angeles. Ten patients (nine males and one female) with diagnoses of primary or secondary alcoholism were chosen as the initial treatment population.

The program was initially designed along the lines of an "Alcoholism Recovery Home" with regular group therapy, individual counseling, "therapeutic games," alcohol education, recreation and pseudovocational activities. Four times a week residents' evenings were spent at meetings of Hispanic Alcoholics Anonymous groups. The clients were under 24-hour supervision by a social worker, program assistants, a paraprofessional alcoholism therapist, and a sociologist whose job title was "acculturation specialist." They were housed in a facility which was administratively linked with, but separate from, a larger psychiatric halfway house program for Cuban refugees.

After nine months' operation, it was clear that this very expensive alcoholism treatment program was a failure. The clients sat in stony silence through all the therapy sessions and games. They assimilated little or nothing of the alcoholism education. Some complained bitterly that they wanted to work and earn money, receive vocational training, or at least study English, and that alcoholism education was an irrelevant bore. Several clients pointed out that they had not had a drink for as long as 10 years, before beginning long stretches of institutionalization. It seemed to them that the therapists and program personnel were obsessed with alcohol. There were frequent relapses and (it was later learned) several clients managed to consume a couple of beers every day before breakfast despite the surveillance. Only a few clients ever admitted to their alcoholism, although several had their stay in the program extended due to repeated drinking incidents.

During these nine months the larger psychiatric program for Cuban refugees had undergone many changes. The paraprofessional alcoholism therapist came into conflict with the Licensed Clinical Social Worker who was also director of the larger program. The issue was the director's own drug abuse problems. The therapist was terminated but the director's post also soon fell vacant. The social worker became involved in the ensuing power struggle and was terminated when an opposing candidate took charge. The sociologist was called upon either to restructure the alcoholism treatment program or abolish it.

Analysis of Initial Program Failure

This nine-month start-up period was a useful learning experience for analyzing what was wrong with the recovery home approach when dealing with institutionalized refugees and for defining ways to restructure the alcoholism treatment program. The first difficulty was inappropriate selection of clients. Many residents of the larger psychiatric program had drinking problems but were not assigned to the alcoholism program due to vocational or other commitments which might have suffered. Others were assigned directly upon arrival after years of institutionalization in federal prison or a maximum security mental hospital. Such institutionalization followed years in Cuban jails so that, in one case, 14 years had passed since the client had had an opportunity to take a drink. Since this client was only 28 years old, his diagnosis of primary alcoholism was very questionable. Several alcoholic clients were unable to benefit from the program's didactic approach due to organicity. Neither staff nor residents were taking the alcoholism treatment program seriously.

It seemed that the only program activities which had any therapeutic impact were the Alcoholics Anonymous meetings. Two in-house meetings were conducted by members of the Hispanic Alcoholics Anonymous Institutions Committee each week and the clients were also taken to two meetings in the community. These activities had elicited a certain amount of interest and participation from the clients, whereas no other program activity had aroused anything more than boredom and hostility.

Establishment of the Hispanic AA Group

In the Spanish-speaking communities of Los Angeles, Alcoholics Anonymous is a rapidly growing organization, with over 100 groups in operation. Hispanic AA follows the 12 AA Traditions for functioning groups of the original Anglo organization and urges members to use the 12-step program for personal recovery from alcoholism. All literature is translated from literature approved by the New York office. AA groups seek to help members promote their own recovery by admitting that drinking has made them lose control over their lives, trusting in a "higher power" than themselves, taking an inventory of their personal faults, making amends to those they have harmed and helping alcoholics who want to stop drinking.

The alcoholism program was restructured around and in cooperation with the Hispanic branch of Alcoholics Anonymous. The components which had been borrowed from conventional recovery homes—the group therapy, the personality games ("positive me exercises," etc.), the alcoholism education, the separate residential facility, and the fruitless attempts to persuade unwilling or illiterate clients to write out personal inventories—were all abandoned. The new program director insisted that the alcoholism program no longer be called a "treatment program" since the traditional elements of alcoholism treatment had been abandoned. She wanted it called "the Alcoholism Prevention Unit" and this name stuck even though there were no components of traditional alcoholism prevention programs. "Alcoholics Anonymous is also for prevention," is a phrase which is commonly heard in Hispanic AA groups, so the sociologist did not think it necessary to engage in polemics over the name. Staff of the alcoholism unit refer to their activities as "the Alcoholism Program." This name was then given to the residents' AA group which was formed later.

The alcoholism recovery home staff was disbanded and transferred to other duties, leaving the sociologist to conduct program activities without help or interference. The new program functioned in the evening, which meant that alcoholic clients who worked during the day could now attend. Residents who presented drinking problems were assigned to attend by their counselors, but the sociologist tried to develop voluntary participation by treating the opportunity to attend meetings as an "outing" or a festive occasion.

The Sociologist's Role

The sociologist, who has not accepted personal defeat by alcohol, is in a marginal condition with regard to membership in Alcoholics Anonymous. However, sociologists are trained to be alert to the unstudied population, to the unseen social phenomenon which is worthy of research attention. In this case the unstudied phenomenon was the transcultural adaptation of the Alcoholics Anonymous program and philosophy to help Hispanic alcoholics. The sociologist adopted the role of the participant observer and ceased acting as a therapist while attending the AA meetings. To the Hispanic AA members in the groups he looked like a driver who was in charge of getting the participants to the groups and taking them home afterwards. Overt acts of supervision in public were reduced to a minimum. Throughout this period the larger program was in turmoil due to power struggles and executive incompetence so the sociologist was free to develop the work of the alcoholism program without interference.

Attendance at AA meetings in the community became the central focus of the restructured program although there were still two in-house institutional meetings each week. Clients were encouraged to participate in structuring program activities and making decisions. For example, whenever an outing was scheduled to an AA meeting in the community, clients would be asked which meeting they wished to attend. The decision would be made on the basis of this preference. Seeing himself as a participant observer, the sociologist tended to treat the clients as helpers and informants rather than as patients. Since he is obviously a "gringo," clients' help in relating to other groups was welcome. It became possible to set aside the mental patient role, at least for those clients who sincerely related to the AA program. However, it was not always possible to get out of the role of social controller for some of the more disturbed residents.

The Residents' Own AA Group

Before long it became clear that the clients would benefit from an AA group they could call their own. One of the goals of the program was to enable the clients to establish friendly, nonalcoholic relationships with members of the Hispanic community. When clients set out to do this at AA meetings, one of the first questions they encountered was: "What group are you from?" A truthful response of the form: "We are from a psychiatric halfway house for Mariel Cubans," would not enhance effective interaction. In fact, most of the clients had no response when confronted with such a question. A more suitable way for the clients to present themselves was needed.

The Hispanic AA Institutions Committee's workers had been able to stress the first step in the AA program: the admission that one's life has become ungovernable due to alcohol abuse. Several of the other steps were also presented, but it is very difficult for an institutional group to work through all 12 of the steps, particularly the last one which involves taking the AA message to alcoholics who still suffer. By operating a group within the "Traditions" it would become possible for those who were ready to work the steps to do so.

One evening during an in-house meeting conducted by members of the AA Institutions Committee, the suggestion was made that the residents might start their own independent group. Hearty agreement was aroused in several Cubans who had accepted the AA program, and they began to discuss the prospect excitedly. The Institutions Committee member soon had second thoughts about his optimistic suggestion that unemployed mental patients could start their own autonomous group, but there was no taking it back. The sociologist facilitated an arrangement to use a building owned by the city for very nominal cost and the clients pooled some of their spending money to start things off.

Establishment of a traditional AA group was a challenge which involved overcoming some of the habits of dependency into which these Cuban refugees had fallen. The objectives were "empowerment" in that residents would have an AA group to invite others to and to provide a definition of self as an AA member with roots in a group rather than as a mental patient. AA Tradition Number Seven requires that each group maintain itself from its own resources—members' contributions. The members arrange their own affairs in accordance with AA traditions, making decisions about expenditures and celebrations without consulting their social workers or the direction of the larger program. Of course the sociologist is still there to offer advice, which is not always taken. The group is open to anyone and is authorized to certify that drunk drivers referred by the courts have attended AA meetings. As many as six persons from the community have attended on a given night and three attend more or less regularly.

The residents' AA group has recently completed its first anniversary. Two members have completed a year's sobriety and have had their anniversary celebrations as well. Five or six others have accepted the AA program and are working the steps to the best of their ability. Another half dozen attend AA whenever they want and have stopped drinking. Ten or 12 residents of the psychiatric facility have occasional drinking episodes and, when they do, are assigned to attend AA meetings for a while. Ten others have run away from the program and it is not known whether they are drinking or not. Four have found employment and have been discharged from the program. At least one of these still has serious drinking problems. While the results are imperfect, they represent an advance over the previous program.

The residents' AA group maintains as much separation as possible from the psychiatric program. When a client has a drinking episode, he or she is given a card resembling those given drunken drivers by the courts. The resident may take the card to any AA meeting and have it stamped. Most residents who are given cards attend the residents' AA group, but some prefer to attend other groups in the community. Attendance is therefore voluntary and any coercion involved comes from elsewhere, not from the AA group itself. The residents' group meets three nights a week.

The participants in AA activities are nearly all males. This reflects the composition of the psychiatric population of Mariel Cubans in the larger program. No females participate in the alcoholism program regularly although one of the four female residents attends AA meetings occasionally. Members' ages range from 25 to 68 years old. Several of the members exhibit some degree of organicity, and more than half are developmentally disabled.

Shortly before the residents established their own group it was decided to enlarge the alcoholism program. A recovering alcoholic from the Hispanic AA Institutions Committee was hired by the psychiatric program and given the task of transporting residents to AA meetings in the community. Activities were scheduled for seven nights a week instead of four. One vehicle proved too small to transport all those who wished to attend AA so two more recovering alcoholics were hired. At present, as many as 25 residents are transported to AA meetings in the community each evening. The sessions of the residents' group are held a few blocks from the psychiatric facility so most members walk.

Not all has been smooth going, however. Some residents resented the fact that the psychiatric program would require them to attend AA meetings after a drinking bout. Several alcoholics who had understood the AA philosophy without accepting it phrased their complaints in convenient rhetoric and expressed their discontent from the "tribuna" or speaker's platform. This seemed harmless until one man began to accuse the sociologist and the employees responsible for transporting and supervising visits to groups in the community of "selling the message."

AA and Professional Roles

In English-speaking AA, the relationship of professionals and paraprofessionals working in alcoholism programs has been clarified. Recovering alcoholics who are AA members can work in alcoholism treatment and prevention but they should not misuse the name of AA. But treatment of alcoholic Hispanics is a relatively new field and Hispanic 12th step workers who maintain their own sobriety by helping others may develop resentments at seeing others getting paid for engaging in rather similar activities. The disgruntled client, who may have been seeking to protect his own drinking, struck a responsive chord in a group run by Central Americans, some of whom were antagonistic to the privileges of Cuban entrants receiving federal resettlement assistance. The sociologist's residual clinical role came under fire as he became the focus of "terapia dura" (confrontive therapy) at a meeting of this group. The sociologist had, for some time, sought to downplay this clinical role in relations with residents attending AA meetings, so the confrontation seemed somewhat misdirected. On the other hand, the participant observer received rich inputs of new data, some of it emotionally charged. It was an uncomfortable learning experience. Program philosophy and procedures were reassessed and the AA literature was searched for precedents and explanations. Fortunately, the English-speaking organization had experienced similar controversy and ample discussion is available (AA, 1957: 109–110). The issue is not professionalism, but anonymity. Of course AA members can work in treatment programs. But AA's name must not be used for fundraising or publicity. Provided the name of Alcoholics Anonymous was not misused we were not doing anything objectionable.

The Sociological Clinician

Straus (1984) points out that sociological intervention at the personal level may involve "directing clients to appropriate support networks to reinforce their definitions, or to peer self-help groups to help them reconstruct their realities outside of a therapy framework" (p. 56).

Borman (1983) notes that human service professionals and researchers have a special role in assisting in the formation of self-help groups and also in learning from them. According to Borman, the helping mechanisms of Alcoholics Anonymous are universality and acceptance, communication, social support, and response to both informational and emotional needs of the clients. "This occurs in settings which are non-coercive, non-threatening, and under the control and management of peers" (p. 105). Altruism—the helper therapy principle—is another beneficial mechanism, in addition to the sharing of common values, development of a sense of hope and having opportunities to talk at great length with others like yourself. One of the reasons these helping mechanisms are too often ignored by conventional therapists is that they do not really require a therapist's involvement. While professionals have frequently played important roles in the formation and development of peer self-help groups, they do not have integral functions in the groups' helping processes.

Brody (1983) examines the contradictory position of the clinician as researcher who seeks to broaden knowledge of the relationships between culture, illness, and healing. Noting that praxis is an "indispensable element" which "characterizes the production of clinical knowledge" (p. 296), Brody explores the uses of the clinical role to obtain cultural information. Noting that fieldwork is a confrontation involving an inevitable disruption of the sense of self, he argues that "clinical work, as well as clinical status, may protect the professional helper from the shift in subjective reality experienced by the anthropologist struggling for acceptance and a new equilibrium in a strange setting."

Pollner and Emerson (1983) point out that "the major threat to observation derives from pressures that dissolve the stance of 'mere observer' by according the researcher some more consequential presence in the ongoing scene. This occurs when fieldworkers become incorporated, for a variety of reasons, into the ongoing social life in some central and consequential way" (p. 236). The authors point to responses that involve full participation on the behavioral level, but withdrawal and distance on the subjective level.

The problem of subjective distance and withdrawal was even more acute for a sociologist charged with developing an effective alcoholism treatment program—especially when analysis of available resources showed that Hispanic Alcoholics Anonymous could provide highly effective assistance. How could the sociologist rationalize his presence at nightly AA meetings? Professional therapists have no legitimate role in developing AA groups. Listening to the histories and testimonials of clients and other AA members with therapeutic intent is inappropriate. Such confessions are expressed for the speakers' benefit and for the benefit of alcoholics in recuperation, not for the purposes of clinical intervention, charting of clients' progress or maintenance of discipline in a psychiatric program. Research on the growth and development of AA as an institution is more appropriate, provided the research focus is on open, public AA meetings. Thus, the subjective stance of a researcher interested in group development and in the transcultural adaptation of AA ideology was useful for handling the dialectic between involvement and detachment. The initial absence of a preliminary struggle for personal equilibrium, of difficulty in finding acceptance and becoming a participant in the society observed, had left anxieties and unresolved conflicts which were exacerbated by the fact that clinicians, as such, do not have a legitimate role in the AA community. Consciousness of the research role made it possible to adopt a more honest personal attitude toward participation in AA and to explain separation from some of AA's central values.

By developing a program approach that would allow for changes in the residents' definition of self and situation from that of coerced inmates of a recovery home to that of (mostly) voluntary participants in an autonomous program, resistance to alcoholism treatment was to some extent overcome. Some radical changes in human relations interventions were necessary, including separation of the residents' AA group from the alcoholism program's interventions in the larger psychiatric program. Thus residents' anonymity in AA meetings had to be respected, even when they might confess to breaking the rules of the psychiatric program.

During the reorganization, the alcoholism program underwent very high staff turnover. The sociologist's job title changed temporarily from "acculturation specialist" to "alcoholism program supervisor." The participant observer role was acknowledged to the recovering alcoholics who were hired to assist with the reorganized program and to colleagues in the academic community, but not to the succession of directors of the strife-torn larger program. After a time the alcoholism program seemed almost to run itself, at least to the extent that the sociologist no longer had to attend so many AA meetings. The "acculturation specialist" role reemerged, and there was also time for reflection on the Hispanic AA experience, writing up the ethnographic data and interviewing the large number of informants developed during participant observation at Hispanic AA meetings.

This intervention did not focus on providing treatment to individuals, but on development of a new, semi-autonomous program which could act as a vehicle for clients to empower themselves by adopting the ideas and practice of the Alcoholics Anonymous self-help movement. Those who failed to relate to AA and who continued drinking fell under the sanctions of the larger program, but the alcoholism program did not coerce anyone to attend meetings. The sociologist felt the need for a subjective refuge in the role of ethnographic researcher while attending meetings at which clinical roles were inappropriate. The psychiatric patients were thus promoted to the status of informants and subjects of research on the process of transcultural adaptation of the AA program to serve Hispanic populations.

REFERENCES

Alcoholics Anonymous
 1957 A.A. Llega a la Mayoria de Edad. New York: World Service.

Alcocer, A.A.
 1982 Alcohol Use and Abuse among the Hispanic American Population, NIAAA Special
     Population Issues. Alcohol and Health Monograph No. 4, Washington, DC.

Amaya, D.
 1983 "The bottom of bottoms: chemically dependant Mariel entrants," Alcohol Health
     and Research World 7, no. 3:37–38.

Borman, L. D.
 1983 "Self-help groups, professionals and the redefinition of pathological states." Pp.
     99–118 in Demitri B. Shimkin and Peggy Golde, eds., Clinical Anthropology.
     Lanham, MD: University Press of America.

Brody, E. B.
 1983 "The clinician as ethnographer: a psychoanalytic perspective on the epistemology
     of fieldwork," Culture, Medicine and Psychiatry 5:273–301.

Hoffman, F.
 1985 "Clinical sociology and the acculturation specialty," Clinical Sociology Review
     3:50–58.

Page, J.B., Lucy Rio, Jacqueline Sweeny and Carolyn McKay
 1985 "Alcohol and adaptation to exile in Miami's Cuban population," in L. Bennett and
     Genevieve Ames, eds., The American Experience with Alcohol. New York: Plenum
     Press.

Pollner, M. & R. Emerson
 1983 "The dynamics of inclusion and distance in fieldwork relations," Pp. 235–252 in
     R. Emerson, ed., Contemporary Field Research. Boston: Little, Brown.

Straus, R.
 1984 "Changing the definition of the situation," Clinical Sociology Review 2:51–63.

Weidman, H. H.
 1975 "Concepts as strategies for change," Psychiatric Annals 8:17–19.
 1983 "Research, service and training aspects of clinical anthropology: an institutional
     overview," in Demitri B. Shimkin and Peggy Golde, eds., Clinical Anthropology.
     Lanham, MD: University Press of America.

Uses of Clinical Sociology in Crisis Intervention Practice

Bryan D. Byers
Adult Protecting Services
Office of the Prosecutive Attorney, St. Joseph County, Indiana

ABSTRACT

Crisis intervention is a practice-oriented set of procedures designed to offer someone experiencing incapacitating stress emotional first-aid. Concepts and ideas found in the sociological tradition are quite applicable to crisis intervention practice. What has been offered are alternatives to the traditional psychological and psychiatric positions.

There are similar characteristics between crisis intervention and clinical sociology as change strategies. Particularly, the ideas found under the sociological social psychology purview serve well when practicing crisis intervention. The interpretation of crisis events is a social act in that the individual experiencing the crisis is influenced through social circumstances. Social circumstances play a vital role in crisis formation and intervention.

Intervention strategies are offered which integrate aspects of clinical sociology while using a case study for application. The crisis intervention steps include crisis assessment, information gathering, control, direction, progress assessment, and referral. Through these procedures, the intervener may work with the client toward the goal of socioemotional stability

For many years, crisis intervention has been a viable helping strategy. Beginning as a formal approach some 40 years ago (Lindemann, 1944), the field began to flourish. Crisis intervention was primarily attached to the medical profession so it employed a medical model. Logically, then, the major emphasis has been on psychiatric/psychological approaches of crisis definition and resolution. Recently, however, it has become apparent that there was a valuable social component to crises, which could be used in crisis intervention theory and practice.

Correspondence to: Bryan D. Byers, Adult Protective Services, Office of the Prosecuting Attorney, St. Joseph County, County-City Building, 10th floor, South Bend, IN 46601.

As a helping strategy, crisis intervention includes theory (how crises are produced, types of crisis, etc.) and practice (skills for effective crisis resolution). This paper will present practical considerations for theory and practice while integrating principles of clinical sociology. The typology of crisis, crisis event interpretation, and crisis formation will be examined. A presentation of crisis intervention strategies will be offered with a case study application. What will follow, then, includes crisis theory and intervention which integrate aspects of sociological intervention.

Crisis Intervention and Clinical Sociology

In approaching crisis intervention, it is useful to integrate some of the ideas of "sociological intervention" (Straus, 1984) and "social behavioral intervention" (Straus, 1982) into the existing operational framework (Byers and Hendricks, 1985; Hendricks, 1984). Clinical sociology is the use of sociological knowledge and concepts for positive change, while crisis intervention is emergency emotional first-aid. Although distinctively different in definition, the two areas can be usefully integrated. The ideas of the sociological tradition are compatible with crisis intervention practice; it should prove beneficial to integrate sociological knowledge with the existing psychological and psychiatric tradition. This will not only broaden the eclectic nature of the approach, it will also offer the client more effective treatment. In other words, using interventionist strategies from different perspectives increases the likelihood that the client will receive appropriate and effective attention. Intervention strategies are situational. No one approach is appropriate at all times. However, coupling sociological practice and crisis intervention allows for an effective effort. The contention that clinical sociology should be used in company with other counseling, therapeutic, change, and intervention strategies was posited early (Jaques, 1947; Lee, 1955; Link, 1948; White, 1947; Wirth, 1931). Furthermore, the utility of sociology in therapy has been suggested in a number of recent publications (Black and Enos, 1980; Church, 1985; Glassner and Freedman, 1979; Hurvitz, 1979; Moreno and Glassner, 1979; Polak, 1971; Straus, 1979a, 1979b, 1982, 1984). A unidisciplinary approach to the problem of personal crisis runs the risk of possibly missing important information that knowledge from another discipline might provide. As Glassner and Freedman (1979:12) have noted, "The work of crisis interventionists can be quite instructive for some aspects of clinical sociological practice." Taking this position a step further, there is a reciprocal benefit to be gained from the combined use of crisis intervention and clinical sociology. Individuals do not experience crises in a psychological vacuum; personal crises must be examined from a perspective which recognizes the role of society and the social forces which influence the individual.

Most people are thrust into crisis many times throughout a normal life cycle.

The intervener must be prepared to tend to individuals in crisis in order to help restore them, at the very least, to a stable level of functioning. This is an explicit goal of crisis intervention. Stable functioning may be defined as a constitutional state where the client is capable of understanding the crisis, demonstrating effective social and psychological functioning, and learning from the crisis and the intervention. This will leave the client better equipped for future crises. Intervention is on the micro level and should entail an understanding of the client's social environment as well as psychological, affective, and behavioral aspects. This understanding of the social realm is evidence of the importance of integration, as are themes that characterize clinical sociology and that are also well suited for crisis intervention. These include a practice orientation, focus on case studies, a diagnostic nature, change-orientation, a humanistic position (Freedman, 1982), and "minimal intervention" (Straus, 1982:63). In a minimal intervention the intervener monitors and keeps at a minimum the span of interventions, the helper's authoritarian role, and the expectations for change placed on clients. (See Straus, 1982:6–7, for a complete description of "minimal intervention.") These concepts help the intervener understand the dynamics that must be dealt with within the client's social environment.

Clinical sociology offers the intervener a wide array of interpretive strategies for problem identification and solution. These include such concepts as socialization, status, role, in-group/out-group, group dynamics, conflict, interactionism, situational analysis, definition of the situation, etc. Through a utilization of the sociological perspective, then, the intervener will gain necessary insight into the social nature and function of interpersonal and intrapersonal crisis. With this understanding, the intervener may step into the crisis situation with more than the customary level of knowledge associated with crisis intervention.

Although the intervener deals directly with the individual, the social reality of the client must be recognized. This may entail intervention which not only leads to change in the individual but also to change within a dyad, a family or a social group. The orientation of the clinical sociological approach affects the group level even when an individual is being treated (Glass, 1979; Lee, 1979; Moreno and Glassner, 1979). This type of influence may be desired as part of the intervention strategy, or it may be a therapeutic by-product of the encounter. The intervener must treat the individual as a social being on the micro level while taking into account the social and/or sociological variables which influence behavior and affect. Crisis intervention and clinical sociology are both intervention strategies, and both can be applied on the micro or individual level. Further, crisis intervention is active rather than passive or neutral, as is clinical sociology. As Fritz (1985) states, "Clinical sociology is intervention work." Both approaches are defined by explicit intervention, that is, intervention for positive change.

Personal Crisis

A crisis might emerge when an individual experiences unpleasant socioemotional feelings, which result from the onset of a perceived insurmountable stressful life event. This is accompanied by an inability to cope with or adjust to the event. These are common components of personal *crisis definition* (Rapaport, 1962; Smith, 1978). The "socioemotional" basis of feelings assumes that there is a close connection between social reality and one's affective state. For our use, a crisis may be defined as:

> The unpleasant psychological and social feelings/sensations, which result from the onset of a perceived insurmountable stressful life event, disrupting stability, and accompanied by an inability to adjust or cope.

According to Morrice (1976), emotional crises may present themselves in two generic forms: "accidental" or "developmental." These typologies aid the intervener in ascertaining the nature of the crisis and the appropriate intervention. The accidental form of crisis has been described by Morrice as those events in life which create an emotional impasse, cause emotional turmoil, and are temporarily incapacitating. Accidental crises are unexpected or unintended. This typology includes crises which result from sudden traumatic stress. Examples include: divorce, relationship conflict, school failure, loss of health, loss of work, death of a loved one. We all have ideals concerning how life should flow; however, the ideal is not always the reality. Even if one expects a crisis to materialize (e.g., a long-troubled marriage, terminal illness), the degree of trauma experienced when the event happens is not necessarily less. For instance, one may know cognitively that a loved one is dying of cancer, but that might not necessarily soften the impact of the stress produced by the loss. On the other hand, experiencing the long-term death of a loved one might produce more stress than the final demise. The death may be a relief rather than an incapacitating experience. Accidental crises include impasses that are not expected during an ideal life course. It is important to remember that individuals respond to stressful life events through a complex socialization process. Learning takes place through a myriad of life experiences and conditions. The response to stressful life events might hinge on how one's life situations and life chances have been formed.

The developmental category of crisis is characterized as consisting of events which are normal life experiences, but which may also produce crisis reactions. Some examples of developmental crises include growing old, getting married, sexual identity, graduating from school (high school or college), children leaving home (empty nest), value conflict, dominant-subordinate relationships. These events will not produce crisis in everyone experiencing them, of course. However, they may produce a crisis reaction under certain circumstances. The social and/or sociological nature of these two types of crisis is obvious. As stated by Burgess and Baldwin (1981:31): "Every emotional crisis is an interpersonal event involving at least one significant other person who is represented in the crisis situation directly, indirectly, or symbolically." Crises are produced in the individual through social circumstances. Social life is, at times, stressful. A certain degree of life stress is required and desirable. On a clinical level, the majority of clients treated by counselors and psychotherapists have stress-related problems (Straus, 1979a). Social circumstances set the stage for individual stress reactions and crisis event interpretation.

Crisis Event Interpretation

Events which occur in one's life do not, alone, produce crisis. An *interpretation of the event* must take place. That is, the situation must be perceived as a crisis before the individual will react to the crisis. The concept of the "definition of the situation" is quite applicable here (Thomas, 1931). (Lydia Rapaport, 1962:211, a prominent crisis theorist, also cites W. I. Thomas as a useful social theorist in this area.) An individual presented with a potential crisis-producing situation must first define the situation or the context of the crisis. The situation may be interpreted as one of crisis or one of normalcy. It is through a definitional process that situations will be interpreted as a threat to emotional stability or as an event which poses no threat. As See and Straus (1985:66) have described, in order to understand another human being one must "discover (a) how he or she actually interprets the meaning of different kinds of situations; and (b) how he or she has come to analyze situations in that particular way." This type of analysis is useful because it enables the crisis intervener to make sense of the situation based on the social characteristics of the case. As mentioned above, the crises which characteristically affect individuals have either social influences or social causes. Individuals react to external stressors by cognitively internalizing the meaning of the crisis precipitator (hazardous event) according to personal interpretation. The crisis precipitator is any social event which has the potential to be perceived as a threat to socioemotional stability. The event is termed a "precipitator" because it precedes the crisis onset. For example, the death of a loved one may not be a crisis event until 1) the death notification has been made, and 2) the information is situationally defined. Points such as these make it important to examine the crisis situation from a clinical sociological perspective.

When describing the onset of crisis and the circumstances that produce the crisis, much of the literature describes the hazardous event, the perception of that event, the resulting feelings, and the inability to find immediate solutions (Smith, 1978). Thus, the nature of the crisis event and its interpretation, although commonly found in the psychological or psychiatric literature, may be described well through the components of interactionism or sociological social psychology. The precipitating event is commonly a social event, or at least has repercussions on the social level, which provides a basis for a social psychological interpretation of the process.

Crisis Formation Process and Intervention

In order to intervene effectively in a crisis situation, one must have an accurate understanding of the process through which a crisis is produced. This is the crisis formation process. Also, the intervener needs to utilize an effective and efficient intervention process, that is, a procedure designed specifically as a guide to intervention while providing help to the client in crisis.

Crisis Formation Process.   This is the course through which the client progresses on the way to emotional instability. Before the process begins, it is often assumed that the individual has a balanced state of affect and thought. As mentioned earlier, this is not always the case. Examples include families which have been slowly destroyed by terminal illness, domestic violence, or an alcoholic family member. In these instances, structural factors within the family must be taken into account as possible and probable contributors to a crisis. Individuals do not go untouched by prior or current events. Crisis is not experienced in a psychological vacuum. Although, the client may have exhibited precrisis emotional stability, other factors often come into play to form a crisis.

Many early crisis theorists referred to the stress-producing nature of crisis situations. Partly due to ties to the medical profession, homeostasis and physiological reactions to stress were used to explain crisis (Caplan, 1964; Lindemann, 1944). It was not until the work of Howard J. Parad that it was recognized that "the event precipitating the crisis must be perceived by the person as a stressful situation before it can become a crisis" (Smith, 1978:397).

The *precipitating event*, or hazardous event, presents a threat to emotional stability. These events come in a variety of forms, such as the death of a loved one, relationship failure (divorce, breakup), interpersonal conflict, unfair social structure, or professional practices. However, it is not the event per se that produces the state of crisis. It is through a *definition of the situation* (Thomas, 1931) that the event is defined as an unpleasant occurrence. The individual first interprets the event in terms of its emotional and social consequences. Different events carry different levels of social and emotional impact depending on the nature of the event and the person experiencing it. For example, a relationship breakup might be very devastating for one person while for another it might be considered a blessing. The death of someone with a terminal illness may be a blessing, a relief, an end to a stressful life period for both the family and the patient. These reactions depend on the circumstances of the event, the actors involved, and situational definitions. Although some events will probably be quite stressful for most persons, the definitional nature of the event largely determines the degree of the emotional reaction. The interpretation of precipitating events and the resulting definition occur on the cognitive level, which, in turn, becomes transmitted to the emotional level. The definition may be made in terms of how the event will affect the individual, how the event will be seen by others, or how the event will influence others' perceptions of the individual. One not only reacts in terms of the emotional component but also according to the interpretation by others. This is most likely when the event could result in some form of social stigma, such as legal arrest, divorce, mental hospital incarceration, cancer, AIDS. Here, one can incorporate Cooley's (1956) concept of the Looking-Glass Self, which claims that people develop self-images through a perception of how others view them. The notion is that individuals mirror, in affect and cognition, the believed perceptions of others. Thus, crisis formation has a major social component, and the sociological perspective offers the intervener a vantage point for examining these social aspects.

The next phase of the process, *internalization of the definition of the situation*, has already been touched upon. Internalization takes place when the client incorporates the definiton of the precipitating event. In other words, the definition becomes part of the individual. The perceived nature of the precipitating event and a weighing of the personal and social consequences are incorporated into the client's behavior and thought repertoire. Once the client tests regular coping mechanisms and discovers that regular adjustment strategies prove inadequate, the emotional turmoil is overwhelming. When this is realized, the client will often engage in self-destructive behavior which only perpetuates the already present emotional hazard. It is at this point that the crisis becomes manifest. The individual knows that the sensations experienced are not normal, but is unable to provide the necessary coping behavior to resolve the crisis and restore emotional stability.

Crisis resolution may take place through active and intentional efforts of the clinician using an *intervention process*. It has been posited that crisis intervention is most effective during the acute, or beginning, levels of crisis (Caplan, 1964; Morrice, 1976). The intervention strategy consists of several steps which enable the intervener to help bring the crisis to resolution. The process may be fairly smooth or extremely complicated depending on the situation, social dynamics, nature of the problem, client abilities, and intervener capabilities. The crisis intervention strategy is active, normally short in duration (usually 1 to 8 therapeutic encounters within 4 to 5 weeks),[1] specifically problem targeted (Caplan, 1964), and involves stabilizing the client while attempting to return the client to a stable socioemotional state. Intervention is a response to the onset of socioemotional crisis. Throughout the encounter, the intervener must remain aware of the purpose and goal of crisis intervention—decisive interventive action which leads the client to a level of stable functioning or crisis resolution.

What will follow includes an integration of the crisis intervention process posited by Hendricks (1984) and Byers and Hendricks (1985) and the clinical sociological approaches of Straus (1982, 1984). A case study will be utilized in order to demonstrate the intervention process. The scenario is an actual one, but intervention was not possible at the time. Nonetheless, the case study offers a challenging set of circumstances for crisis intervention with a clinical sociological emphasis. A step-by-step process for crisis intervention will be introduced, utilizing sociological intervention strategies while integrating the case study information to demonstrate what could have been done.

Case Study[2]

Mrs. F is a white, married, 30-year-old woman living in a small town. The community is predominantly middle-class, rather affluent, and has a strong protestant work ethic. Individuals there are often held responsible for their own life situations. Mrs. F has been divorced once and widowed once. Her current husband is incapable of working due to severe mental illness. Mrs. F has a job which pays minimum wage and has no advancement possibilities. She has an untidy appearance, does not appear intelligent, and has a nonassertive demeanor. She has been characterized as a member of the lower-class (SES).

Mrs. F has two children (both under 4 years old) and recently gave birth to a third. This baby was born in a local hospital; after the delivery, Mrs. F and her child were sent home. The baby was born with, and was sent home with, a jaundice condition. After a few days at home, the baby began to vomit, appeared sick, and lost weight. Mrs. F contacted her physician (Dr. P) and informed him of the developments. Mrs. F then took the baby to the office of Dr. P, per his instructions, for an examination. Dr. P recommended that she take the child to a specialist. She did. The baby was hospitalized for 2 weeks and showed improvement during the stay. The child gained 8 ounces in weight. At this time, the baby was diagnosed as having malabsorption. In this case, it was determined to be a genetically transmitted disorder—the patient cannot physiologically take and use nourishment. The social definition is the Failure to Thrive Syndrome. In this condition, the child appears malnourished, which sometimes has the social connotation that the mother has not properly cared for the child. With much improvement, the specialist released the baby from the hospital.

After about a week at home, Mrs. F noticed that the baby was developing the same symptoms again. She took the baby to the nearby hospital, and the child was admitted. During a stay of 3 days, the child maintained its weight. Dr. P released the child. Soon after the hospital stay, the child became sick with the same symptoms. Mrs. F contacted Dr. P again. He told her to bring the baby to his office. It was discovered that the child had lost 14 ounces since the second hospital stay. Mrs. F was very concerned over the welfare of her baby. Dr. P told Mrs. F to take the child home; if the child weren't better by the next week, he would call the specialist again. Dr. P wanted Mrs. F to care for the child for 1 week at home before growing concerned. Mrs. F, very worried, obeyed the doctor's orders and took the baby home. During the week, the baby grew sicker. The mother called Dr. P, who said to take the baby back to the specialist. The baby died en route to the hospital. It was eight weeks old.

The coroner's report indicated that the mother must have been inadequate in caring for the child. This coroner claimed that Mrs. F was not even aware that the child was dead upon arrival due to her deficient mental capacity. Mrs. F, in fact, was aware that the baby died en route.

Mrs. F has another child 2 years, 6 months old. The child has developed the same symptoms of malabsorption. She is aware that this child may have the same genetic disorder, but she appears to lack the assertiveness and influence to pressure Dr. P, or any other physican, to give the care which she feels her child needs. She is currently in a confused, self-blaming crisis state not knowing what to do.

Crisis Assessment

Crisis assessment is an ongoing activity in the intervention process (Smith, 1978). One of the main purposes is to arrive at decisions to facilitate the intervention process. It is an evaluative procedure between the client and the intervener; collaboration between counselor and client is essential during assessment and throughout the intervention process. The nature of the collaboration consists of beginning the therapeutic relationship, providing an atmosphere for open and honest talk, and maintaining a commitment for a positive outcome. In order to begin therapy, the intervener must "get a handle on" the problem through problem focusing. When focusing on the problem, the intervener should remain committed to the present difficulty, working in the "here and now." Through this activity, the helper will gain an essential understanding of the client's crisis. The activity of problem identification may prove to be therapeutic in itself. Through identifying the problem, the client may begin better to understand the situation.

From the data in the above case study, the intervener may gain valuable information (however, such chronological information is seldom available) in order to ascertain the overt nature of the problem. Mrs. F has been traumatized by her baby's death, which has been compounded by the possibility that her youngest child might be afflicted with the same disorder. Furthermore, she may have been victimized by medical personnel, and she lacks the personal and financial resources to improve the situation. Through an assessment of this information, the intervention can be planned. New information is likely to emerge throughout an interventive encounter. Thus, assessment must be an ongoing intervention activity.

Intervention Steps

Information Gathering.   This begins with the client referral. It may be a self-referral, a referral from another person (such as a concerned individual or significant other), or a referral from an agency. In this case, we will assume that the referral was made by a concerned friend. If the referral has been made from sources other than the client (e.g., friends, family, police, hospital personnel, etc.) valuable information about the case may be obtained from these sources. However, the helper should use this type of information cautiously, being attuned to possible bias, stereotyping, labeling, and stigma. These sources of information are valuable, but it is necessary to exercise caution when using them.

The primary activity in this stage is interviewing the client.[3] This is similar in practice to the gathering of information in Straus' (1982:64) Social Behavioral Intervention Assessment Phase. Close interviewing with the client is also important. The intervener would want to speak with Mrs. F personally and engage in active reflective listening (Rogers, 1951), while recognizing the need to be attentive to possible class differences. It is important to remember that one of the roles "of the therapist is to match the individual with the social systems in which he participates" (Costello, 1972:421). In addition to these points, and important from a sociologist's position, the intervener will wish to use such concepts as symbolism, role, presentation of self, and interaction patterns (Blumer, 1972).

Interaction with the client (such as Mrs. F) is designed to get to know the client personally in order to build a trust relationship and to gain an understanding of the client's situation. The intervener should adopt a warm, empathic approach when interacting with the client. Role taking is applicable (Mead, 1934). By taking the role of the other, the intervener may better understand the client's social world. It should be understood that Mrs. F has been through much trauma. By demonstrating a caring demeanor, the helper reflects his/her understanding of the crisis, as assessed, back to the client in order to verify understanding. The intervener might say, "You seem to be in pain and confused about what to do next" or "I can understand that all of this is difficult and sad for you." If the intervener is not interpreting or understanding the situation accurately, the client will likely let it be known. Also, the intervener might wish to "negotiate a mutually acceptable definition of the situation with the client" (Straus, 1982:64). This will facilitate understanding and effective therapeutic interaction.

Always understand that the client has experienced a traumatic situation (or, in the case of Mrs. F, many situations). Through information gathering the intervener should get to know the client, get a handle on the presenting crisis, and seek all relevant information concerning the client's social and psychological world.

Control.   The main emphasis here is on rationality and stability. That is, rationality of thought and stability of affect. Once the crisis has been identified and stability introduced, the intervener may wish to devise a set of intervention goals with the client (when the client is capable of doing so) designed to foster positive growth and change. This will serve as a good reference from which interventive efforts can be launched. Mrs. F and the intervener may decide to talk about the crisis. The intervener may emphasize alternatives to her current emotional state.

The degree or amount of stability utilized is dependent upon the lethality of the situation; of paramount importance is the reduction of potential danger. This might mean danger to the social-emotional self or to the physical self. It is in this stage that the *crisis is addressed.* The nature of the crisis is identified, by the intervener, through the collaborative efforts of both counselor and counselee. At this point, Mrs. F may tell the intervener that she cannot bear the sadness of losing her baby. She might even say, "I should have done more for the baby" or "It's all my fault; I should have left the baby in the hospital." These positions are reinforced by the nature of this situation, namely, the social connotation of the disorder, the appearance that the attending physician did all that could be done, the response of the coroner, and possibly the devalued nature of the social group to which she belongs. In this case, blame, although subtle, seems to be placed on Mrs. F. Here, the intervener may wish to draw on the individualistic nature of American society and how responsibility is meted out based on that structure (Ryan, 1971). It is understandable that she might blame herself given these social patterns.

When the nature of the crisis is identified, the *crisis is defined and this information is conveyed to the client.* What the intervener is dealing with, then, is the "operational definition of the situation" (Straus, 1984:32). When the crisis is defined by the client, the definition is based on precipitating factors and how they are interpreted and internalized. This results in unpleasant feelings or a state of crisis. Given the nature of our case study, this could be expected. Challenging a physician is not an activity which many feel comfortable with; this is especially true for our nonassertive client. As outlined above in the crisis process, crises do not suddenly materialize. Crises are produced in the individual through a "definition of the situation" (Thomas, 1931). For Mrs. F, the death of her child was defined, internalized, and reacted upon based on self-blame. It is normal for guilt to be present; however, Mrs. F needs to be guided away from this self-destructive pattern. The client is encouraged to understand his/her ideation and the feelings being experienced. Intervention, at this point, might be done by sharing with Mrs. F the nature of physician-patient relationships, how authority tends to operate, and specifically, how socialization seldom advocates questioning authority. The intervener must, in this instance, be cognizant of physician-patient relationships and how they are formed (Kallen and Pack, 1985). Also, Mrs. F needs to be reminded of the steps that she did take when caring for her child, in light of the dynamics between key players in this situation. Futhermore, the intervener might wish to educate Mrs. F on the social interpretation and the genetic reality of the disorder. The above tasks may be accomplished through gentle encouragement and role taking designed to help the client understand the thoughts and emotions being experienced. Any form of open ventilation should be allowed here. This is not only a stage that emphasizes definition and control but also exploration and open catharsis.

The intervener may demonstrate control and emotional stability by being a strong and confident "role model." The client might need someone that she can learn from. In this capacity, Mrs. F may be shown that a stable emotional constitution is attainable. Intervention should be marked with a demonstration of confidence, patience, purpose, trust, competence, compassion, and empathy. This conveys to the client that socioemotional stability and control are possible. Warmth, positive regard, unconditional acceptance, and respect (Rogers, 1951) should be demonstrated continuously; the client must be treated as a feeling human being. Clients need to be assured that their ideas and feelings are not "abnormal" and that there are many adjustments and stressors which one must contend with in life. The labeling process has no use here and should be avoided. Labeling the client with a diagnostic category has the potential of being destabilizing.

The intervener needs to examine, with the client, the definitional nature of the crisis. That is, the crisis intervener, using the sociological method, may help the client to identify any inaccurate, faulty, or self-destructive definitions of the situation. This is necessary because of the nature of personal definition in the formation of crisis. It is not just the situation itself that produces crisis; it is the definition of that situation that contributes to crisis formation. For example, Mrs. F might believe that she was at fault for her baby's death because she defined the situation in terms of total personal responsibility. Mrs. F should be made aware of the strength of authority, prestige, and status when responsibility is meted out. Is Mrs. F defining herself as a failure? Based on situation definitions, she may have perceived the situation in a self-destructive way. Once the client has been introduced to the definitional nature of the crisis, it is then necessary to show the client that he or she has the ability to *redefine the situation* (Straus, 1979a, 1984) in ways which may be more emotionally productive. The client can be helped to interpret and act upon the situation in a way that does not have self-destructing or self-limiting features. This is similar to what Straus (1982:69) refers to as "teaching control." In the present context, this includes suggestions or tactics designed to alleviate the client's stress and crisis. Through a redefinition of the situation, the client is given the skills to reduce levels of stress and crisis.

Direction.   This step has an emphasis of decisive action. It is the step which puts into action the situation redefinition process. The main emphasis in direction is to encourage the use of alternatives to unpleasant thoughts, feelings, and behavior. The explicit goal is to help the client reach a level of socioemotional stability that promotes self-assured independence. It is important that this take place without an excessive time-lag. If this is not the case, the client runs the risk of falling deeper into the self-destructive behaviors that the therapeutic encounter was meant to change. When change does not take place within a relatively short time (1–8 encounters), one is no longer practicing crisis intervention. The development of direction is an important therapeutic goal. The intervener, during this and all stages, must be open, honest, and genuine. Above all, the intervener needs to be attentive (an active and caring listener) and intentional (devoted to a positive therapeutic outcome). With these points in mind, a productive encounter may ensue.

Direction puts into practice the redefinition process. A "direct mode" of intervention deals with the actual problem and tends to be "expedient" (Straus, 1984:55). When changing the definition of the situation, it is, of course, essential that the client understand the definition he or she already has. This clarification should take place during the "control" stage. Clients should be helped to understand self-destructive, self-defeating, self-limiting, and counterproductive definitions. Clients are then encouraged to define the situation in more positive and manageable terms. In other words, the intervener will attempt to reframe the situation through collaborative efforts with the client (Straus, 1982). Let us, again, take the case study example. Mrs. F defined the situation in such a way that she had taken the burden of the child's death. Through this reaction, Mrs. F was defining herself as a failure in mothering, irresponsible, and to blame. Our client can be guided through a redefinition process. Mrs. F needs to be shown that she is considering herself a failure due to the child's death. It can be demonstrated that thinking she is a failure will result in a "self-fulfilling prophecy" (Merton, 1968:477). This concept states that by falsely defining a situation one may evoke new behaviors that make the false definition true. The client can be shown that the definition, which may not necessarily be accurate, is causing pain. Mrs. F needs to be helped to understand that she cannot hold herself accountable for a genetic disorder and, furthermore, that she *did* take action on behalf of her child. The client may respond, "It's easier said than done" or "I just can't forgive myself." However, it is possible that once the client understands that her definition of reality has produced the emotional state being experienced, personal empowerment will take place to alter existing definitions.

Progress Assessment. Once the situation has been defined in "control" and redefined in "direction," the intervener may wish to engage in progress assessment. This form of assessment is different than the aforementioned type. Here, the intervener examines the progress which has been made between the intervener and client toward the desired end. This may entail an examination by the intervener or a joint assessment between intervener and client. This is also a good opportuntity to compliment the client on progress made; positive reinforcement will work to the advantage of the client and the desired therapeutic outcome. Also, if the therapeutic encounter was not successful in its goal, the intervener will wish to approach the crisis again. This would mean returning to the control step. If deemed appropriate, the intervener may wish to introduce confrontation with the client, such as that explained by Jones and Polak (1968). For instance, it may be necessary to confront the client if, in the intervener's judgment, the client is not taking the necessary degree of responsibility in the relationship. One must, however, use caution when introducing confrontation. Client ability to manage confrontation must be assessed in order to avoid a reaction marked with defensiveness and resentment. In short, then, this stage gives the client and intervener the opportunity to review the progress, or lack thereof, in the encounter.

Referral. The final step in the crisis intervention process is referral. At this time, the client is either referred to another helper or agency for more specialized treatment, or the case is closed. Referral is made for more specialized services and assistance that cannot be provided by the intervener. Referral should be made as the situation warrants it. A referral might have been made, in our case study, to an agency specializing in bereavement counseling, a local health department, or to legal aid (the latter due to possible legal encounters with Dr. P). Most important would be to ensure that the surviving child, which had developed the same symptoms, received medical attention. This should be sought from a different physician, if possible. Often some form of follow-up is useful, beneficial, and therapeutic. The separation of intervener and client need not be stamped with a seal of finality. If it is desirable for both parties, continued contact has a place in the therapeutic relationship as long as the contact does not evolve into dependency, namely, client dependency on the intervener. However, it is a beneficial practice to address separation issues early. These should be attended to early in order to avoid problems of dependency when separation becomes a reality. The crisis intervener has a limited role in providing aid to those in emotional turmoil. This role has, as its main emphasis, the tasks of gathering information, providing control and direction, and arranging referral.

Summary

Many sociological concepts are applicable to crisis intervention practice. The two approaches are quite compatible. Individuals are social beings, affected by social circumstances. Crisis is not experienced in a psychological vacuum; social forces aid in the formation of crisis. Personal crisis is formed through an interpretive and definitional framework. Precipitating events are given meaning through interpretation which, in turn, leads to a crisis state through a perceived threat to socioemotional stability. It is through the precipitating events and the definition of the situation that the crisis is produced.

Once the clinician understands the social psychological basis of crisis formation, effective intervention strategy can be developed. The intervention process includes crisis assessment, information gathering, control, direction, progress assessment, and referral. A case study illustration was used to clarify suggested crisis intervention strategies. Through these steps, the intervener will be able to work with the client in order to reach stable socioemotional functioning.

NOTES

1. Beyond this duration, one might be practicing brief psychotherapy or beginning an extended therapeutic relationship.

2. The images of the client, which are presented, are not intended to be demeaning or stereotypical. The author believes the information to be important for understanding the case.

3. The intervener may find it useful to review interviewing skills (especially the proper uses of open and closed ended questions). This information is available in many qualitative sociology texts. Also, *The Helping Interview* by Alfred Benjamin (1981) offers a good presentation of effective communication skills.

REFERENCES

Benjamin, Alfred D.
    1981   The Helping Interview, 3rd ed. Boston: Houghton-Mifflin.
Black, C. M. and R. Enos
    1980   "Sociological precedents and contributions to the understanding and facilitation of individual behavior change: the case for counseling sociology," Journal of Sociology and Social Welfare 7:648–664.
Blumer, H.
    1972   "Symbolic interaction: an approach to human communication," in Richard Budd and Brent Ruben, eds., Approaches to Human Communication. Rochelle Park, NJ: Hayden.
Burgess, A. W. and B. A. Baldwin
    1981   Crisis Intervention Theory and Practice. Englewood Cliffs, NJ: Prentice-Hall.
Byers, B. D. and J. E. Hendricks
    1985   "Suicide intervention with the elderly: analytical and interactional aspects." Unpublished manuscript.

Caplan, G.
    1964   Principles of Preventive Psychiatry. New York: Basic Books.
Church, N.
    1985   "Sociotherapy with marital couples: incorporating dramaturgical and social con-
                structionist elements of marital interaction," Clinical Sociology Review 3:116–128.
Cooley, C. H.
    1956   Social Organization: A Study of the Larger Mind. Glencoe, IL: Free Press.
Costello, D. E.
    1972   "Therapeutic transactions: an approach to human communication," in Richard Budd
                and Brent Ruben, eds., Approaches to Human Communication. Rochelle Park, NJ:
                Hayden.
Freedman, J.
    1982   "Clinical sociology: what it is and what it isn't," Clinical Sociology Review
                1:34–49.
Fritz, J. M.
    1985   Colloquium on Clinical Sociology. Bowling Green State University, October 7.
Glass, J.
    1979   "Renewing an old profession: clinical sociology," American Behavioral Scientist
                22:513–530.
Glassner, B. and J. A. Freedman
    1979   Clinical Sociology. New York: Longman.
Hendricks, J. E.
    1984   "Death notification: the theory and practice of informing survivors," Journal of
                Police Science and Administration 12:109–116.
Hurvitz, N.
    1979   "The sociologist as a marital and family therapist," American Behavioral Scientist
                22:557–576.
Jaques, E.
    1947   "Social therapy: technocracy or collaboration?" Journal of Social Issues 3:59–66.
Jones, M. and P. Polak
    1968   "Crisis and confrontation," British Journal of Psychiatry 114:169–174.
Kallen, D. J. and C. A. Pack
    1985   "Medical sociology: the clinical perspective," in Roger A. Straus, ed., Using
                Sociology: An Introduction from the Clinical Perspective. Bayside, NY: General
                Hall.
Lee, A. M.
    1955   "The clinical study of society," American Sociological Review 20:648–653.
    1979   "The services of clinical sociology," American Behavioral Scientist 22:487–511.
Lindemann, E.
    1944   "Symptomatology and management of acute grief," American Journal of Psychiatry
                101:141–148.
Link, E. P.
    1948   "A note on sociosomatics," American Sociological Review 13:757–758.
Mead, G. H.
    1934   Mind, Self, and Society. Chicago: University of Chicago Press.
Merton, R. K.
    1968   Social Theory and Social Structure. New York: Free Press.
Moreno, J. D. and B. Glassner
    1979   "Clinical sociology: a social ontology for therapy," American Behavioral Scientist
                22:531–541.

Morrice, J. K. W.
    1976   Crisis Intervention: Studies in Community Care. Oxford: Pergamon.
Polak, P.
    1971   "Social systems intervention," Archives of General Psychiatry 25:110–117.
Rapaport, L.
    1962   "The state of crisis: some theoretical considerations," Social Service Review
                36:211–217.
Rogers, C. R.
    1951   Client-Centered Therapy. Boston: Houghton-Mifflin.
Ryan, W.
    1971   Blaming the Victim. New York: Pantheon.
See, P. and R. Straus
    1985   "The sociology of the individual," in Roger A. Straus, ed., Using Sociology: An
                Introduction From The Clinical Perspective. Bayside, NY: General Hall.
Smith, L. L.
    1978   "A review of crisis intervention theory," Social Casework 59:396–405.
Straus, R. A.
    1979a   "Clinical sociology: an idea whose time has come . . . again," Case Analysis
                1:21–43.
    1979b   "The reemergence of clinical sociology," American Behavioral Scientist 22:477–485.
    1982   "Clinical sociology on the one-to-one level: a social behavioral approach to coun-
                seling," Clinical Sociology Review 1:59–74.
    1984   "Changing the definition of the situation: toward a theory of sociological interven-
                tion," Clinical Sociology Review 2:51–63.
Thomas, W. I.
    1931   The Unadjusted Girl. Boston: Little, Brown.
White, L. A.
    1947   "Culturological vs. psychological interpretations of human behavior," American
                Sociological Review 12:686–698.
Wirth, L.
    1931   "Clinical sociology," American Journal of Sociology 37:49–66.

Looking Closely at Quality Circles: Implications for Intervention

Martin L. Abbott
Seattle Pacific University

ABSTRACT

This article explores quality circles (QCs), a popular type of work group employed extensively in business and industry. It is noted that several empirical studies point out the failure of QCs to achieve desired outcomes. On the basis of the findings of a study involving QCs in an electronics manufacturing firm, three categories of QCs are identified: management dominated QCs; stable QCs; and QCs in crisis. The article suggests that practitioners should recognize the complexity of QCs and focus intervention efforts upon individual, QC group, and organizational levels of analysis.

A relatively new and innovative type of work group known as Quality Circles (QC) has become increasingly popular in American business and industry. It has been reported (Main, 1984) that over 2000 American companies hold membership in the International Association of Quality Circles (IAQC). Lawler and Mohrman (1985:66) estimate that over 90% of Fortune 500 companies have QC groups, including, "IBM, TRW, Honeywell, Westinghouse, Digital Equipment, and Xerox." Smeltzer and Kedia (1985:30), citing the *Quality Circle Journal*, note that more than 7000 American companies have started QCs within the past 5 years.

Quality circle practice is not limited to industry, but is represented in such widely varying contexts as: banking, health care (e.g., Goldberg and Pegels, 1984; Orlikoff and Snow, 1984), branches of the armed forces, and is especially

This paper is a revision of a paper presented at the Fourth Annual Clinical Sociology Association Collaborative Conference, San Antonio, Texas, August 23–26, 1984. The study was originally reported in an unpublished dissertation (Abbott, 1984).
Correspondence to: Martin L. Abbott, Department of Sociology, Social and Behavioral Sciences, Seattle Pacific University, Seattle, WA 98119.

growing in educational institutions (e.g., Bonner, 1982; Chase, 1983). It would appear that the phenomenon known as Quality Circles is geometrically progressing and, according to Ouchi (1981:261) is "in danger of becoming the management fad of the eighties."

This paper has several aims. First, QCs are explored in order to provide practitioners and clinicians with current information about this increasingly popular form of work group. Second, the findings of a study of QCs in an electronics manufacturing plant are reported in order to contribute to the scarce empirical data on QCs. Third, the primary focus of the paper is to suggest specific intervention approaches which are linked to different analytical levels of QC programs (individual, QC group, and organizational levels). Although QC use is expanding, much of the literature speaks to the potential for failure to achieve the intended outcome. By looking closely at QCs, researchers, practitioners, and clinicians may come to understand them better, and thus be better prepared to intervene for constructive and positive change.

THE PRACTICE OF QUALITY CIRCLES

Although there are various definitions of quality circles, the following by Gibson (1982) may be considered standard:

> Quality circles are small groups of individuals who do similar work, who volunteer to meet on a regular basis to be trained to identify problems in their work areas, analyze causes, implement and track solutions, measure results and communicate recommendations and results to management. (from Gibson, 1983:487)

It is difficult to account for the stylishness of QCs; however, their popularity may be loosely attributed to two factors: 1) the attempt to bolster productivity, improve work satisfaction, and reduce other job-related costs (e.g., absenteeism, and inferior product quality); and 2) the attempt to promote the ideals of industrial democracy.

A review of the recent literature on quality circles reveals a paucity of empirical analyses. Although there are many published accounts on the subject, few studies have approached QCs using systematic social science methodology (see Ferris and Wagner, 1985:155; Mohrman and Novelli, 1985:93).

Several empirical studies point out the failure of QCs to achieve desired outcomes. For example, Mohrman and Novelli's (1985) study of QCs in a warehousing operation concludes that the assumed links between QC participation and attitudinal and productivity outcomes are not well established. The authors suggest that attitudinal improvements due to QC participation may not lead to "improvements in productivity and attitudes of the workforce as a whole"

(p. 109). In like manner, Ferris and Wagner's (1985) analysis based upon social science research, challenges some widely held assumptions regarding QCs. They conclude that assumptions about the linkage between QCs and group performance, productivity, and desire for participation, cannot be made without reservation.

The disparity between the limited research activity and the widespread use of QCs is most noticeable in the many anecdotal accounts of the effects of QC programs. Most of these accounts are reports by practitioners discussing the benefits of QC, or at least the elements of the program which can lead to success. Although many of these accounts cast QCs in a positive light, many conclude that QC programs can, and do, fail to achieve positive outcomes. Problems with QCs are not confined to this country. For example, according to Cole (1981), only about one third of the circles established in Japan are doing well.

Most of the recent literature on QCs attempts to identify the potential reasons for failure and to prescribe procedures for success. Among the key elements of success noted by various authors are: gaining management support, and provision of adequate training for managers, leaders and facilitators (Metz, 1982); development of adequate communication (Ingle, 1982); and creation of the proper "atmosphere" for the programs (Ingle, 1982; Widtfeldt, 1981).

Management is frequently implicated in both success and failure. Many of the recent reviews of QCs note that management is a crucial link in the ability of the QC to produce significant results. Speaking broadly of the work ethic in the American workplace, Yankelovich and Immerwahr (1984) point out that it is management which has failed (but which is needed for success) in implementing programs which can garner worker commitment. The authors suggest that managerial resistance is linked to matters of authority, status and fairness. Ingle (1982) and Jones (1983) also note that management fears loss of authority and power.

The IAQC report by Gibson (1983) is more specific in identifying potential reasons for managerial difficulties in QC programs. In this report, the author lists the following problem areas: lack of support by middle management; slow management response to circle recommendations; apprehension or suspicion about management motives; and problems chosen by management. Other accounts point out that managers may be using QCs for their own purposes (Thackray, 1982).

A STUDY OF A QUALITY CIRCLE PROGRAM

Several research questions were explored in a study of quality circles in an electronics manufacturing organization. Data were collected through questionnaires, interviews, and observations, to test the widely held assumption of an automatic linkage between worker participation and outcomes such as job satisfaction and increased productivity. Blumberg's (1968) analysis represents a classic statement of this relationship. More recently, the studies by Ferris and Wagner (1985) and Mohrman and Novelli (1985) challenge this assumption, and suggest that these assumed benefits of participation provide the rationale for many QC programs. Locke and Schweiger (1979) also address this issue, concluding that about 40% of laboratory, correlational, and field studies demonstrate no superiority of participation in decision making upon satisfaction.

Data for the current study were obtained from two production areas within a major division of a large electronics manufacturing firm. These production units manufacture various electronic display systems and electronic peripheral processing equipment. Although each area produces different instruments, the areas are linked to a common management structure, and job classifications are the same.

The study site has used the quality circle worker participation program since 1979. Quality circles emerged largely from another worker participation program which began in 1975. Since their inception, QCs grew steadily until workforce reductions and reorganizations occurred during the Fall of 1981. From then until now, QCs have been reduced in number to about twenty. The study was based upon ten circles which were involved in all phases of the production process (assembly, test, and inspection) of various electronic instruments. Membership ranged between three and twelve with a mean size of about five. The groups differed in terms of how long they had functioned, with a mean length of about thirteen months.

Findings for this study can be analyzed by reporting both questionnaire data and data based upon interviews and observation. An analysis of this information is then used as a basis upon which to propose a meaningful avenue for clinical intervention into QCs.

Questionnaire Findings

Data analysis showed no clear linkage between QC participation and job satisfaction. QC members and nonmembers did not differ on these measures, suggesting that the assumption of an automatic linkage between participation and satisfaction is unwarranted. This finding is supported by the studies of Ferris and Wagner (1985) and Mohrman and Novelli (1985), which were reviewed earlier.

In addition to the overall participation-satisfaction test, several analyses addressed the issue of the mediating effects of desire for, and attitudes toward, participation. These findings led to the emergence of several suggestions regarding the overall relationship between worker participation and job satisfaction. First, there appeared to be positive regard for worker participation programs in general; however, the QC program in place was unable to promote general job satisfaction. Second, the management structure may have partially obstructed the QC program from reaching its full potential. Third, "desire for participation" was found to be an important variable in terms of the overall relationship between QC participation and job satisfaction. This suggests that subsequent tests of this relationship should take this variable into account. Dean's (1985) study of QCs in a manufacturing corporation supports this finding. Dean concluded that those people who were more likely to join QCs desired greater organizational involvement and believed that circles would be instrumental in making improvements.

Taken together, the questionnaire data challenge the assumption of a simplistic relationship between QCs and such outcomes as job satisfaction. Further, it is apparent that workers' attitudes toward the QC must be taken into account in order to provide an accurate indication of QC success. The connection of this individual level of analysis of worker attitudes with QC program intervention is addressed more fully below. First, however, data from interviews and observations are discussed.

Interviews and Observations

One finding that clearly emerged from the interviews and observations was the extent to which workers viewed themselves in contradistinction to managers, with respect to participation in decision-making activity. Although workers desired participation both because of their direct contact with the work and because it had an impact on their subjective definitions of importance, they nevertheless accepted, in theory, the legitimacy of a management-controlled decision-making structure. This finding is consonant with Witte (1980:38) who noted "workers' natural acceptance of hierarchical authority and their perception that obedience to authority is an integral part of one's job." Leitko et al. (1981) also spoke to this point in their conclusion that workers learn situational adjustment attitudes at work, one of which is the notion that it is the manager's job to manage, and that workers have limited job information from which to make decisions.

The apparent paradox in workers' attitudes—on the one hand desiring participation and on the other hand accepting the legitimacy of a decision-making structure which may not deliver—may be partially explained by the domination by (or unresponsiveness of) managers over decision making at this location. In a sense, managers may have been partially perceived by workers in this study as an active hindrance to decision-making ability.

The primary advantages of QCs included the perception by workers that they could provide a convenient problem-solving mechanism, and that they could provide common ground upon which management and workers could communicate and share information. Among the disadvantages noted were management domination, unmotivated members, and the choice of inconsequential problems.

Ongoing observations of the QC program resulted in the identification of three categories of QCs: 1) management dominated; 2) stable; and 3) those in crisis. It should be noted that these categories are based upon a small number of circles and cannot adequately capture the dynamics of QC activity. In addition, the issues discussed cannot be considered mutually exclusive, but interactive.

Management Dominated Circles

In a majority of the QC groups observed, manager domination was present in some guise. Many groups could be designated "management dominated," since the managers interfered with the QC meeting process either by overt intimidation or by leadership style. This usually resulted in one or more of the following consequences: 1) obviation of the QC leader's role; 2) suppression of group interaction; and 3) assumption of the central focus by the manager.

Stable Circles

A QC which met regularly, kept on task, maintained good attendance, had fairly open communication, and in which manager domination did not preclude the occurrence of these events was identified as stable. Although the QC members may have had negative attitudes and management domination was present in varying degrees, the groups maintained somewhat steady progress. The stability of these QC groups may be explained in part by the presence of leaders who exhibited good group interaction skills. They maintained a pleasant atmosphere, encouraged open participation, kept the group on task, and, in differing degrees, maintained control in the presence of dominant managers.

Circles in Crisis

Several of the QC groups were largely ineffective and appeared inert. Although these QCs continued to meet with varying degrees of regularity, the overall group process deviated from the initial intent of quality circles (according to the definition of QCs). This was evidenced by the following factors: group meetings were irregular or frequently cancelled; attendance was erratic; membership was shrinking or very low; the group had difficulty attracting new members; there was considerable difficulty choosing new projects, or finishing current ones; participation in ongoing projects waned; leadership appeared uncommitted; and the membership was generally lethargic in terms of their overall motivation.

Discussion

Based upon this study of a QC program, it is suggested that practitioners need to address QCs as a multifaceted process. As noted, QCs do not necessarily lead directly to assumed outcomes. The attitudes and perceptions of individual workers toward QCs must be taken into account. Further, QCs develop different activities and dynamics. Successful QC programs must recognize these differences, as well as the organizational conditions which are intimately related to QC groups. Quality circles represent an important potential for workers and the organization which supports them. However, successful programs require ongoing critique, and analytical techniques which can be provided by clinical interventionists. The next section of this paper addresses QC intervention through an analysis of problems and solutions which arise at each analytical level of a QC program.

QC INTERVENTION

Attempts to intervene in QC processes for constructive change must begin with the recognition of different levels of analysis. Quality circles are primarily a group phenomenon. However, they are comprised of individual workers, and they take place within an organizational context. As noted earlier, little attention has been directed toward individual workers' attitudes. Recent studies have addressed other levels of analysis, especially the organizational structure. Goldstein's (1985) analysis of "organizational dualism," Meyer and Stott's (1985) three different analytical perspectives of QCs, and Smeltzer and Kedia's (1985) discussion of organizational culture all attest to the importance of viewing the QC as integrally related to its organizational environment.

Constructive intervention may be achieved by considering empirical evidence and suggestions from the literature regarding the QC on individual, group, and organizational levels. Although considered separately, it must be recognized that each level is related to the other in a very complex fashion. Smeltzer and Kedia's (1985) analogy of a rope comprised of single, interwoven strands (used to describe the different aspects of organizational culture) is an apt way to view the interrelationship of the various levels of QC programs. It must also be recognized that each level has its own problems, and therefore, its own specific conditions for solutions.

Problems and Solutions on an Individual Level

Little empirical analysis has been done that focuses upon the individual worker's attitudes toward QCs. Notable exceptions to this lack of research are the study by Dean (1985), discussing the reasons workers give for joining QCs; Mohrman and Novelli's (1985) analysis of the effects of QCs on workers' attitudes; and an article by Ferris and Wagner (1985) reviewing the assumptions underlying workers' desire for participation (among other considerations).

The results of the study discussed in this paper thus join others that focus on the importance of individual attitudes in understanding QCs. If, on the one hand, workers are committed to the QC process and are satisfied with its operation, the QC will probably have a much greater chance of success. If, on the other hand, workers are not committed to, and satisfied with, the process, the QC will be more likely to experience difficulty, and the nature of the group may change from its initial purpose.

Constructive intervention requires an ongoing program of evaluating individual workers' attitudes. The attempt to ensure salient QC participation would require that practitioners answer such questions as: To what extent do workers feel satisfied with their QC group? To what extent do workers feel manipulated or tricked? How do workers view the contribution to, or domination by, managers in the QC process? To what extent do workers feel that problems chosen are either trivial or significant and meaningful?

The advantage of monitoring individual attitudes is two-fold. First, practitioners would have a knowledge of how workers perceive the program. Although this may appear trivial, it is a crucial issue since QCs are often installed "from the top down," thus effectively obscuring individual commitment to the program. Second, an ongoing check of attitudes would serve as a barometer of QC change. QCs evolve and change. A ready understanding of individual attitude changes would provide valuable insight into potential reasons for QC success or failure. QC groups may also affect individual attitudes, and it is important to establish a plan for assessing these attitudes.

A plan of this nature would require a financial commitment on the part of the host organization. However, the potential increase in understanding and subsequent program changes would have to be considered among financial assets.

Accomplishing this type of intervention program would require specific research expertise and might profitably include a number of different providers. Outside sources, such as a research consultant who is sensitive to the complexities of clinical intervention, is one such provider. Organizational development (OD) staff could profitably be utilized, however, the same sensitivity to intervention issues would be necessary. Gutknecht's (1984) analysis of OD and its implications for clinical sociology provides an excellent discussion of issues which can be related to intervention on an individual level in QC programs.

Problems and Solutions on a QC Group Level

Careful analysis is also crucial on the QC group level since their success or failure, from the organization's point of view, is most commonly identified with group "output." Several studies have suggested that QC groups have "life cycles," or pass through certain stages (e.g., Lawler and Mohrman, 1985; Meyer and Stott, 1985), usually ending in decline. The study reported in this paper also indicates that (perhaps as they evolve) QCs develop their own distinctive styles. That is, at any point in time, QCs are characterized by different activity levels, participation, and interpersonal dynamics. The different QCs noted earlier (management dominated, in crisis, and stable) represent different QC group typifications. This is an important distinction as QCs will not only experience problems as they evolve, but also problems specific to their type.

Given this distinction, solutions to QC programs need to be customized to the group, and to be dynamic as QC groups change. As with the individual level, careful monitoring is crucial, especially to detect changes in QC functioning. Knowing the QC composition and character can make possible a range of intervention strategies streamlined for a given group. For example, attempts to revitalize QC groups in crisis may include the following: coupling the members with stable QC group members in order to help them observe and model the strengths of other approaches; integrating members from stable QC groups into QC groups in crisis to provide fresh insight into problematic group elements; providing a specific work problem that members of QC groups in crisis may be adept at solving.

Other intervention attempts would, in similar fashion, take as their starting point the specific nature of the QC group. Management-dominated QC groups would profit from specific intervention to change the managers' approach to QC group process. This could be accomplished by training in group dynamics and problem-solving techniques, with the specific intent of allowing QC groups to operate autonomously, apart from managerial obstruction. Stable QC groups would best be left alone, to the extent that they do not experience internal difficulties.

Several studies in the literature have suggested additional approaches to intervene constructively in QC group operation. These suggestions would be especially helpful if coupled with specific QC types. Meyer and Stott's (1985:42) suggestion of a charter or steering committee may be important here. Discussing the impact of different "interest groups" upon QC operation, the authors note that charters or steering committees can provide support, establish priorities, and prevent QCs from becoming ends in themselves. Viewing this suggestion in light of group differences may yield a strategy of assigning different priorities and involvement that are specific to each type of QC group. For example, stable QC groups might be left to operate autonomously, while the other groups would be given more structured direction.

Due to the specific nature of the overall QC group process, Goldstein (1985:510–514) makes several suggestions regarding the "boundary conditions" for QCs. Among these are the ideas of rotating membership from outside groups; restricting QC activity to idea generation only (and not implementation of ideas); and preference for a convener chosen from the membership to lead, rather than imposing a formal leader upon the QC. While these are excellent suggestions, it would appear that they would be especially efficacious if matched with different types of QC groups.

Along a different line, some studies indicate that QC groups could profitably be merged into different group structures, especially ''Self-Managing Teams'' (Sims and Dean, 1985), along with other forms of worker participation (Lawler and Mohrman, 1985). Again, viewing this merger of QC groups in light of their specific nature could provide the organization with flexible and dynamic worker participation groups.

All of these ideas imply the existence of a specific organizational structure that can monitor, oversee, and constructively intervene in groups, depending upon their specific circumstances. The same recommendations for experts in the area of clinical intervention is indicated here as with individual-level concerns. The analysis, identification, and facilitation of change for QC groups requires a special sociological fund of knowledge that can be brought to bear upon a concrete set of individual, group and organizational problems.

Problems and Solutions on an Organizational Level

Since the majority of my research was done on the levels previously discussed, this section is based primarily upon observation of QC groups in industry, and suggestions from the literature. Realistically, this may be the most crucial level of analysis since QC groups are vitally linked to the entire organizational environment. Intervention into individual and QC group processes requires some organizational commitment and restructuring. Specifically, attention to the following issues appears to be crucial for the overall success of the QC program: the management role; appropriate organizational climate; rationale for QC program.

The studies cited earlier dealing with problems in management are joined by similar analyses from other authors (Lawler and Mohrman, 1985; Meyer and Stott, 1985; Smeltzer and Kedia, 1985; Thompson, 1982). From my own observation, and drawing from sociological theory, the problem of managers (especially middle- and first-level managers) stems from a problem of meeting multiple, competing expectations (''role strain''). On the one hand, managers are expected to provide and promote greater decision-making power on the part of individual workers. On the other hand, managers must somehow engineer ''success'' in terms of the criteria for QCs established by upper management, often in the absence of specific training or support. Thus, managers and supervisors fear erosion of their control over the work process because of QCs, but at the same time have come to equate success in the workplace with QC success.

Solutions to this problem are complex, due to authority structures which are frequently based upon hierarchical systems of decision making. Aside from the decision to address the structure of power in organizations, QC programs could profit from providing organizational support and training to managers in terms of QC purpose and operation. The qualified clinician could provide specific training and resources for managers in the following areas: recognizing different management styles; the nature and dynamics of QC groups; decision-making styles; matching individual managerial style with specific tasks; the philosophy of worker participation; communication skills; and different techniques for resolving role strain.

Organizational-level intervention must take into account the entire nature of the environment in which QCs operate. Smeltzer and Kedia's (1985) analysis of organizational culture specifies several different elements that should be addressed in analyzing QCs: organizational structure, management style, decision making, adaptation to change, labor relations, and commitment. Other studies (e.g., Meyer and Stott, 1985) specify organizational components that must be addressed in order to assess the practicability of QC group success. The addition of individual and group-level knowledge would combine with this macrolevel analysis to provide a comprehensive data base from which to consider QCs. With this information and perspective, the decision to maintain or dismantle QCs, or to phase them into other forms could be more successfully negotiated.

Ultimately, the issue of the rationale for the QC program must be addressed. Solutions to specific QC problems depend upon the reason QCs exist at the particular site. If they have been installed by management, the clinical interventionist must ask a series of important questions. First, were QCs developed due to their fadishness, and must be forced to fit a particular upper management agenda? If this is the case, QC success is more a function of how closely they conform to this agenda than a function of their own dynamics or products.

The overall question to be answered prior to any intervention, however, is whether the QC program has been established to increase true decision-making ability for workers, or for some other purpose. The fact that many QC programs are installed by management without input from workers is testimony to the nonparticipative environment within which QC programs must operate. Rinehart's (1984:89) discussion of QCs as schemes to raise productivity and reduce costs "through the cultivation of cooperation on the shop floor and the appropriation of workers' knowledge" speaks directly to this point. The clinical interventionist must assess the extent to which QCs may be a way of engineering success at the workers' expense, rather than as a legitimate, participative work form. At this level, solutions take less of a specific character and rest with the ability of the clinician to articulate the specific rationale of the program.

CONCLUSION

Quality circles have the potential for both success and failure. Though very popular, QCs have not been subjected to sustained empirical scrutiny. Thus, practitioners are only beginning to identify the dynamics of QCs and the elements that can lead to meaningful and successful work programs. This paper has suggested several directions for intervening into QC programs. First, QC programs must be viewed as comprising several different levels of analysis. Successful intervention must take each of these levels into account. Second, each of the levels presents the practitioner with a distinct set of problems. Third, constructive intervention requires the clinical skills of researchers who are able to address creatively the problems emerging from each of these levels. Last, clinical intervention requires, first and foremost, an analytical way of viewing QCs, which includes proposing specific solutions and asking difficult questions at each level of the program.

REFERENCES

Abbott, Martin L.
    1984   "The outcomes of a quality circle program in an electronics manufacturing firm."
            Unpublished dissertation, Portland State University.
Blumberg, Paul
    1968   Industrial Democracy. New York: Shocken.
Bonner, James S.
    1982   "Japanese quality circles: can they work in education?" Phi Delta Kappa 63, no.
            10:681.
Chase, Larry
    1983   "Quality circles in education," Educational Leadership 40, no. 5:18–26.
Cole, Robert E.
    1981   "Japan can but we can't." March 1981 IAQC conference presentation. Cited in
            Edmund J. Metz, "Caution, quality circles ahead," Training and Development
            Journal, Aug.
Dean, James W., Jr.
    1985   "The decision to participate in quality circles," Journal of Applied Behavioral
            Science 21, no. 3:317–327.
Ferris, Gerald R. and John A. Wagner, III
    1985   "Quality circles in the United States: a conceptual reevaluation," Journal of Applied
            Behavioral Science 21, no. 2:155–167.
Gibson, Price
    1982   "Quality circles and quality of work life: suggestions, myths and facts, problems,
            and advice." Dec. 1982. Paper prepared for first IAQC Executive Briefing, cited
            in Price Gibson, "Highlights from 1981 and 1982 quality circles research," 1983
            IAQC Conference Transactions.
    1983   "Highlights from 1981 and 1982 quality circles research," 1983 IAQC Conference
            Transactions, 486–502.
Goldberg, Alvin M. and C. Carl Pegels (with the special assistance of Elaine C. Rendall)
    1984   Quality Circles in Health Care Facilities: A Model for Excellence. Rockville, MD:
            Aspen Systems.
Goldstein, S.G.
    1985   "Organizational dualism and quality circles," Academy of Management Review
            10, no. 3:504–517.
Gutknecht, Douglas B.
    1984   "Organizational development: an assessment with implications for clinical sociol-
            ogy," Clinical Sociology Review 2:94–108.

Ingle, Sud
    1982   "How to avoid quality circle failure in your company," Training and Development
                Journal 36, no. 6:54–59.
Jones, W. G.
    1983   "Quality's vicious circles," Management Today, March: 97–102.
Lawler, Edward E., III, and Susan A. Mohrman
    1985   "Quality circles after the fad," Harvard Business Review Jan-Feb.
Leitko, Thomas A., Arthur L. Greil and Steven A. Peterson
    1981   "Lessons at the bottom: worker participation as situational adjustment." Paper
                presented at the Society for the Study of Social Problems, August.
Locke, Edwin A. and David M. Schweiger
    1979   "Participation in decision-making: one more look." Pp. 265–339 in Barry M. Staw,
                ed., Research in Organizational Behavior, vol. 1. Greenwich, CT: JAI Press.
Main, Jeremy
    1984   "The trouble with managing Japanese-style," Fortune, April 2.
Meyer, Gordon W. and Randall G. Stott
    1985   "Quality circles: panacea or Pandora's box?" Organizational Dynamics 13, no.
                4:34.
Metz, Edmund J.
    1982   "Do your quality circle leaders need more training?" Training and Development
                Journal Dec: 108–112.
Mohrman, Susan Albers and Luke Novelli, Jr.
    1985   "Beyond testimonials: learning from a quality circles programme," Journal of
                Occupational Behaviour 6:93–110.
Orlikoff, James E. and Anita Snow
    1984   Assessing Quality Circles in Health Care Settings: A Guide for Management. Chi-
                cago: American Hospital.
Ouchi, William
    1981   Theory Z: How American Business Can Meet the Japanese Challenge. Menlo Park,
                CA: Addison Wesley.
Rinehart, James
    1984   "Appropriating workers' knowledge: quality control circles at a General Motors
                plant," Studies in Political Economy 14:75–97.
Sims, Henry P. and James W. Dean, Jr.
    1985   "Beyond quality circles: self-managing teams," Personnel 62, no. 1: 25–32.
Smeltzer, Larry R. and Ben L. Kedia
    1985   "Knowing the ropes: organizational requirements for quality circles," Business
                Horizons 28, no. 4:30.
Thackray, John
    1982   "U.S. labor: the quest for quality work," Management Today, March: 66–69.
Thompson, Philip C.
    1982   Quality Circles: How to Make Them Work in America. New York: AMACOM.
Widtfeldt, James R.
    1981   "Jumping on the quality circles bandwagon," Data Management, Oct:32–35.
Witte, John F.
    1980   Democracy, Authority, and Alienation in Work. Chicago: University of Chicago
                Press.
Yankelovich, Daniel and John Immerwahr
    1984   "Putting the work ethic to work," Society, Jan-Feb:58–76.

Sociological Strategies for Developing Community Resources: Services for Abused Wives as an Example

Mary C. Sengstock
Wayne State University

ABSTRACT

There has been increased concern for the problem of family violence in recent years, and an accompanying interest in providing services to meet the needs of victims. This has led to research efforts, as well as to the development of new community services. Clinical sociologists can do much to assure that the development of community resources and empirical research in this area procede hand in hand. This article reports on the work of a committee, chaired by the author, which used social research and knowledge of sociological principles in the development of services for battered wives in a major metropolitan area. Three major intervention strategies were employed in the committee setting: provision of information about social structure and its consequences to enable members to develop more effective plans; use of sociological principles and data to make people aware of aspects of the situation of which they had not been aware; and involvement of group members and other individuals in the planning process to maximize the likelihood of an investment in the outcome. Committee activities are discussed as a means of indicating both successes and difficulties with these strategies.

During the past decade, there has been a growing recognition of the problem of family violence on the part of social scientists and the general public alike. In

The author wishes to express appreciation to the members of the planning staff of United Community Services of Metropolitan Detroit, for their untiring service to the committee. Margaret Ball was the staff worker who worked most closely with the committee at the beginning. Eben Martin has proven extremely helpful over the entire length of the group's operation. Basilio White and Margaret Mitzel also served with the committee for shorter periods of time.
Correspondence to: Mary C. Sengstock, Ph.D., C.C.S., Professor and Chair, Department of Sociology, Wayne State University, Detroit, MI 48202.

the field of research, a number of studies have focused on this topic (Gelles, 1972; Straus et al, 1980; Dobash and Dobash, 1979; Giles-Simms, 1983). In the social service fields and in the general public, there has been a growing awareness of the need for the development of services for victims of domestic abuse (Roy, 1977; Campbell, 1984).

Unfortunately, in many instances, these two lines of activity may develop independently of each other. Consequently, social research may proceed with little recognition of community needs, and community resources may be developed with little knowledge of the research data available or the contribution which social research may make to the understanding and solution of community problems. Clinical sociologists can do much to integrate these two fields, with beneficial consequences for both social science and community resource development. Community needs can be served more effectively when solutions are founded on a firm basis of social scientific knowledge. And social science becomes more refined through contact with the data found in community social settings.

A Community Planning Example

This article describes an example of a community planning activity in which social science principles and data were brought to bear in the design and implementation of a social service plan for abused wives in a major metropolitan area. The group, to be known as the Implementation Committee, was charged with implementing a service plan which had been developed by a prior research and planning committee. Both committees were chaired by the present author, and operated under the auspices of a United Fund supported community planning agency. The chairship of these committees occurred as a result of the author's prior service on a variety of volunteer committees, as well as several years of experience as a sociologist, including research on family violence.

The Implementation Committee was faced with a task which many believed was far too advanced for its time. They began their work in 1980, at a time when few services for such victims existed, when there was little public sympathy for their plight, and when neither professionals nor the general public possessed much knowledge about the problem. The odds against their success were high, but their eventual accomplishments were also considerable.

The committee chair was responsible for working with staff members of the planning agency in the selection of committee members, as well as for insuring that the charge to the group would be accomplished. Analysis of the activities of this committee provide an opportunity for illustrating the manner in which sociological strategies can be brought to bear in the solution of community needs.

INTERVENTION STRATEGIES IN A COMMITTEE SETTING

Throughout the process of selection of committee members, establishment of committee goals and objectives, and determination of methods for accomplishing these tasks, three major clinical strategies were employed:

1. Provision of information about social structure and its consequences, enabling individuals and groups to use knowledge of social structure to develop more effective plans for group action;
2. Use of sociological principles and data to make people aware of aspects of the social situation of which they had previously been unaware;
3. Involvement of the individuals/group members in the planning process, to maximize the likelihood that they will have an investment in the outcomes.

In reality, all three processes occur at once. Principles and data relating to the social structure are provided to key individuals in a manner designed to integrate them into the planning process. This results in the development of a sense of involvement on the part of those actors most able to effectuate change in the social structure. In the interest of clarity, however, each of these strategies will be explored separately.

1. Social Structural Analysis to Develop Effective Action Plans

The consideration of key social structural components in the development of an approach to the problem can be observed in the selection of committee members, in the establishment of task forces, and in the hearings which were sponsored. Each process involved the identification of those segments of the social structure which were central to the solution of the problem and of individuals who held critical positions in those social structures. Pressure could then be exerted on these individuals to enlist their assistance in accomplishing the task. In some instances the pressure was political; in other instances it was more subtle—a topic which will be discussed in the third section of this paper focusing on personal involvement.

Use of Social Structural Factors in Member Selection. Prior to the establishment of the committee, the committee chair and two staff members from the planning agency, both of whom were trained social workers, spent considerable time in the selection of committee members. Since the committee's charge was to implement a program of services for abused wives, it was necessary that the committee include not only persons with sufficient interest to work on the problem of spouse abuse, but also persons whose professional or other social structural contacts would place them in a position to influence the establishment of those services. Consequently, we attempted to select individuals who were part of or had influence with agencies whose services were needed by abused wives.

Research has shown that spouse abuse victims require a wide variety of services, including financial support, housing, legal assistance, counseling, and job placement (Dobash and Dobash. 1979; Spouse Abuse Project Committee, 1980). Members were chosen to insure that key agencies providing these types of services would be represented. These included personnel from the police department and prosecutor's office, an attorney active in women's rights, and individuals who worked in mental health and family service agencies. Wherever possible, an effort was made to locate individuals from these agencies who had already developed some sensitivity to the problems of battered women; where persons friendly to the cause were not available, other representatives were sought. In some instances, it was clear that the individuals invited were not anxious to participate, but felt that it was politically impossible to refuse to attend, or at least to send a representative.

In addition, there were representatives of educational institutions, and of various women's social groups and church organizations. All of the shelters for battered wives in the local area were also invited to send representatives. The resulting committee consisted of two major categories of members: individuals who had an intense empathy for the needs of abused wives and a strong commitment to assisting them, and others who may not have shared these feelings about the problem of spouse abuse but whose position in the social structure was such that they held the key to some type of assistance or service which would be helpful to spouse abuse victims. It was the organizers' hope that participation in the group discussion at committee meetings would influence these critical role players to use their positions in the service of abused wives.

Establishment of Task Forces.   The same approach was taken in the establishment of the task forces which developed out of the committee and, later, in the hearings which some of the task forces undertook. Here again, the clinical sociologist can direct the group's attention toward key aspects of the social structure of the community, indicating those segments of the social structure that can help the group to accomplish its goals. The committee spent considerable time discussing research related to the problem of spouse abuse, a topic that will be discussed in the next section on the provision of sociological principles and data. From this discussion emerged the view that three major types of services were needed by the women. The committee decided to form three task forces, focused around each of these needs: services from the criminal justice system (Justice System Task Force); services focused on the special counseling and shelter needs of battered women (Specialized Services Task Force); and improved information about spouse abuse, both for professionals and the general public

(Education Task Force).

Members of these task forces were selected by a process similar to that used for the committee as a whole. The process was based on the assumption that key actors in the community social structure could be co-opted if they could be induced to become members of the task forces. Consequently, the Justice Task Force included key figures in the police force and the prosecutor's office, and the Specialized Services Task Force included directors and representatives from family services and counseling agencies, as well as central figures from the county offices of the state department of social services. Although some of these persons attended reluctantly at first, their public image required that they give at least lip service to the goals of the committee. Many eventually became committed to the group and came to use their positions to assist in attaining the group's goals. Some examples of the manner in which these changes in attitude and behavior came about will be provided in the third section on the development of personal commitment through individual involvement.

The Use of Hearings.   There are some key individuals, however, whose time commitments are such that it is unlikely that they can be brought into a committee or task force on an ongoing basis. Directors of large agencies are an example of such individuals. Yet their involvement was critical if the process of restructuring the service network was to be successful. The Specialized Services Task Force dealt with this problem by holding hearings on key topics, with agency personnel being invited to attend and present their views. Since it was only a single meeting, there was a greater chance that an agency director would participate. The hearings covered critical service needs for battered wives, and the individuals invited to appear were persons whose position in the community structure was key to the attainment of such services. Agencies invited to participate included the local office of the state department of social services, family service agencies, mental health agencies, and substance abuse counseling agencies.

The earliest success of this task force is an example of the value of the hearings approach. The members were concerned about the problem of obtaining financial support for abused wives, whose fear for their safety often forces them to take their children and flee their homes, but with neither financial resources nor means of making a living. They find they are ineligible for welfare since their husbands' incomes are usually used as the test of eligibility. The latent function of this process is to force women to remain in a violent marriage. A change in state law had obviated this rule; however, most state caseworkers were unaware of the change, and bureaucratic red tape prevented the women from getting attention to their special problems.

The county director of social services was invited to attend a hearing and report on his department's efforts to assist battered wives. Members of the task force were prepared for an intense, perhaps even a bitter battle to make social services procedures more responsive to the needs of abused women. At the outset of the hearing, the director surprised everyone by announcing the appointment of a special caseworker to whom all cases of battering would be referred. This would insure prompt and sympathetic treatment, in accordance with the new state guidelines.

Committee members were convinced that the long-sought change in department procedures had come about largely because the director had to make a public statement before a concerned community group, a technique which is often effective in achieving long-term attitude and behavior change (Mayer et al, 1980; Kerr and MacCoun, 1985). Since the task force represented a planning agency with some standing in the community, he could hardly refuse to appear. Neither did he wish to appear callous toward the needs of abused women. His appearance allowed him to play the hero role, solving a major problem of battered wives by a simple change in bureaucratic procedure.

Avoiding the Pitfalls.   The technique of placing key role players on the committee and its task forces generally worked to great advantage, but it was not without its dangers. For example, one task force member took considerable issue, not with the goals of the group, but with the program plans it developed. The director of a major women's rights oriented group, she attended committee meetings on an irregular basis, usually sending an alternate in her place. When she did attend, she frequently questioned the actions enacted in her absence, pointing out that her organization was empowered to conduct many of these activities.

In retrospect, it is apparent that this member's behavior should have been handled more forcefully by the committee chair. She should have been informed that the actions taken in her absence were valid, that her alternate had been present, and that no one had the right to call these issues into question at a later date. She should further have been given the option, either to arrange her schedule so as to attend more regularly, or to appoint an alternate who could serve as the regular committee member, with full rights to represent the group in the committee. Lacking firm action on the part of the committee chair, the committee as a whole was frequently stymied in its action by a single member's behavior.

The failure to deal more effectively with this member probably stemmed from two factors. First, her leadership role in a key women's group led us to be too concerned with gaining her support. Second, we had anticipated opposition from traditionally oriented groups, but not from the leader of a women's rights group. Consequently, we were unprepared for the difficulties this individual caused. Had we been more alert, we would have recognized that groups such as hers might see our committee as a major competitor for community resources and recognition. Our lack of foresight allowed her to delay the actions of this task force for nearly an entire year, until she finally resigned from her position with the organization, and consequently, from the committee as well.

2. Providing Knowledge of Sociological Principles and Data

From the outset, it was important to focus the group's attention on the task at hand by means of written and/or oral materials relating to their task. In sociological terms, this essentially constitutes a "definition of the situation," as originally defined by Thomas (1931). As the group defines its task, the clinical sociologist encounters a critical point for inclusion of sociological principles and data. Sociological insights and data can guide the group as it defines the problem and selects specific goals to pursue. (See Straus, 1984:57–58, for a discussion of different levels of definition of the situation.)

The Implementation Committee was comprised of professionals whose training had occurred at a time when the existence of domestic violence was not even recognized, and of eager but unskilled volunteers. Many members lacked information about various aspects of the problem of wife abuse: they knew little about the men who perpetrate it or the women who are its victims. They did not understand the dynamics of family violence or the problems which victims have in obtaining services from medical and social agencies. They needed assistance in redefining their conceptions of appropriate role structures for the family, as well as the manner in which families should be served by the health and social service organizations.

It was important for committee members to increase their knowledge of the nature and dynamics of spouse abuse. They should know, for example, that spouse abuse is rather widely accepted in the population, that many people consider hitting one's spouse to be necessary and normal (Gelles, 1972:58–61; Stark and McEvoy, 1970:52; Straus et al., 1980:47–48). They should also be made aware of the consequences this situation frequently has for victims, most of whom know their friends and relatives ignore their plight and excuse their husbands' abusive behavior (Gelles, 1972:59–60; Giles-Sims, 1983:59). Committee members also needed an introduction to the suspected causes of spouse abuse, including the role of stress (Giles-Sims, 1983:55–56), and the patriarchal nature of Western society (Davidson, 1977; Dobash and Dobash, 1977, 1979). They also considered the common view that wife abuse is victim precipitated, and learned that most authorities now question that assumption (Straus, 1976; Gelles, 1972:159).

Since the committee's charge focused on a service plan, it was critical that members understand the service needs of abused wives and the problems they encounter in getting these services. Studies indicate that battered women receive little help, whether from doctors, the police, ministers, social workers, or counselors, all of whom tend to ignore or excuse the problem, or worse, to suggest that it is the woman's fault (Michigan Women's Commission, 1977; Dobash and Dobash, 1977, 1979). With this knowledge, the committee would realize that, without alteration, the existing system of social and health services could not alleviate the problems of abused wives.

Techniques for Providing Information.   In providing this information to committee members, four major techniques were used. First, and most obvious, they were provided with references to appropriate books and articles, such as those cited above, and the most committed members probably made an effort to obtain them. However, it should also be recognized that most members of a volunteer committee are unlikely to make the effort necessary to track down such materials. Consequently, the second approach was to provide copies of important materials at committee meetings whenever the cost was not prohibitive. The report of the predecessor committee, which summarized important research and service needs of abuse victims in the local area, was an important source in this regard (Spouse Abuse Project Committee, 1980). Professional journal articles were also distributed, if they were not too methodologically or theoretically complicated. Articles from the mass media could also be used, provided that the information they contained was factually correct and sociologically valid.

Both of these approaches, however, assume that the members are sufficiently committed to do the outside reading. Those who lack this level of commitment require group discussion of important information to help alter their views (Asch, 1948; Janis and Mann, 1977). Hence, the third approach used with the committee was to hold group discussions on a number of issues, particularly with relation to the types of services available in the local community.

Similar discussions also formed the major part of the hearings, to which agency representatives were invited. Guests were asked to discuss the degree to which they saw wife abuse among their agency clientele, and how they handled these cases when they saw them. The hearings were an eye-opening experience, both for the agency representatives and for the members of the committee. It became obvious that few agencies had any method for determining the presence of violence among their clients. Unless the client pointedly informed the worker that violence was a problem, most workers simply assumed that it was not present.

One committee member, a long-time director of a family service agency, expressed concern as to the situation in his own agency. He announced his intention to ask his workers how they determined the presence of abuse among their own clients. He later reported to the committee that the caseworkers' estimates of the number of clients in violent marriages was far lower than the number of cases they found when clients were asked this question directly. Such incidents helped committee members to become aware of the need for constant questioning of their assumptions about violent families.

The fourth and final technique is especially effective for providing accurate information. It requires that the clinical sociologist remain alert during group discussion for evidence of inaccurate information or invalid assumptions on the part of committee members or guests. For example, a common assumption is that alcohol operates as a causal factor in spouse abuse. Many people assume further that the violent behavior will be cured automatically if the alcoholism can be brought under control. These views were expressed by several of the substance abuse counselors who attended our hearings, as well as by some committee members themselves. Authorities question this assumption, however, suggesting that alcohol may be a method by which violent individuals excuse their behavior, rather than an actual cause of the violence (Gelles, 1972:113–117). Furthermore, an alcoholic often experiences greater levels of stress at the outset of a period of abstinence, leading to an even greater tendency toward violent outbursts. Thus the assumption that treatment need not be specifically directed toward the violence is invalid. Substance abuse counselors and committee members alike had to be dispelled of this myth.

It is important that the clinical sociologist be alert to the expression of such inaccuracies, for these incidents offer an opportune occasion for providing new information to correct the inaccuracies. This must be done with sensitivity, lest members and guests be insulted or offended. One effective technique for providing new information is to invite members of the group to check the literature and report back to the group. This increases the members' level of participation and makes them more likely to be persuaded by the arguments (Fazio and Zanna, 1981; Sherman et al, 1983; Taylor et al, 1978; Watts, 1967). Other techniques for involving members in group process may also be effective in generating commitment to group goals, a topic which will be discussed in the next section.

3. Developing Personal Commitment through Individual Involvement

The role of group relationships in attitude stability and change has formed an important part of social psychological theory for some time (Asch, 1948; Newcomb, 1943; Lewin, 1951). Since the goal of the planning activities was to alter the manner in which community agencies operated, it was critical to include key members of these agencies in the planning process, and to obtain their commitment to the group and its goals. In employing this strategy, we combined the use of social structural knowledge, which helps to identify key roles and role players in the social system, with social psychological principles, which remind us that attitude and behavior change is more effectively produced when the individual becomes personally involved in the change process (Sherif, 1966; Janis and Mann, 1977). This approach, which has been termed "cooperative intervention," seeks to involve the individual who will be affected by the change in the change process itself (Straus, 1984).

By encouraging group discussion and allowing members and guests to express their concerns or objections, the group should be able to resolve major objections as they arise. By their involvement in the decision-making process, it was hoped that participants could be induced to accept the group's views on the needs of battered wives. Examples of the effectiveness of this process can be seen in the behavior of several individuals who were assigned to the Justice System Task Force, many of whom were originally reluctant to become involved. It was strongly suspected that only the orders of their superiors or the fear of bad publicity for their departments brought about their participation.

One individual, a staff member at a local prosecutor's office, had once been criticized publicly by women's rights' groups for his insensitive treatment of abused wives who sought his help. After serving for several months as a member of the task force, he initiated a review of his own department's procedures to insure that abused wives would be handled properly. Other members were police officials with a reputation for ignoring the concerns of battered women. After serving for a time on this task force, they often astounded their listeners by supporting changes which they once had vigorously resisted.

This strategy can be used not only with group members, but also with outsiders whose support the group must generate. The success of the group in understanding the philosophies of others and accommodating their goals to these philosophies can be illustrated by one of the more difficult projects which the Education Task Force assumed. This group had placed a high priority on the training of professionals whose services were needed by abused wives. As noted earlier, most had been trained when there was little recognition of the problem of family violence, and their professional training reflected this lack. This is true of law enforcement officials, but since these officials operate under the direction of the courts, task force members became convinced that changes in the police and prosecuting attorneys' offices would be of little value if a concurrent change could not also be produced in the judiciary. Hence the group placed a high priority on training judges in the proper procedures of handling spouse abuse cases. They also recognized that generating judicial support for such a training program would be no small task.

Analysis of the issues occurred in the context of data on the most effective settings for accomplishing attitude and behavior change. Social psychology has long indicated that influence is more effective when exercised by individuals of high status or prestige, or to whom an individual feels attracted (Asch, 1948; Mullen, 1985; Walker et al, 1980). Members of the group realized that judges considered themselves the authorities on legal issues and were not likely to accept training which came from a source outside of the legal profession, or even outside of the judiciary. They would be more likely to accept training regarding spouse abuse if it came from another member of their own peer group, particularly some of the more influential judges. Members of the task force then analyzed the local judicial system and held interviews with judges who were known to be sympathetic to the problems of battered women. They learned that there was an annual, statewide judicial institute, which included seminars on a variety of subjects.

Further analysis of the judicial training institute indicated that the judges with major responsibility for this program tended to be highly conservative men who prided themselves on their support of the traditional family institution. They were likely to oppose programs which appeared to threaten the traditional family in any way, and some had opposed assistance for abused wives because they believed that this assistance necessarily involved divorce. The committee considered this fact and concluded that these judicial leaders might support training with reference to spouse abuse if they could be convinced that such training would support rather than distract from the strength of the family.

Consequently, they developed an argument which emphasized an important characteristic of most abused wives, namely, the fact that they usually do not want to get a divorce, but only to have the beatings stop (Campbell, 1984:257, 264, 266; Giles-Simms, 1983:62, 137–139; Pagelow, 1984:306, 318). Committee members met with a representative of the judges and tried to convince him that the judicial system would support the stability of the family rather than detract from it if it could help prevent wife abuse. Their arguments were effective; the judges were persuaded, and the judicial training was established. Some of the judicial leaders became staunch supporters of the program. This was accomplished largely because the committee took care to identify key role players in the social structure, to consider their personal values and commitments, and to adapt the group's arguments to fit these philosophical positions.

This strategy of developing personal commitment through individual involvement in group action can be an effective clinical tool in other applied or evaluation research settings as well. Professionals whose careers are primarily action oriented are frequently resistant to the use of social research and often distrust its findings. They are convinced that their own professional judgment as social workers, nurses, and others, is a more valuable guide to effective social action. Consequently, they resist using either the methodology or the results of social research projects. This resistance can be overcome somewhat by involving such professionals as key participants in the research project itself.

CONCLUSION

This article has provided an example of the manner in which a volunteer community planning committee, made up of concerned members of the general public and professionals in key fields, can alter community social processes toward the solution of a community problem. That they were able to accomplish what they did may be attributed, in part, to the employment of sociological strategies, including analysis of the social situation, written and oral presentations of social scientific data, observation of key segments of community social structure and its role players, and involvement of influential individuals in the planning process. A major drawback of the committee approach, however, is the possibility that some members may subvert the group's activities for their own ends, and clinical sociologists who use this approach should be alert to this concern.

REFERENCES

Asch, S.
    1948   "The doctrine of suggestion, prestige, and imitation in social psychology." Psychological Review 55:250–276.
Campbell, Jacquelyn
    1984   "Abuse of female partners." In Jacquelyn Campbell and Janice Humphreys (eds.), Nursing Care of Victims of Family Violence. Reston, VA: Reston.
Davidson, Terry
    1977   "Wifebeating: a recurring phenomenon throughout history." Pp. 2–23 in Maria Roy (ed.), A Psychosociological Study of Domestic Violence. New York: Van Nostrand Reinhold.
Dobash, R. Emerson and Russell P. Dobash
    1977   "Love, honour, and obey: institutional ideologies and the struggle for battered women." Contemporary Crisis 1:403–415.
Dobash, R. Emerson and Russell P. Dobash
    1979   Violence Against Wives: A Case Against the Patriarchy. New York: Free Press.
Fazio, Russell and Mark Zanna
    1981   "Direct experience and attitude-behavior consistency." In L. Berkowitz (ed.), Advances in Experimental Social Psychology, Volume 14. New York: Academic Press.
Gelles, Richard J.
    1972   The Violent Home. Beverly Hills, CA: Sage.
Giles-Simms, Jean
    1983   Wife Battering: A Systems Theory Approach. New York: Guilford.
Janis, Irving L. and Leon Mann
    1977   Decision Making: A Psychological Analysis of Conflict, Choice, and Commitment. New York: Free Press.
Kerr, N. L. and R. J. MacCoun
    1985   "The effects of jury size and polling method on the process and product of jury deliberation." Journal of Personality and Social Psychology 48:349–363.
Lewin, K.
    1951   Field Theory in the Social Sciences. New York: Harper.
Mayer, F. S., S. Duval and V. H. Duval
    1980   "An attributional analysis of commitment." Journal of Personality and Social Psychology 39:1072–1080.
Michigan Women's Commission
    1977   Domestic Assault: A Report on Family Violence in Michigan. Lansing: State of Michigan.
Mullen, B.
    1985   "Strength and immediacy of sources: a meta-analytic evaluation of the forgotten elements of social impact theory." Journal of Personality and Social Psychology 48:1458–1466.

Newcomb, T.
    1943   Personality and Social Change. New York: Holt.
Pagelow, Mildred Daley
    1984   Family Violence. New York: Praeger.
Roy, Maria, ed.
    1977   Battered Women. A Psychosociological Study of Domestic Violence. New York:
                Van Nostrand Reinhold.
Sherif, M.
    1966   In Common Predicament. Boston: Houghton-Mifflin.
Sherman, Steven J., C. C. Presson, L. Chassin, M. Bensenberg, E. Corty and R. Olshavsky
    1983   "Smoking intentions in adolescents: direct experience and predictability." Person-
                ality and Social Psychology Bulletin 8:376–383.
Spouse Abuse Project Committee
    1980   Spouse Abuse in the Tri County Area: The Problems and Some Answers. Detroit:
                United Community Services of Metropolitan Detroit.
Stark, R. and J. McEvoy
    1970   "Middle class violence." Psychology Today 4:52–65.
Straus, Murray
    1976   "Sexual inequality, cultural norms, and wife-beating." Victimology 1:54–76.
Straus, Murray, Richard Gelles and Suzanne Steinmetz
    1980   Behind Closed Doors: Violence in the American Family. New York: Doubleday.
Straus, Roger A.
    1984   "Changing the definition of the situation: toward a theory of sociological interven-
                tion." Clinical Sociology Review 2:51–63.
Taylor, D. G., P. B. Sheatsley and A. M. Greeley
    1978   "Attitudes toward racial integration." Scientific American 238, no. 6:42–49.
Thomas, W. I.
    1931   The Unadjusted Girl. Boston: Little, Brown.
Walker, M., S. Harriman and S. Costello
    1980   "The influence of appearance on compliance with a request." Journal of Social
                Psychology 112:159–160.
Watts, William
    1967   "Relative persistence of opinion change induced by active compared to passive
                participation." Journal of Personality and Social Psychology 5:4–15.

The Sociological Practitioner as a Change Agent in a Hospital Setting: Applications of Phenomenological Theory and Social Construction of Reality Theory

Clifford M. Black
Richard Enos
John A. Holman
North Texas State University

ABSTRACT

This article contains a discussion and a rationale for the use of phenomenological theory and social construction of reality theory in sociological practice. It also presents examples of the application of these theories via sociological practice in a hospital setting, and describes the role of a sociological practitioner in this setting.

In a paper on cultural relativity as a counseling paradigm in clinical sociology, Black and Enos (1982) emphasize the role of the clinical sociologist in individual counseling. In the process of justifying that role, they also present considerable support for the role of the clinical sociologist as a change agent within groups. Glassner and Freedman posit that groups are the focus of all clinical sociology. It is their contention that when the sociologist, as clinician, works with individuals, it is with the end of developing "effective strategies for group living" (1979:288). In a discussion of the clinical sociologist on the micro level, Lee

Clifford M. Black, Ph.D., is Associate Dean, School of Community Service; Richard Enos, D.S.W., is Chairperson, Department of Social Work; John A. Holman, Ph.D., is Director, Institute of Criminal Justice Programs—all of The School of Community Service, North Texas State University, Denton, TX 76203.

details the use of "first-hand observation and interviews to investigate and assess the significance of social influences on small group activities," as well as on personal development and actions (1979:490). Black and Enos (1980) underscore the importance of the latter. Glass designates the group as the focal point in counseling, even when the client is an individual: "Individuals as clients are seen sociologically in a group context as engaged in social interaction with others" (1979:514). He describes the role of the clinical sociologist as "a social therapist whose clients are individuals seen as part of some social system. Relationship and social structure become the focus of scrutiny and the locus of change" (514).

This article illustrates the role of the sociological practitioner in what Capelle refers to as "changing human systems" (1979:37). The example used is a hospital bureaucracy. The sociological practice model described in this article draws heavily upon the work of Black and Enos (1980, 1981, 1982; Enos and Black, 1983) on the utility of phenomenological theory and social construction of reality theory in clinical work.

The unifying factors for these theories are two-fold. First, both focus on perceptions of reality. Phenomenology focuses on the meaning of an act for the actor, that is, the individual perception of reality. Social construction of reality analyzes the involvement of the individual and the group in the development of perceptions of reality. Second, both models are consistent with the clinical sociological perspective as articulated by the major practitioners in this field (Black and Enos, 1982). They lend themselves to goals which are humanistic, holistic, and multidisciplinary. Both theories posit the significance of the individual in understanding human social interaction. Both are historically grounded in a concern for the value of the human being. Each theory considers the total person in an attempt to understand human behavior. This includes recognition of such factors as biology, environment, socialization, and psychology.

The sociological practice discussed here was an attempt at interpretation and understanding of inner meanings (or *verstehen*) and life perceptions (or social constructions of reality) of the clients. Its main goal was the idea that all members of the group (including the sociological practitioner) would "come to know themselves, and in process, come to know the other group members" (Martindale, 1960:269). In addition, the intervention was designed to reveal the process of reality construction, its effect on knowing self and others, and the creation of perceptions of self and others.

The purpose of the paper is two-fold: First, to demonstrate the utility of two different models in sociological practice and, second, to describe the role of the sociological practitioner in a specific setting. The article is divided into two parts: a general and systematic presentation of the two theoretical paradigms; and a case example and analysis of the work of a sociological practitioner in a hospital bureaucracy.

THEORETICAL PARADIGMS

The sociological practice outlined here, and the evaluation of that change process, were based upon phenomenological theory. The phenomenological perspective advances the idea that human behavior can only be comprehended from the vantage point of the perceptions of the actors. Further, these perceptions are composed of an inner personal dimension in behavior as well as an inner personal dimension in the observation of behavior (Matson, 1966:238). Phenomenology is also a method of introspection for "controlled examination of awareness itself" and "for the downward reduction of experience through successive stages toward what is most directly experienced as social reality" (Martindale, 1960:269, 277). The phenomenological perspective was used as "a method for obtaining insight about society and its component parts through inspection" (Martindale, 1960: 269; Black and Enos, 1981:35). Using these perspectives from phenomenology, the intervention sought to elicit interpretations and understandings of inner meanings *(verstehen)* and life perceptions (the process of social constructions), to the end of self-knowledge and knowledge of other group members.

A second model used in the intervention drew from the social construction of reality. Berger and Luckmann (1966) define reality construction as a dialectical process involving three phases: externalization, objectivation, and internalization. The emphasis on one phase to the exclusion of others will result in a distortion of the actual reality (Freeman, 1980; Black and Enos, 1982). This distortion of reality frequently creates problems for specific groups and individuals, and in this case, led to seeking help from the sociological practitioner. The practitioner, in turn, needed to create a process which helped the client understand how reality was constructed.

A sociological practice model based on social construction of reality posits that: understanding the process by which the social realities of societies, cultures, institutions, organizations, groups, roles, and statuses are constructed better equips the individual and the individual group members to interact within the confines of these social realities. Specifically, it enables them to resolve the critical issues necessary for survival as individuals, as individuals as members within specific groups, and as individuals who are members of various groups. The purpose of this model is, therefore, to help persons become aware of the process of constructing social reality and socialization (Enos and Black, 1983:11).

The method derived from this theoretical perspective is best characterized as a dialogue, discussion, or debate which involves the sociological practitioner and the person(s)-in-situation(s) in an ongoing, teaching-learning process, focused on helping the client(s) understand how reality is constructed (Enos and Black, 1983:12). It includes providing information, questioning, directing, supporting, reflecting, and confronting, as appropriate.

Enos and Black (1983:14) cite several specific treatment objectives for the social construction of reality. These include aiding the individual and individuals as members of a specific group:

1. To see and understand the process of reality construction;
2. To comprehend the process by which a person defines objects and situations;
3. To understand her/his(their) own explanation(s) for behavior;
4. To see and understand her/his(their) role in constructing her/his(their) collective enactment of it;
5. To define, understand, and select the games s/he(they) are playing.

Two key concepts in this theoretical perspective are: imitation and experimentation. Life experiences are utilized as opportunities for selective modeling and imitation. Experiences drawn upon and utilized in the sociological practice can be from other societies, cultures, and subcultures. The experiences can be personal (practitioners or client) or vicarious. Such experiences provide the basis for transmitting information about social structures, institutions, organizations, groups, statuses, and roles. Finally, they can be utilized for critical evaluation of behavior options. In this sense, they represent experimentation and practice problem solving.

The concept of reinforcement also shapes the techniques of this work. The practitioner and the client(s) are viewed as the most important elements in the sociological practice process, as opposed to the ideas, information, or other content generated within or outside the practice encounter, or any other construction of reality. Reinforcement may occur in the practitioner's use of techniques grounded in the notion that client self-direction, self-management, and the acquisition of information for individual and group survival provide reinforcement and learning. Other elements of the client-practitioner relationship, such as support, encouragement, acceptance, reassurance, and a positive evaluation, may also provide reinforcement.

The concept of incorporation (internalization) also influences and shapes sociological practice techniques. Experiments in constructing social reality and problem solving within everyday individual and group reality are utilized. Success in these can also provide reinforcement. Self-direction, self-management, and the ability to apply essential information for survival in society by individuals, and the individuals as members of a specific group, are considered evidence of incorporation. Also, such behaviors are considered to be, by themselves, potential reinforcements.

CASE EXAMPLES

The examples used to illustrate the usefulness of the two theoretical approaches to practice are taken from an intervention with a hospital. The hospital board of trustees saw difficulties in the administrative process of the hospital, as exemplified by interpersonal communication problems between the hospital administrator and staff. The trustees' solution was to engage the sociological practitioner to teach a formal course in human relations. All department heads and supervisors would be required to attend this course. This a priori definition of the problem and its solution is not uncommon in industrial and service organizations.

The definition of the problem and its intended solution presented problems for the practitioner. It is a basic tenent of clinical sociological practice that the clinician or practitioner and the clients jointly have the freedom to define the problem and to initiate the appropriate intervention. Furthermore the board's decision to require attendance of all department heads and supervisors is at odds with the clinical norm of client self-determination. The practitioner negotiated with the board of trustees so that the full range of administrative and communication problems could be explored. In addition, it was agreed that staff participation in the treatment program would be voluntary.

A total of 22 department heads and supervisors was included in the intervention process. A final written report of the entire process was prepared in consultation with group members and the administrator and presented to the board of trustees. Much of the material in the present study comes from that final report.

The specific sessions reported here are taken from both the initial 12-week intensive phase, which involved weekly meetings, and the less intensive 5-month follow-up phase, in which the groups met twice monthly. The first sessions included the mechanics of the process, the establishing of rapport, and the development of trust. Examples are taken from the first, second, and fourth sessions. The eighth session is used as an example of the middle stage, while the final two sessions demonstrate the work of the final stage.

The sessions in the follow-up phase are similar to those in the intensive phase. Hence, they are summarized with regard to structure, process, goals, and outcomes. Particular emphasis is given to the agenda developed by the supervisors and department heads, the success of the administrator in dealing with these agenda, and the evaluation of the administrator in following through on the agenda set by the group. The materials selected for presentation are representative of the work done in these stages; they are illustrative rather than exhaustive.

Session 1

The first session drew heavily upon the phenomenological paradigm for direction. The intent of the session was to initiate the processes of understanding: 1) the perception(s) of the actor(s); 2) the inner personal dimensions of the actors' behavior; 3) the inner personal dimensions in the actors' observation of others' behavior; 4) that which was most directly experienced as social reality; and 5) the inner meanings of that social reality for the actors. In other words, the goal of this session was predicated upon the phenomenological goal of knowing self and others, and understanding the meaning of experience, power, forces, and facts of social life. The method was phenomenological in its use of introspection and inspection. Social construction of reality was also utilized as a paradigm in the first session. The goal was to begin to teach and learn the process of reality construction. The session drew upon the everyday group life settings of the clients. Dialogue and discourse were used to help members construct their social realities. The practitioner provided role modeling in his self-evaluation and revelation, and through his acceptance of evaluation by group members. Reinforcement was also used in analyzing potential strengths of individuals and the group.

As a technique, each member of the group was asked to write one or two questions about the course or the sociological practitioner. The purpose of this exercise was to provide an anonymous means of expressing their perceptions of the meaning of the program. After discussing their written questions, suggestions for the practice work were invited. This discussion elicited strong feelings on the part of the participants, both in support of and in opposition to the purpose of the program.

These techniques provided an opportunity for the clients to better understand the goals of the instruction. They also demonstrated the process of evaluating oneself in order to understand others and, thus, better understand oneself.

Session 2

The goal of this session was to give group members an opportunity to come to know the practitioner better and, in the process, to know themselves better. Drawing upon both paradigms, the session used techniques to expose the clients to the phenomenological method of introspection and inspection of meaning as a method of knowing or understanding. The personal experiences of the clients were used in designing an appropriate behavior for the practitioner, which could also serve them later in their own group interaction. These techniques were designed to provide experimentation and problem solving in the everyday reality of group life.

This session began with the sociologist communicating to the group his perceptions of what they meant by their critical ideas, suggestions, and emotional responses in the prior session. The group then discussed the practitioner's emotional responses to and his intellectual perceptions, observations, and meanings of the situation. The individual members of the group attempted to understand the meaning of the situation for the sociologist in order to come to better understand him. In the process, they learned something about themselves in a similar kind of situation. Later, they could draw upon his experience vicariously or imitate his behavior. Both of these techniques are consistent with social construction of reality.

Each member of the group was then asked to describe a situation in which they had an experience and perceptions of meaning similar to those described by the sociological practitioner, and to indicate how they responded in that situation. It is possible that both experiential and insight learning could occur, since members of the group might become aware of the fact that solutions used elsewhere might be applicable here, and that the role-played solutions might be of use in the future. This use of teaching and learning by role-playing and insight and experience is based upon a social construction of reality model for socio-logical practice.

As a conclusion to this session, an outline for the continuing practice work, incorporating critical ideas and suggestions of the group from session 1, was presented. Several options for participation in the group and for evaluation of the process were provided. This emphasis upon self-direction and self-manage-ment is based upon the teaching-learning model in the social construction of reality paradigm and, in particular, upon reinforcement and incorporation. In addition, it demonstrated problem solving and construction of social reality by the group in their everyday group reality.

Session 4

Session 4 was designed to teach about the social construction of bureaucracies and, in particular, the bureaucratic structure of the clients' own hospital. An attempt was made to elicit both helpful and hindering elements of the organi-zational structure of the hospital. One example of the learning that occurred came in the discussion of informal structure. There was an identification of certain behaviors in the hospital that indicated that a status differential existed (for the most part an informal development) with respect to the departments. Housekeeping and laundry indicated that their personnel seemed to be at the bottom of the status hierarchy. Employees in these departments found that the reality of this social fact resulted in a variety of forms of discrimination, including how they were treated in the halls by personnel from other departments. The nursing staff were considered the most serious offenders. The negative effects of this type of interaction were discussed along with potential solutions.

Session 8

Communication, a key consideration in phenomenological theory, was the focus of this session. What is communicated and how it is communicated is important. The communication of meaning and the importance of understanding the meaning of action and behavior for the individual are given a position of prominence.

A specific model for communication and listening was outlined. The nature and significance of feedback and listening was considered. Group members used their own group position in the hospital as a reference for selecting some important communication. They then experimented with new communication. For example, the head of maintenance used this as an opportunity to communicate to other department heads some of the specific problems they created for him in refurbishing or remodeling situations. Not only was this an opportunity to learn about communication, imitate the skills of others, role-play, and use personal experience but, as indicated, it also drew upon situations of everyday reality of group life for problem solving. These techniques were based upon the social construction of reality paradigm.

The sociologist provided feedback on his observation that, on the whole, the group appeared to be more successful in communicating about their own situations and experiences than they did in listening and providing feedback to others. This phase of the communication process continued to be a focus in a later session.

Session 11

One purpose of this session was to teach something about the nature of group characteristics which affect group interaction. This has added significance when one analyzes one's own group in this manner. Lippitt (1961:32–34) listed 10 characteristics of groups: 1) background; 2) participation patterns; 3) communication patterns; 4) cohesion; 5) subgroups; 6) atmosphere; 7) standards; 8) procedures; 9) leadership; and 10) member behavior. He discussed the significance of each of these in group interaction. Each of these characteristics was used as a vehicle for analyzing and working with this group of department heads and supervisors.

The specific characteristic used to demonstrate this technique is what Lippitt (1961) labels "member behavior." In discussing this characteristic of groups, he notes, "To get genuine group thinking and group action there must be shared responsibility on the part of the members. Members of the group must want to contribute to the task of reaching the set goals" (34). The sociological practitioner focused the group upon their own behavior with regard to attaining the goals of the group. Goals for the group were arrived at unilaterally by the administrator and/or one or two other individuals. Goals were not always clear. The individual group members could articulate some general goals of the hospital, as could the administrator, but when asked for specific application, they could not articulate these goals. There was no annual goal setting in which group members and the administrator discussed goals, set priorities, communicated departmental needs, and engaged in setting specific goals. Thus, it was often not clear to members of the group how specific goals set by the administrator or others related to the overall goals of the hospital. For example, the position of Inservice Education Director had been created and filled with no consultation with this group as to the nature or purpose of this position. The administrator indicated to the sociologist in his individual sessions that his method of operation was that the less communicated the better for his supervisory personnel. The group, however, expressed the need for sessions in which they could communicate their own departmental or supervisory goals and needs, and could relate these to the needs and goals of other departments and to the total organization.

Session 12

In this session, use was made of self-direction, self-management, support, encouragement, and acceptance. The session drew extensively upon the social construction of reality theory techniques of reinforcement and incorporation. It also included incorporation in its use of experimentation, problem solving, and social construction in the reality of everyday group life. One goal in this session was teaching the process of constructing social reality.

   This session included an evaluation of the group process up to this point. The members evaluated: how the group and the sociological practitioner had functioned; what processes had been most and least helpful; what had been omitted; and what should have been omitted. The group was also asked if they wanted to continue the last 10 sessions. The sociologist indicated that if they chose not to continue, it would be made clear to the administrator and trustees that this was an appropriate step. After evaluating the practice work and the practitioner, the group voted unanimously to continue the work. The structure for this decision provided group members with complete anonymity and secrecy.

Follow-up Sessions: 13–22

The follow-up sessions were basically given over to a continuation of and building upon earlier sessions. For the most part, the goals and outcomes of these sessions can be said to have culminated in three proposed agenda for department head/supervisor meetings and a final group evaluation of the administrator. The three agenda were prepared as examples of the type of meetings the department heads and supervisors wished the administrator would conduct. These agenda reflected and summarized the work the group had done with respect to the needs of the group and the administrator. The agenda were prepared by the sociologist under the direction and with input from the group members. The administrator was invited to deal with what the group had, thus, designated as critical issues. This was an attempt to both facilitate communication between the administrator and the group members, and to provide the administrator an opportunity to rehearse patterns of interaction designated by the group as helpful to their own roles. The group and the administrator also assisted in preparing the final report to the board of trustees concerning an evaluation of the practice work.

Despite the use of the prepared agenda, the group members and the administrator still demonstrated several of their original patterns of interaction. The administrator did not explore the meanings of these issues for the members of the group. At the same time, group members were reluctant to communicate to the administrator both the perceptions they had about these issues and the meaning they attached to them.

In fact, the responses of the administrator and group members are not surprising. Berger and Luckmann (1966:47, 53) cite the significance of "institutionalization" and "habitualization" in the maintenance of socialized or learned behavior patterns. This issue is also treated by Enos and Black (1983:87). Although the actual clinical work had been completed, only eight months had passed since its inception. Expectation of total or drastic behavior change would have been premature. The administrator was still reluctant and, in private, expressed anxiety about giving the group much input in the administrative process. Group members resisted revealing their feelings and perceptions about their work, colleagues, and supervisors in the presence of certain colleagues and the administrator. They expressed concern over possible retaliation. It might have been helpful to provide some sessions in which group members role-played the position of the administrator and he, in turn, role-played some of their positions. This might have eliminated increased anxiety resulting from directly focusing on his work as administrator in front of the entire group. In this sense, he might have been able to concentrate more on alternative approaches. In addition, this would have provided some opportunity for imitation and modeling. Reinforcement and incorporation would also have been underlying components of this technique. Finally, it would have created a setting in which each individual might have gained a clearer understanding of the perceptions of other group members and the administrator.

SUMMARY AND CONCLUSIONS

The purpose of this paper was three-fold: to demonstrate the use of phenomenological theory and social construction of reality theory in sociological practice; to demonstrate the practice of sociology in a hospital setting; and to describe the role of the sociological practitioner in one specific setting. Actually, the summary of the sociological practice and any conclusions drawn from it are, to a great extent, embodied in the three agenda and the group evaluation of the administrator already referred to. The three agenda and the evaluation represented the successful efforts of the group to conceptualize and articulate the problems of the hospital, as they perceived them. The inability of the administrator to effectively conduct meetings in which the group sought to resolve expressed problems and concerns reflected his failure at communicating with his administrative staff and in drawing upon their expertise. This failure was addressed in subsequent action taken by the board of trustees following the sociologist's final report.

The last intervention sessions resulted in the group articulating two critical issues which they felt needed to be resolved within the next year: 1) what the hospital, and specifically supervisors and department heads, could do to increase patient census; and 2) an assessment of the financial status of the hospital and its long-term stability. It was recommended to the administrator, by the group, that these two issues be treated as priority items for the department head/supervisor meetings for the next year.

Several other questions raised by the group and placed on the agenda reflect their perceptions of the hospital, its problems, and the administrator. The development of the agenda demonstrates the ability of the group to work together, to plan, and to identify problems and solutions. These questions did, in fact, reflect several key problems in the hospital. The group wanted the administrator to clarify how decisions were made in the hospital. Group members felt that the process was exclusive and that decisions were imposed rather than being, in any sense, mutually arrived at. The group wanted the administrator to clarify the importance of communication in the hospital. It was their perception that it was strictly from the top down and that they were not informed of important issues. A third question, related to the first two, dealt with the role of department head/supervisor meetings. They asked the administrator to specify the significance or function of these meetings since he made most decisions and did not communicate essential information at the meetings. A common theme throughout the practice work dealt with the feelings of the group that the administrator had never clarified the purpose of the sessions conducted by the practitioner.

The evaluation which the group made of the administrator was shared with him by the sociologist in the presence of the group. This served as the focus of the final session. The administrator was provided time and support to respond to this evaluation and to present his evaluation of the supervisory personnel as a group. In fact, the administrator was unwilling to provide any meaningful evaluation of the group. The group made the following evaluation of his administrative role:

1. That his efforts to be open and his desire to change his administrative style appeared to be genuine.
2. That he needed to initiate yearly planning (goal setting) in the department head/supervisor meetings. Each department head and supervisor should have an opportunity to present needs and goals of their own department to the group and to hear those of other departments. Discussion should occur here with respect to how all of these related to the overall picture of the hospital for the coming year. The group should then have an opportunity to prioritize

these needs and goals for the coming year. Ultimately, of course, the administrator would make the final decision.

3. That decisions related to the annual goal setting needed to be made explicit. Reasons why the final decision was reached should be clarified. This should include follow-up communication to the total group.

4. That, too often, it was assumed that a particular decision would not affect a specific department or individual. However, most decisions have far-reaching implications. In some cases, people perceive a decision affecting them even if it does not. It would be better to be more inclusive in considering who will be affected by a specific decision and consult and follow-up from this perspective.

5. That he needed to share as much information as possible, rather than as little as possible.

6. That department head/supervisor meetings should focus less on information dissemination and announcement of decisions already reached, and, instead, provide more opportunities for discussion and input into the administrative process.

7. That it might be helpful to implement democratic decision making, or to at least clarify how decisions for the group would be made.

8. That he needed to work hard at facilitating group discussion, ideas, suggestions, criticisms, questions, and comments.

The techniques used in these sessions were predicated upon imitation, modeling, reinforcement, and incorporation. It was the intent of the sociological practitioner to demonstrate, to the group, ways of interacting with the administrator with regard to his strengths and weaknesses in his role behavior. Likewise, the sessions were an attempt to model certain leadership and group interaction processes to the administrator. Positive responses for both the group and the administrator, and such responses from each, serve as reinforcers. It was, of course, anticipated that some of this learning would be incorporated by the group members and the administrator. All of these techniques were predicated upon the significance of group members and the administrator interpreting and understanding each other's inner meanings and life perceptions.

An additional phase of this sociological practice was the report to the board of trustees by the sociologist. This report was reviewed and clarified by him with both the group and the hospital administrator. This report resulted in two major observable actions. First, the board of trustees hired an assistant administrator who was charged with improving communication and planning. Second, the board of trustees initiated monthly meetings in which members of the board came to the hospital to communicate about the status of the hospital, goals, and decisions, and to get feedback from the staff, department heads and supervisors.

Finally, one year later, follow-up sessions were held with the group. The group reported that they were working well together and that this enabled them to overcome some of the administrative deficiencies. In addition, the work of the assistant administrator had improved the situation considerably.

One aspect of the clinical process needs to be underscored. Much of what occurred in the group sessions was made possible or, at least, more productive by the one-to-one counseling which the sociological practitioner conducted with each group member and the administrator. In addition, the two theoretical perspectives used are appropriate in both individual and group work. Each also contributes to positive group atmosphere. Both had considerable utility for generating productive techniques in this hospital setting. Finally, both lend credibility to the validity of the role of the practicing sociologist in such settings.

REFERENCES

Berger, P. L. and T. Luckmann
    1966   The Social Construction of Reality. Garden City, NY: Doubleday.
Black, C. M. and R. Enos
    1980   "Sociological precedents and contributions to the understanding and facilitation of individual behavior change: the case for counseling sociology." Journal of Sociology and Social Welfare 7(September):648–664.
    1981   "Using phenomenology in clinical social work: A poetic pilgrimage." Clinical Social Work Journal 9(Spring):34–43.
    1982   "Cultural relativity as a counseling paradigm in clinical sociology: a theory and case studies." Humanity and Society 6(February):58–73.
Capelle, R. G.
    1979   Changing Human Systems. Toronto: International Human Systems Institute.
Enos, R. and C. M. Black
    1983   "A social construction of reality model for clinical social work." The Journal of Applied Social Sciences 7(Fall/Winter):83–97.
Freeman, R. C.
    1980   "Phenomenological sociology and ethnomethodology." Pp. 113–154 in J. D. Douglas (ed.), Introduction to the Sociologies of Everyday Life. Boston: Allyn-Bacon.
Glass, J. F.
    1979   "Clinical sociology: renewing an old profession." American Behavioral Scientist 22(March/April):513–529.
Glassner, B. and J. A. Freedman
    1979   Clinical Sociology. New York: Longman.
Lee, A. M.
    1979   "The services of clinical sociology." American Behavioral Scientist 22(March/April):487–511.
Lippitt, R. L.
    1961   "How to get results from a group." Pp. 31–36 in L. P. Bradform (ed.), Group Development. Washington, DC: National Training Laboratories and National Education Association.
Martindale, D. F.
    1960   The Nature and Types of Sociological Theory. Boston: Houghton-Mifflin.
Matson, F.
    1966   The Broken Image. Garden City, NY: Anchor.

Salvador Minuchin: A Sociological Analysis of His Family Therapy Theory

Mark Kassop
Bergen Community College

ABSTRACT

Various academic disciplines are involved in the analysis of marriage and the family (e.g., anthropology, economics, history, psychology, psychotherapy, social work, sociology), but they frequently work in ignorance of the research and theoretical findings of their sister disciplines. This paper is an attempt to establish a theoretical bridge between sociology and family psychotherapy.

Although these disciplines have been working independently, they have much in common. For this paper, the work of one prominent family psychotherapist, Salvador Minuchin, has been analyzed using two of sociology's theoretical constructs: structural functionalism and symbolic interactionism.

This analysis suggests that a fruitful dialogue could be established between these two disciplines which often use different concepts to make the same points and to reach very similar conclusions. Additionally, an exchange of ideas between these two disciplines could potentially foster new and important insights into classical studies, and promote valuable joint research projects.

One of the most unfortunate gaps for the field of family therapy is its separation from the field of family theory as found in sociology.
(Hansen and L'Abate, 1982:296)

In the course of reading a text by James Hansen and Luciano L'Abate (1982), the above quotation aroused my attention. As a trained sociologist who has taught marriage and family courses for the last 15 years, I had been surprised at all of the theorists and researchers who are involved in family therapy who

---

Correspondence to: Mark Kassop, Social Sciences Division, Bergen Community College, Paramus, NJ 07652.

were rarely mentioned in sociological literature, and I was equally surprised to discover how infrequently sociological researchers were noted in psychotherapy literature. Hansen and L'Abate's statement suggested that it might be useful to create a theoretical bridge between the related fields of family psychotherapy and sociology of marriage and the family.

The following article attempts to create that bridge by showing how the theory of one important family psychotherapist, Salvador Minuchin, fits into two major sociological theoretical constructs: structural functionalism and symbolic interactionism. This paper does not purport to be a thorough examination of every facet of Minuchin's theory; only an emphasis on its sociological content.

One of the serendipitous effects of engaging in this project was the discovery that although these two somewhat isolated schools of thought had been working independently for many years, they had developed many of the same ideas, but had simply used different labels in their work.

SALVADOR MINUCHIN AND STRUCTURALIST THEORY

> Minuchin's theory reads like a sociology textbook on structural func-
> tionalism. Even before he presents his theory, he talks about the
> social context of the individual. . . . Minuchin is concerned with
> family as an interlocking set of small groups arranged hierarchically.
> The task of the therapist is to restructure these small groups (sub-
> systems) so that the whole (family system) can function adequately
> (i.e., adapt to the demands placed on it by internal and external
> forces). (Hansen and L'Abate, 1983:142)

Although he is not a trained sociologist, Salvador Minuchin's version of family therapy is very sociological. He primarily represents the school of thought that sociologists have named structural functionalism, but his theory also includes smatterings of symbolic interactionism. Structural functionalism was developed by Talcott Parsons, Robert Merton, Kingsley Davis, and others, and it is one of the three major perspectives used by sociologists today (the third perspective is conflict theory). Many sociologists feel this perspective is inherently con-servative, emphasizing maintenance of the status quo, and thereby discouraging social change (Robertson, 1981:17–18). However, some sociologists and Min-uchin use the basic outlines of the approach in a more dynamic fashion.

Parsons (1951:27) analyzes a social system on three levels: the individual, the group, and the cultural. His views mirror the gestalt position in that "a gestalt is an organized entity or whole in which the parts, although distinguishable, are interdependent" (Eshleman, 1981:51). The essential premise of the structural functionalist perspective is that social structures, such as the family and society, are systems with interdependent parts, with each part making some contribution to overall group stability. The component elements of a given structure are analyzed in terms of their specific function for that system's maintenance. Critics of this approach argue that a practice that is functional for equilibrium at one level may be dysfunctional at another level, and that change is an inherently disruptive process (Abrahamson, 1981:61–62). Minuchin's theory would represent a revision of the traditional structural functional model in that it is dynamic and that it considers disequilibrium to be potentially functional for the social group.

Family Therapy

Salvador Minuchin's family therapy is based on a highly developed theory of family structure and dynamics that recognizes most of the fundamental concepts in the structural functionalist position as outlined by Parsons. In particular, as Goldenberg and Goldenberg state about Minuchin,

> The structuralists are interested in how the components of a system interact, how balance and homeostasis is achieved, how family feedback mechanisms operate, how dysfunctional communication patterns develop, and so forth. Beyond that, they are especially attentive to family transaction patterns because these offer clues to the family's organization, the permeability of the family's subsystem boundaries, the existence of alignments or coalitions. (1985:178)

In Minuchin's view, the family is a social structure with a variety of subsystems or coalitions (e.g., husband-wife, mother-child, father-child). When the family unit encounters pressures from internal sources (developmental changes) or external sources (the cultural level in Parsons' schema), it must make "adaptations," which may create dysfunction within the family. Dysfunctioning families are the result of structural problems, thus therapy is aimed at changing the organization or structure of the family unit (Minuchin and Fishman, 1981:69–71). Therefore, part of the therapeutic procedure is to induce family interaction.

Symbolic Interactionism

The family's structure organizes the ways in which family members interact with each other, and creates *transactional patterns,* which can only be viewed when the family subsystems are interacting. These transactional patterns regulate the behavior of family members, and they are maintained by two systems of constraint: generic and idiosyncratic. *Generic constraints* are based on universal "rules," such as the traditional hierarchical relationship between parents and children, and the *idiosyncratic constraints* are based on the unique "rules" that evolve in every family as the result of "explicit and implicit negotiations among family members (Minuchin, 1974; Minuchin and Fishman, 1981:78–79).

Minuchin's concern with idiosyncratic constraints parallels the interests of symbolic interactionists. Symbolic interactionists, such as Erving Goffman, George Herbert Mead, and Charles Horton Cooley, address themselves to two questions, both of which are of importance to family theorists: socialization and personality. "The first—socialization—focuses on how the human being obtains and internalizes the behavior patterns and ways of thinking and feeling of the society. The second—personality—focuses on the way in which these attitudes, values, and behaviors are organized" (Eshleman, 1981:55).

Gilbert Nass and Gerald McDonald summarize the symbolic interactionists' concern with the family in a manner that is consistent with Minuchin's approach:

> Interactionists examine the internal workings of the family. They attempt to analyze both observable behavior and the attitudes and expectations family members have regarding each other. In so doing, they consider symbols used in interpersonal communication, the meanings these symbols have for different family members, and how such shared meanings create, sustain, and change "definitions of situations" for families and individual family members. (Nass and McDonald, 1982:50)

It is also worth noting that there are several subdivisions of symbolic interactionism, and that one of these subdivisions, ethnomethodology, addresses the analysis of the unwritten rules and regulations that guide our everyday behavior and the social construction of reality (Douglas et al., 1980). Some important points developed by ethnomethodologists include: human beings actively shape their own behavior; human behavior is constructed in the course of its execution; and, most importantly for us, "an understanding of human conduct requires study of the actors' hidden behavior" (Manis and Meltzer, 1978).

The emphasis on rules is, on one hand, part of the family's structure (and therefore a characteristic of structural functionalism). On the other hand, the reference to rules that govern the system is a clear reflection of symbolic interactionism and, specifically, the ethnomethodologists' concern with the unwritten rules that organize our everyday lives. Part of the ethnomethodologists' concern is to discover these unwritten rules and regulations (Robertson, 1981:23; Douglas et al., 1980; Manis and Meltzer, 1978).

Manis and Meltzer (1978) indicate that rules governing any system are created by the systems' members, and that in order to understand the behavior of the system's members, one must uncover these "hidden behaviors." Symbolic interactionists also emphasize that the stability of any social group or relationship is dependent upon three interdependent factors: an individual's norms (personal standards of behavior, which are learned in a cultural context); the definition of the situation (certain behavior is learned to be appropriate in some situations but not in others); and the perception of the definition of others (how we think other people are expecting us to act) (Robertson, 1981; Douglas et al., 1980).

In line with the previous statements, the therapeutic goal of Minuchin is to change the family's organization. As previously noted, the family is a rule-governed system with homeostatic tendencies. Its resistance to change is organized around rules that are frequently not conscious or explicit, and it is the function of the therapist to discover these rules and to restructure the family so that it is more capable of satisfactorily managing stress (Hansen and L'Abate, 1982:148). This is a good example of both structural functionalism, a homeostatic system, and symbolic interactionism, rules that may not be conscious or explicit that govern people's behavior.

One last reference to the symbolic interactionists and their concern with the social construction of reality is warranted here. These theorists note that "all analysis of everyday life . . . begins with an analysis of the members' meanings. . . . 'Meaning' is used to refer to the feelings, perceptions, emotions, moods, thoughts, ideas, beliefs, values, and morals of the members of society" (Douglas et al., 1980). Similarly, Minuchin focuses his attention on *framing* and *reframing*, which are fundamental aspects of the therapeutic process. Therapy starts with the therapist and the family, its individual members, and the therapist having different definitions of reality, different "frames" in Minuchin's words. "The family's framing is relevant for the continuity and maintenance of the organism more or less as it is; the therapeutic framing is related to the goal of moving the family toward a more differentiated and competent dealing with their dysfunctional reality" (Minuchin and Fishman, 1981:74).

Subsystems

Returning to structural functionalism, Parsons and Minuchin stress that the family unit is not an isolated entity. The family of procreation has a history and it must be viewed within a cultural context. Minuchin notes that the first subsystem formed in the family, and in many ways the most important one, is the *spouse subsystem*. This subsystem can reconcile different sets of values brought by the spouses to their new relationship from their families of orientation, or these values may be retained by each spouse to maintain a sense of self (Minuchin and Fishman, 1981:16; Minuchin, 1974). Any dysfunctions in this subsystem that emphasize complementarity and mutual accommodation have significant consequences for the family's other subsystems, as children may be scapegoated or co-opted into alliances with one parent against the other. In addition, the spousal subsystem is important for serving as a model for appropriate male-female interactions when the children create their own families (Minuchin, 1974:56–57).

The second subsystem that is formed is the *parental subsystem*. The partners "must now differentiate to perform the tasks of socializing a child without losing the mutual support that should characterize the spouse subsystem" (Minuchin, 1974:57). In this and the other subsystems, partners often expect that roles will be performed similarly to the way they were performed in their respective families of orientation. Negotiations and renegotiations characterize the family as parents attempt to establish transactional patterns that borrow from their own backgrounds, that are the product of their negotiations, and that are constrained by generic and idiosyncratic rules (Hansen and L'Abate, 1982:136).

The last subsystem to be formed, according to Minuchin is the *sibling subsystem,* but this may actually consist of several subsystems in a large family, as siblings may divide along lines created by developmental stages (Minuchin and Fishman, 1981:19). This subsystem is a social laboratory for children, who may use this social environment to safely experiment with peer relations, exercise their right to privacy, have their own interests, and be free to make mistakes (Minuchin, 1974:59; Hansen and L'Abate, 1982:132–133).

Several assumptions are made by Minuchin about these subsystems. First, each subsystem has a threshold of tolerance, and any behavior that goes beyond this threshold will cause the system to adjust and return to a more comfortable state of equilibrium; this parallels Parsons' discussion of social control and system maintenance (Hansen and L'Abate, 1982:133; Parsons, 1951:297–298). Second, family subsystems are not as neat as the first impression may impart. Although there are only three subsystem categories, the family may subdivide into a variety of dyads, triads, and larger groups which are limited only by family size, but which can be labeled with one of the subsystem categories that have already been explained. It is an important part of the therapeutic process for the therapist to delineate the relevant subsystem groupings that exist in a given family and the dysfunctioning that exists within and between each. Third, individuals may be members of more than one subsystem at any given time, and they may play different roles and have different transactional patterns in each subsystem. Once again, this is an important concern for the therapist.

Finally, each subsystem establishes *boundaries* to separate it from other subsystems within the family.

> A boundary of a subsystem is described as the rules that define who participates and how. The function of boundaries is to protect the differentiation of the system. All in all, the composition of subsystems organized around family functions is not nearly as significant, according to Minuchin, as the clarity of the subsystem boundaries. (Hansen and L'Abate, 1982:133)

These boundaries may vary from extreme rigidity to extreme diffuseness. In the former case, *disengagement* is likely. In disengaged families, communication across subsystem boundaries is difficult and family members may function separately and autonomously. They lack the ability to be interdependent. When a family member is under stress, the disengaged family has difficulty in coming to that individual's assistance (Minuchin, 1974:51–56; Goldenberg and Goldenberg, 1985:69). In the latter case, *enmeshment* is likely. The family turns in on itself and away from the cultural level discussed earlier, and the boundaries between family members become blurred. Family members in enmeshed families become overinvolved and overconcerned in one another's lives. "Members of enmeshed subsystems or families may be handicapped in that the heightened sense of belonging requires a major yielding of autonomy" (Minuchin, 1974:55).

Hansen and L'Abate make several important statements about "enmeshed" and "disengaged" families. First, they are labels for different transactional styles. Second, a normal family displays characteristics of each style at various times. Third, a pathological family is one that continually operates in an extreme "enmeshed" or "disengaged" manner. Fourth, a strong family is capable of mobilizing either transactional pattern to suitably meet internal pressures from the individual level, or external pressures from the cultural level (1982:133–135). In addition, Nichols notes that it may be functional for families to be enmeshed or disengaged. These interactional styles are not a problem in and of themselves. Problems occur only when families fail to modify their structure to fit changing circumstances (1984:65–66).

Causes of family dysfunctioning may emanate from one of four sources that may be related to the structural model developed separately by Minuchin and Parsons. One source of stress is extrafamilial and initially affects one individual, but this stress may, in turn, necessitate accommodating behavior on the part of one or more family subsystems or the family as a whole. A second source of stress is also extrafamilial, but it impacts on the entire family rather than on one member. A third source of family dysfunctioning is related to the natural developmental tasks that evolve during the course of a family's history. The fourth source of stress is "idiosyncratic" problems (e.g., retardation, handicaps, addiction) that overload the family's coping mechanisms (Hansen and L'Abate, 1982:135).

Therapeutic Strategies

Minuchin's therapeutic strategy flows logically from his structural conceptualization of the family. He is primarily concerned with the flexibility of the family's boundaries, their developmental stage, and sources of stress and support. The identified patient's symptoms are equally important, as are the functions and dysfunctions of these symptoms within the family unit. The primary goal of therapy is to change family organization, which the therapist does by creating a *therapeutic system*—a social unit composed of the family and the therapist. Hansen and L'Abate diagram Minuchin's view of therapy in the following manner: "(family) + (therapist) = (family + therapist) = (family + therapist's ghost) − (therapist)" (1982:138). As a result of changing the family structure, the subsystem members will undergo a change in transactional patterns that will enable them to better cope with various forms of family stress. Minuchin interprets the therapist's role as "extremely active," "confrontive," and "involved," and as emphasizing the present rather than the past (Minuchin and Fishman, 1981:20–22).

It is interesting to note that Minuchin makes reference to Parsons in one of his early works, *Families of the Slums.* Minuchin is discussing the initial contact with a family and what features one looks for in the interactional patterns of that group that might be indications of structural dysfunctioning. He quotes the following passage from Talcott Parsons, that focuses on structural determinants of family behavior:

> The structure of the nuclear family can be treated as a consequence of differentiation on two axes, that of hierarchy or power and that of instrumental vs. expressive function . . . these two axes of differentiation as symbolized by the two great differentiations of generation . . . and sex, overshadow other bases of differentiation within . . . a 'typical' nuclear family. (Minuchin et al., 1967:218)

There are two intervention strategies that are used by Minuchin: *coupling,* or joining the family to increase therapeutic leverage; and *restructuring,* strategies aimed at changing the family's transactional patterns (Minuchin and Fishman, 1981:28–49, 142–145; Minuchin et al., 1978:94). *Coupling* takes place through the use of three techniques: maintenance, or supporting the family; tracking, or showing interest in the family; and mimesis, or modeling therapist behavior on the family's mood, tone, speed of speech and mannerisms (Minuchin, 1974:123–129).

Once Minuchin has established the therapeutic system, he attempts to *restructure* the family by a variety of techniques that vary according to the characteristics of the therapist, the family, and the symptoms. Some of the restructuring techniques relevant to us here include: "actualizing family transactional patterns"—the family enacts typical transactions for the therapist, and the therapist observes the patterns (structure) rather than the behavior; "marking boundaries"—the therapist helps the family to recognize subsystem boundaries and subsequently their importance; and "escalating stress"—the therapist blocks typical transactional patterns (Minuchin, 1974:138–157).

In conclusion, Minuchin is concerned with the family's structure and the functions and dysfunctions of that structure for the family's members. The family is just one social unit situated in a hierarchy composed of individuals and increasingly more inclusive social structures. Minuchin moves from the family unit level down to the subsystem level, then down to the individual level; he may also move from the family level up to the cultural level in his analysis. The aim of therapy is a flexible family, one that has neither exceptionally rigid nor diffuse boundaries between its subsystems, and one that is capable of shifting the composition of its boundaries to manage different types of stresses.

CONCLUSION

As I have proceeded through the literature, I have become aware that several different individuals or groups of individuals active in the field of family therapy have attempted to develop typologies for creating some order in this theoretical field. It was of interest to me as I was involved in the early stages of research for this paper, that in some of these typologies Minuchin was included in different categories depending upon the criteria used by the typologist.

Specifically, in the Group for the Advancement of Psychiatry (GAP) model, Minuchin was designated as a therapist who used a systems approach (Goldenberg and Goldenberg, 1985:123). Guerin, however, places him in a subgroup of systems theorists: "structural therapists" (1976). L'Abate and Frey classify Minuchin as an "activity" theorist (Goldenberg and Goldenberg, 1985:124–125). And, Goldenberg and Goldenberg classify Salvador Minuchin as a structural therapist (1985:126–127).

The typologies noted above are interesting both for what they tell us and for their inconsistencies, which are the result of focusing on different aspects of a therapist's approach or style. The purpose of this paper was to discuss the family therapy theory of Salvador Minuchin and to place him within a sociological context. As we can learn more about the various family therapy theories by placing them within the typologies noted above, it is hoped that the sociological classification system that has been used in this paper sheds new light on important aspects of this theory. By emphasizing the structural functional characteristics of Minuchin's theory, it is hoped that the work of this important theorist has been clarified and extended in a significant manner.

Further research could place other family psychotherapists within appropriate sociological constructs. For example, Jay Haley, Murray Bowen, and Mara Selvini-Palazzoli could also be analyzed using both structural functionalism, and, particularly, symbolic interactionism, and the work of Gerald R. Patterson and other social learning theorists could be interpreted in light of the exchange theory developed by George Homans, Peter Blau, and others. These efforts to cross traditional academic boundaries give promise of shedding new light on these theories and of promoting cooperative efforts in a field of mutual interest.

REFERENCES

Abrahamson, Mark
    1981   Sociological Theory: An Introduction to Concepts, Issues, and Research. Englewood Cliffs, NJ: Prentice-Hall.
Douglas, Jack D., Patricia A. Adler, Peter Adler, Andrea Fontana, C. Robert Freeman, and Joseph A. Kotarba
    1980   Introduction to the Sociology of Everyday Life. Boston: Allyn and Bacon.
Eshleman, J. Ross
    1981   The Family: An Introduction. Boston: Allyn and Bacon.
Goldenberg, Irene, and Herbert Goldenberg
    1985   Family Therapy: An Overview. Monterey, CA: Brooks/Cole.
Guerin, Philip J., ed.
    1976   Family Therapy. New York: Gardner Press.
Hansen, James, and Luciano L'Abate
    1982   Approaches to Family Therapy. New York: Macmillan.
Manis, Jerome G., and Bernard N. Meltzer
    1978   Symbolic Interaction: A Reader in Social Psychology. Boston: Allyn and Bacon.
Minuchin, Salvador
    1974   Families and Family Therapy. Cambridge, MA: Harvard University Press.
Minuchin, Salvador, and H. Charles Fishman
    1981   Family Therapy Techniques. Cambridge, MA: Harvard University Press.
Minuchin, Salvador, Braulio Montalvo, Bernard G. Guerney, Bernice G. Rosman, and Florence Schumer
    1967   Families of the Slums. New York: Basic Books.
Minuchin, Salvador, Bernice G. Rosman, and Lester Baker
    1978   Psychosomatic Families. Cambridge, MA: Harvard University Press.
Nass, Gilbert D., and Gerald W. McDonald
    1982   Marriage and the Family (2nd ed). Reading, MA: Addison-Wesley.
Nichols, Michael
    1984   Family Therapy: Concepts and Methods. New York: Gardner Press.
Parsons, Talcott
    1951   The Social System. New York: Free Press.
Robertson, Ian
    1981   Sociology (2nd ed). New York: Worth.

The Clinical Sociologist as a Health Broker

John G. Bruhn
The University of Texas

ABSTRACT

One of the key aspects that distinguish clinical sociologists from other sociologists is the former's more active role in intervention and change. The clinical sociologist performs several functions of a broker. This paper discusses the role of health broker and the opportunities it provides for clinical sociologists, especially in large organizations.

Clinical sociology entails the use of sociological knowledge and the sociological perspective in providing consultation and technical assistance to social units ranging in size from single individuals to large-scale organizations (Rossi and Whyte, 1983). The precise role of the clinical sociologist depends upon the situation and the nature of his/her involvement in it. Indeed, the clinical sociologist's role may change or he/she may function in several different ways while involved in a given situation. One of the key aspects that distinguish clinical sociologists from other sociologists is the former's more active role in intervention and change. The clinical sociologist may facilitate, advocate, negotiate, consult, advise, innovate, observe, or perform several of these functions as part of his/her role as broker. A broker is an agent or middleman, an essential third party in an interaction in which some type of change, involving two or more parties, is planned. The purpose of this paper is to discuss situations in which clinical sociologists might function as health brokers.

John G. Brahn, Ph.D., Professor of Medicine and Community Health, and Dean, School of Allied Health Sciences, The University of Texas Medical Branch, Galveston, TX 77550.

Newell (1984) has suggested that brokered partnerships will be a growing option for reducing health costs. The brokered partnership brings providers and purchasers of health care together into one self-regulating group. The group becomes a true broker, negotiating price, use, and quality of health care services from a competitive position, with both buyers and sellers participating in the decision making.

Brokering is not new to the health field. Third-party payers are probably the largest and most common of brokers. Nurses have functioned informally as brokers, providing health information to patients, assisting patients in making health care decisions, and matching the needs of patients with the resources of the health care system (Fine, 1982). Brokering has also been an integral function of other health professional groups such as social workers. The social worker seeks to match family realities and community resources with patient needs (Pruger, 1982). Brokering is not new to sociologists either, especially those involved in criminology (Alinsky, 1984), marriage and family counseling (Voelkl and Colburn, 1984; Church, 1984), organizational development, and employee assistance programs in industry and large business organizations (Gutknecht, 1984), and in universities (Miller, 1985). Health brokering is, however, a new role option for clinical sociologists. It can involve brokering health information to enhance health among employees in large corporations; assisting individuals and groups in accessing health care resources; facilitating change in the health behaviors of individuals or families; or helping to ameliorate intraorganizational or interagency problems which affect the availability or quality of health care. Brokering health is an important and, as yet, unfilled gap in the health care system and in society at large. The clinical sociologist is in an excellent position to help fill this gap.

The Health Broker and the Concept of Health

The clinical sociologist must have a view of health that goes beyond treatment and rehabilitation and includes health promotion and disease prevention. Brokering health involves helping to create optimal or maximal opportunities for the well-being of individuals, groups, and organizations. The health broker is concerned with the social definition and implications of health and normality (Bruhn, 1974). Health and normality are not discrete states and their determination is not a completely objective process. Before a broker can intervene to create change, a determination of what is to be changed, why, and the possible effects of the change must be made. Since health is a continually changing process, no single intervention is likely to have a permanent effect. Indeed, health and human behavior have continually changing interactive effects. One job for the clinical sociologist is the delineation of those aspects of human behavior and lifestyle that facilitate the degree and duration of stages or phases of "positive health." This is important to health maintenance organizations and to businesses and industry with health programs for employees.

The clinical sociologist broker must be familiar with and comfortable in working with a variety of health models, i.e., medical model, wellness model, epidemiological model, nursing model, and others. Since the broker must often facilitate multidisciplinary teamwork, it is advantageous for the broker to have an interdisciplinary perspective and a degree of optimism about interdisciplinary outcomes. Perhaps even more challenging is the need for the broker to be knowledgeable about strategies and tools for assessing change and measuring outcomes related to a variety of data types and sources. Finally, if the broker is brokering health, it is important that he/she provide a personal model for positive health behavior. For example, a broker who smokes tobacco may not be the appropriate person to facilitate an organization's consideration of a non-smoking policy.

An excellent example of brokering health in an organization is that in which curricular changes that incorporated the teaching of health promotion and disease prevention were implemented in a school of allied health sciences with the help of a clinical sociologist (Bunker et al. 1986). A federal grant provided the initiative and fiscal support for the effort, with strong support from the school's administration. Over a period of three years, Bunker and a committee of colleagues developed 14 student learning modules on health promotion topics. These were incorporated into the curricula of different disciplines through existing courses. The modular format allowed for flexibility by enabling faculty to select modules relevant to a particular profession or to a particular course and, after completion of two core modules, to select them in any order. The same committee initiated a health-screening clinic and health-risk appraisal for all faculty in the school. Faculty in various allied health disciplines performed different aspects of the screening. About 80% of all faculty participated. Clinic participants were given feedback on how to reduce their health risks. The school initiated an exercise program composed of a variety of types of exercise, a smoking cessation course, and a stress management course. The committee led an initiative for a stricter smoking policy in the school, which was endorsed by the faculty. In all of these efforts, a clinical sociologist and a faculty team acted as brokers with an emphasis on advocacy, facilitation, coordination, counseling, and evaluation.

Brokering—Aspects of the Role

Cousins (1985) described four types of sociological practitioners. The consultant offers advice to individuals, groups, and organizations about issues ranging from interrelationships to the purpose, function, and structure of groups and organizations. The counselor is more concerned with interindividual and group relationships and issues surrounding role, status, power, decision making, and

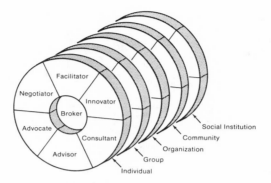

Figure 1. Aspects and Levels of Complexity of Broker Role

adjustment to change. The internal analyst is concerned about the internal "climate" of groups or organizations. The external analyst is concerned about how groups or organizations relate to other social configurations with which they have contact. In all of these roles, the sociological practitioner performs the dual role of inquirer and implementor. These roles require the sociological practitioner to view participants as amenable to change and enlightenment, to utilize strategic reasoning, to adopt a practitioner model compatible with his/her personality, and to be sensitive to ethical issues and able to resolve them (Cousins, 1985).

The more generic term "health broker" includes these and other roles for clinical sociologists. The term "broker" is advantageous because the act of brokering is necessary in situations in which inquiry is a goal, as it is in sociology. The term "health broker" is appropriate for the clinical sociologist who is concerned with problems of health and disease in the broadest sense; it incorporates a unified conceptual view of health and disease that is not fragmented by nosology or diagnostic labels (Engel, 1960). In addition, brokering conveys an active, innovative role for the clinical sociologist in health promotion and community health planning (Rogers, 1968; Rice, 1985).

Figure 1 shows the interrelationships of various aspects of the broker role with different levels of social interaction in which the clinical sociologist may act as a broker. The figure shows how a broker may perform several different aspects of brokering which cut across more than one level of interaction at any given time.

Brokering—Levels of Interaction

Figure 2 provides examples of possible broker involvement at different levels of social interaction.

	Individual	Group	Organization	Community	Social Institution
Individual	• Marital counseling • Divorce arbitration	• Family therapy	• Stress management • Employee assistance programs	• Environmental design and planning	• Health promotion programs
Group		• Understanding of role and function of new specialties in hospitals	• Acceptance and use of PA's in hospitals and private practice	• AIDS education and prevention programs	• Health needs of refugees
Organization			• Interaction of community agencies with similar goals	• Environmental protection groups	• Mothers Against Drunk Drivers (MADD)
Community				• Area-wide emergency medical services • Joint disaster planning	• Family planning, adolescent pregnancy, child abuse
Social Institution					• Programs to meet the needs of the poor, elderly, or homeless

Figure 2. Matrix Showing Examples of Possible Broker Involvement at Different Levels of Social Interaction

At the individual level, the broker commonly interacts with two people, together or separately. The purpose of brokering at this level is to decipher commonalities and differences which might be producing interpersonal conflict or obstructing progress in reaching an organizational goal. The broker seeks and gives information and, as such, is a facilitator, counselor, or coordinator. The two parties may be brought together to achieve reconciliation, to force confrontation, to correct misinformation, or to plan further steps. The recruitment of a broker at this level is usually initiated by the individuals concerned, their supervisors, or friends and peers. The broker is usually perceived as a "neutral" but helpful party.

Brokering at the individual level is often done either to "get people together" or to "keep people apart." For example, a broker, who is a neutral party, might be asked by the leader of an organization to determine the barriers that are preventing a proposed policy change from being accepted, or to offer observations and advice as to why certain individuals in the organization are disenfranchised or isolate themselves. A broker at this level offers perspectives to individuals about barriers and potentials that they may not perceive or know about due to their position in an organization. Because brokers often have "nothing to lose," they can be valuable resources to individuals in planning, problem resolution, thinking through the effects of proposed policies, examination of new markets, etc.

The group level involves brokering in two types of situations: between an individual and a group, and between groups. The former elicits the common example of family therapy in which an individual family member might be the focus of concern or the precipitant for the family to meet as a group. Although brokering for groups involves some of the same types of approaches used in brokering for individuals, it is more complex due to the number of individuals involved. There are numerous examples in which brokers could be used to facilitate the formation of group coalitions, such as providing daycare services to the elderly, or assisting in accepting new groups into existing social institutions, such as the use and hiring of physician's assistants in hospitals. Brokering for groups is also complicated by the fact that group members may change. Hence, the broker may be the primary provider of continuity. One of the difficult aspects of performing the broker role under these circumstances is the need to avoid assuming a leadership position in the group, taking responsibility for group decisions or indecisiveness.

An example of dependence upon the broker-consultant for solving problems was experienced by the author. The "outsider" (broker) was asked to meet with two groups of health workers in a medicine outpatient clinic—clerks and professional nurses—who were at odds with each other. Clerks controlled the patient flow through appointments, and sometimes more patients were scheduled than could be seen by available physicians. The control clerks had over patient appointments was often interrupted by "no-shows," walk-ins, or patients who came on the wrong day or at the wrong time. Physicians were not always available even to see scheduled patients on time due to emergencies, meetings which ran overtime, etc. Nurses, who were the link between the patients and the physicians, caught the wrath of the clerks if the patients who could not be seen were asked to rebook an appointment or were given a return appointment without the clerk's knowledge. Nurses felt ineffective in controlling the availability of physicians, especially to see unscheduled patients. The clerks and nurses actively sabotaged each other's functions, and the patients were often the victims of the clerks' and nurses' angry outbursts and rudeness. The broker was asked to meet with the clerks and nurses together to see if they could work out their differences. Open discussion occurred when the two groups met with the broker, but the broker's suggestion that these groups meet directly with their clinic supervisors was rejected. Members of both groups did not want to risk their jobs by confronting their supervisors with complaints or suggested solutions. The level of distrust between clerks and nurses was such that anyone seen talking with a supervisor was thought to be either "feathering his/her own nest" or complaining about certain individuals. Short- and long-range solutions were only possible when the broker insisted that the supervisors become part of weekly group meetings with the broker. When paranoia lessened, tension lessened, and the groups began to work together for the benefit of the patients.

The broker may be involved in several different types of situations when working with organizations. The broker may interface between an individual and an organization (usually management), between a group or groups inside or outside of the organization and representatives of the organization, or between organizations. Perhaps one of the more frustrating aspects of brokering at the organizational level is the usual delay in decision making, although this will vary with style of management. Communication channels and established lines of power and authority may complicate the broker's role, especially if one of the groups or organizations did not support the involvement of a broker.

Committees, especially in universities, are a way of life (Bruhn, 1981). Committees often function as brokers themselves between the administration, the community and alumni; between administration, faculty, and students; between faculty groups; or between faculty and students. Committees can facilitate or obstruct progress. A broker, especially one outside of the organization, can often provide advice about whether a committee is necessary in accomplishing an objective, and suggest a workable committee structure. When committees bog down, the problems are not always obvious to the involved parties. A broker may be valuable in facilitating compromise, especially if factions have ceased communication with each other. Brokers often perform their role best as listeners and reporters of observations. It is not the broker's job to make a committee work effectively or to accomplish its goal. It is the broker's role, when asked, to comment on behavior and offer suggestions.

Brokering at the community level is a comfortable role for the sociologist as a researcher; however, as an innovator or change agent, the clinical sociologist may become a focal point for individuals, groups, or organizations who might feel threatened by what they perceive the broker's role to be. There may be many different perceptions of the broker's role and, as these create misunderstanding, the perceived threat of a broker may become more real. A broker at the community level requires a variety of skills. He must have the broad perspective of a systems analyst, observing norms and values, interpreting groups dynamics, and facilitating individuals and groups having different attitudes. The broker must have a sensitivity to timing when working at the community level, especially when acting as an innovator or change agent. Often, a broker is employed as a consultant, so personal involvement in community change is limited. The broker can become the focus of anger for community groups, and his/her advice can be used as an excuse should the community fail to achieve its objective.

The current epidemic of Acquired Immune Deficiency Syndrome (AIDS) offered the opportunity for brokering in the author's community. While Texas ranks fourth in the total number of diagnosed AIDS cases in the United States, Galveston (City and County) has only 25 cases. Yet, the university hospital, as a multicategorical referral center, receives AIDS patients from across Texas, especially those without financial resources. This created a community problem and the opportunity for a broker. AIDS patients who could be discharged to outpatient status had no place to go in the community. Apartment owners would not rent to AIDS patients; therefore, patients were kept in the hospital, further escalating hospital costs. The broker, with the assistance of a university admin-istrator, met with the mayor and county judge to inform them of this problem and its likelihood of increasing as the number of AIDS patients grows. The broker first had to educate the officials about AIDS, which was seen by the officials as a problem of larger cities. The officials also resented the idea that the local community should have to cope with housing problems and resultant costs created by patients who were not residents of Galveston County. Both officials finally agreed to appoint a task force to examine the problem and to suggest immediate and long-range solutions, one of which was a half-way house for AIDS patients. The broker, in this example, was able to educate, initiate action toward solving a community problem, and emphasize prevention and planning rather than wait until the problem reached a crisis.

Perhaps the most difficult situation in which to act as a broker is that which might occur at the level of the social institution. This may involve one or more individuals, groups, organizations, or communities in interaction with a social institution. The most common examples are the issues surrounding busing in the public schools, drug use and law enforcement, abortion and religious institutions, and mentally ill transients and mental health institutions. Brokering at the social institutional level undoubtedly involved politics and special interest groups. So-cial institutions are not easily changed. They usually have a public image based on long-standing traditions and are sources of support and stability for their members and advocates. Usually, it is not possible for one person to serve as a broker between institutions because of the complexity of the situation. A team of colleagues would provide a more effective approach to brokering at this level.

Brokers at the institutional level are more likely to be perceived as advocates or change agents, especially if they have an active and visible association with individuals and groups who are known for creating change. While brokering for change can occur within a social institution, the area of change must be viewed as a high priority by gatekeepers or it will not be permitted to be addressed. A well-known technique for stalling change in social institutions is the appointment of a study committee. The nature of the problem or issue may change substantially by the time a committee drafts its findings and recommendations, or the problem may have resolved itself.

Brokering to create change in social institutions is, perhaps, most timely when an institution is experiencing change. Universities provide an example of a social institution that generally undergoes little change except, perhaps, when a new president is appointed. If the appointee is an outsider, considerable anxiety may be created among insiders, whose jobs may be altered or eliminated. Yet, new leadership also provides an opportunity to advocate and help create change. Brokers are often used by new administrative appointees to "sense the environ-ment" and assemble facts about relevant information from components of the institution. In this way, brokers can be especially helpful in program development. This has been done in many universities in developing, for example, health promotion and gerontology programs. A distinguished professor might be recruited to provide leadership in getting a program off the ground. The professor serves as a broker in coalescing divergent components that could not get the program moving without an outside stimulus. Brokers are of key importance in developing most interdisciplinary programs.

The Health Broker as a Lifecycle Interventionist

Another way in which to view the health broker is as a lifestyle interventionist. All organisms have lifecycles and undergo change. Change, or the lack of it, creates dysfunctions in systems at various points in their development and, often, creates the need to seek special advice, direction, or support. A broker can help to alleviate problems in adjusting to change that occur in the process of growth and development, whether it be that of an individual, group, organization, community, or institution. One cannot intervene in a situation without considering the interaction between the demands on a system and its resources for coping at any point in time. French et al. (1974) refer to this as "person-environment fit." The person-environment fit framework considers the consequences of interaction in terms of growth and dysfunction. Much of the initial empirical work using this framework has been in the domain of organizational stress and studies of the effect of the work environment. The person-environment fit concept has the advantage of simultaneously considering individual differences, environmental factors, and their interaction in the development of dysfunction. In this view, a broker could help to predict and, hence, to prevent problems in changing systems.

If we view organizations as entities that are never static, but are experiencing various degrees of decline or growth at any point in time, it is reasonable to expect that there will always be parts of an organization that are not in complete synchrony with other parts. In the same manner, individuals only rarely achieve a state of homeostasis. The ability of an organization to predict problems related to its growth or decline, and thereby minimize the problems associated with decline and maximize the opportunities associated with growth, may be enhanced by the services of a broker. A broker who is concerned with the total health of an organization, and not only with its problems or ills, may call upon colleagues in other disciplines to add to the skills needed to deal comprehensively with organizational health (Coelho et al., 1974).

Table 1 shows various types of needs organizations often have during periods of growth: the needs to reorganize, redevelop, and/or resocialize its employees. These needs may affect the entire structure of the organization, require modifications in its philosophy, or involve role redefinition among employees. A clinical sociologist has several tools or skills to assist the organization's leadership

Table 1

BROKERING IN ORGANIZATIONS:
SOME NEEDS, APPROACHES AND METHODS

Brokering Needs	Level of Intervention	Brokering Methods*
For Organizations Experiencing Growth		
Reorganization and Redevelopment	Structure and organization Employees	Role redefinition New skills training program Reward system Problem-solving groups
Resocialization	Philosophy of organization	Value clarification (individual and organizational)
For Organizations Experiencing Decline		
Revitalization	Financial structure External relationships Product or service	New markets Create new demands Public relations program Involvement in local community organizations
Rehabilitation	Physical and social environment or organization	Quality circles Incentive programs Health maintenance program Involvement in local community organizations

*These methods may be applicable in more than one area.

in coping with needed readjustments. Methods include: organizing problem-solving groups; discussing and clarifying issues related to power, authority, delegation, and reward systems with management and employees; and individual and group counseling.

When organizations undergo periods of decline, they need revitalization and rehabilitation. If an organization's survival is threatened, the basic structure of the organization—its financial system, external relationships, and even its product or service—may need to be reworked. Sometimes, an organization merely grows out of touch with its physical and social environment and its relationships with other organizations. The clinical sociologist can assist the organization in learning new or revamping old survival skills.

The Limitations of Health Brokering

The possible role of a health broker is very broad and, indeed, encompasses the spectrum of concerns in sociology. A health broker is a specialist with specialized interests and skills. A broker is not a universal problem solver, and must be aware of the limits of his/her knowledge and skills. A broker must be aware of, and willing to work with, other professionals who are also knowledgeable in human behavior in dealing with complex issues. Hence, the broker must be comfortable working in interdisciplinary teams. Finally, the broker must be willing to accept failure. Expectations of brokers and consultants are often excessive, especially when a broker is sought as a last resort. Brokers should be careful about setting forth what they can and cannot do at the onset in working with any social unit.

Conclusions

The role of the health broker provides an opportunity for clinical sociologists to play a significant part in coping with the effects of change in a variety of social units, ranging from individuals to social institutions. Brokering requires active involvement or intervention to enhance the health, and minimize the risks to health, among individuals, groups, and organizations. Health brokering is a positive, action-oriented, and futuristic role for clinical sociologists; it directly involves clinical sociology in such current health trends and issues as prevention and gerontology.

REFERENCES

Alinsky, Saul
    1984   "A sociological technique in clinical criminology." Clinical Sociology Review
                2:12–24.
Bruhn, John G.
    1974   "The diagnosis of normality." Texas Reports on Biology and Medicine 32:241–248.
Bruhn, John G.
    1981   "On the care and feeding of committees." Southern Medical Journal 74:133–135.
Bunker, John F., Guy S. Parcel, Billy U. Philips, and Denise Simons-Morton
    1986   "Curricular implications of health promotion and disease prevention in allied health
                education." Journal of Allied Health 15:329–337.
Church, Nathan
    1984   "Sociotherapy with marital couples: incorporating dramaturgical and social con-
                structionist elements of marital interaction." Clinical Sociology Review 3:116–128.
Coelho, George V., David A. Hamburg, and John E. Adams, eds.
    1974   Coping and Adaptation. New York: Basic Books.
Cousins, Albert N.
    1985   "The sociological practitioner: an adjunctive role model." Sociological Spectrum
                5:361–379.

Engel, George L.
    1960   "A unified concept of health and disease." Perspectives in Biology and Medicine,
              Summer:459–485.
Fine, Ruth B.
    1982   "Health information brokers." Nursing Management 13:39–40.
French, J.R.P., W. Rogers, and S. Cobb
    1974   "Adjustment as person-environment fit." In George V. Coelho, David A. Hamburg
              and John E. Adams (eds.), Coping and Adaptation. New York: Basic Books.
Gutknecht, Douglas B.
    1984   "Organizational development: an assessment with implications for clinical sociol-
              ogy." Clinical Sociology Review 2:94–108.
Miller, John S.
    1985   "Sociologists as mediators: clinical sociology in action." Clinical Sociology Review
              3:158–164.
Newell, Lawrence
    1984   "Brokered partnerships: a new way to cap health costs." Business Insurance, Oc-
              tober 1:28.
Pruger, Robert
    1982   "The good bureaucrat." Pp. 385–392 in Hiasura Rubenstein and Mary Henry Block
              (eds.), Things That Matter: Influences on Helping Relationships. New York: Mac-
              millan.
Rice, Thomas J.
    1985   "American public policy formation and implementation." Pp. 153–171 in Roger
              A. Straus (ed.), Using Sociology. Bayside, NY: General Hall.
Rogers, Edward S.
    1968   "Public health asks of sociology. . . ." Science 159:506–508.
Rossi, Peter H. and William F. Whyte
    1983   "The applied side of sociology." Pp. 5–31 in Howard E. Freeman, Russell R.
              Dynes, Peter H. Rossi and William Foote Whyte (eds.), Applied Sociology. San
              Francisco: Jossey-Bass.
Voelkl, Gary M. and Kenneth Colburn, Jr.
    1984   "The clinical sociologist as family therapist: utilizing the strategic communication
              approach." Clinical Sociology Review 2:64–77.

Teaching of Clinical Sociology

Habermas' Sociological Theory as a Basis for Clinical Practice with Small Groups

Valerie Ann Malhotra
Texas Woman's University

ABSTRACT

Jurgen Habermas' sociological analysis of "power-distorted" communication, of "instrumental action vs. symbolic interaction," and his theory of "universal pragmatics," involving an analysis of the "ideal speech situation" or "communicative competency," was used as a basis for clinical practice with 53 women students divided into five small groups.[1] Habermas' theory provided the basis for the assessment of the need for clinical intervention, as well as the model for structuring the communication processes in the groups to alleviate the effects of the distorted communication characteristic of life in post-capitalist society.

The groups of students were involved as participants in a self-reflective process which involved discussions that were videotaped on the second and fifteenth of 16 sessions. The women also submitted autobiographies, kept four-week-long time schedules and daily diaries, wrote narratives describing their experience of time, tape-recorded and transcribed family interactions and submitted several standardized scales. The analysis of Habermas' "communicative competency" as exhibited in these groups and in their at-home conversations is presented here based on the field observations of the researcher and on qualitative and quantitative analysis of the data.

RESEARCH DESIGN

This paper presents an analysis of those aspects relevant to clinical practice with groups of a larger study of women students, especially those age 25 and over. The overall purpose of the study was to gain an in-depth understanding of life

Correspondence to: Valerie Ann Malhotra, Department of Sociology, Texas Woman's University, Denton, TX 76204.

experiences of "older" female students, who typically have multiple role obligations such as wife, mother, and employee, as compared with students entering college directly after high school. Prior to the start of the semester, letters were written to a random sample of 250 women students age 25 and over who were enrolled at a state university, inviting them to participate in the research by enrolling in a course called Social Psychology of Women. In addition, participation was solicited by word of mouth and the use of bulletin boards. The result was 53 women enrolled in five sections of the course, 60% of whom were age 25 and over.

The women met in five small groups weekly for 16 weeks. These groups were structured to foster what Habermas called "communicative competency." They were to function as therapy/support groups and as a focal point for data collection. The women were told they could withdraw from the course at any time without grade penalty. They were told they would all get an A as long as they continued with the group. They were free not to provide any aspect of the data with which they were not comfortable without penalty. Participants signed consent forms and were assured that all data collected would be filed only by number, protecting their anonymity. They were aware that all papers and reports which may result would use disguised identifying information.

Multiple triangulation (Denzin, 1978), both theoretical and methodological, was employed since the purpose was an in-depth understanding of the women's life experiences. The primary theoretical perspectives used were those of George Herbert Mead, Alfred Schutz, and Jurgen Habermas. The data collection included the following: autobiographies, stressing relationships with significant others from early childhood to the present, daily journals, four-week-long time schedules, time-memory studies, videotapes of group process early and late in the term, audiotapes of dinner-time conversations in the home, Kuhn's "Who Am I" scale, and a household division of labor scale. Teams of researchers provided "communicative competency" ratings both early and late in the semester for each group member based on Habermas' criteria. The focus of this paper is limited to those aspects of the data which have a bearing on Habermas' concepts.

What is of particular relevance to clinical sociology is that Habermas' theoretical corpus was fruitful as applied to working with groups. His concepts are sensitizing to areas of life experience which proved to be of crucial importance to the participants. In addition, Habermas' insights about power and distorted communication provided a framework for conducting practice. Clinical sociology from a Habermasian perspective seeks to alleviate and overcome distorted communication and its effects. Habermas draws his key insights from critical theory and its Marxian/Freudian analysis of the effects of power on social relationships. He also integrates the important insights of other theoretical perspectives such as developmental theory (Piaget, Kohlberg), structural/functional/systems theory (Parsons, Luhmann), structural linguistics (Saussure, Chomsky), Weberian theory, symbolic interaction (Mead, James, Pierce) and phenomenology (Husserl, Schutz, and Luckman). Since these theoretical frameworks also provide the basis for existing theories of psychotherapy, it should not be surprising if Habermasian clinical sociology resembles existing therapeutic frames of reference. Actual practices always are rich and multifaceted and can only be partially captured by any theoretical explanation.

Habermasian-based clinical sociology will resemble other practices which are sensitized to power issues as they affect clients. It is not at issue in this paper, however, to show what existing practices may interface with Habermasian practice. Rather, the paper will illustrate that Habermas' concepts lead in and of themselves to effective clinical practice (see Farris and Marsh, 1982). This paper will present a brief overview of some of the relevant concepts of Habermas. It will address how these concepts were applied in the clinical setting with the groups of women. Finally, data will be presented which assess the success of this attempt to base group practice on Habermas' concepts.

HABERMAS' THEORY AS RELATED TO CLINICAL PRACTICE: A BRIEF OVERVIEW

A theme that runs throughout Habermas' work is that of power in relation to communication. To Habermas, the powers of the state, linked with the ideologically buttressed forces of modern science and technology (1970:81f) have greatly distorted communicative processes. Much of what passes for communication is really "pseudocommunication" or "power-distorted communication." In such interchanges, persons are involved in deliberating about means to attain predetermined ends ("instrumental action"). By contrast, in true discourse, or "symbolic interaction," persons discuss ends as well as means. Symbolic interaction or discourse allows for the social creation of meanings (1970:93, 1983:366f).

In communication freed from power distortions, persons can become aware of their true interests and concerns (Habermas, 1972). That one could be unaware of one's own interests is symptomatic in current mass society (see also Stivers, 1982). The forces of rationalization and bureaucratization have produced a "power-saturated" society characterized by instrumental or strategic communication. Increasingly, according to Habermas, society is divided into two groups, the administrators or "professionals" and their clients. Or, to borrow from Goffman (1961), institutions are becoming increasingly like "total institutions," whereby virtually all aspects of one's life come under bureaucratic control. Any communicative action which decreases instrumentalization and increases meaningful symbolic communication would be "therapeutic" given Habermas' analysis. Because of the medical model implicit in the term "therapeutic," however, Habermas would be more likely to use the term "emancipatory."

According to Habermas, the capitalist state has "colonized" the home. This happens as the media intrude upon every waking "free" moment. It occurs as one must account for everything one does in terms of how it will affect one's income tax reports. It increases as jobs demand more and more of the time, life, and energy of both marriage partners. As schools become more like prisons, and children attend caretaking institutions at younger ages, the "colonization" of the world of everyday life intensifies (see Denzin, 1977; Suransky, 1982). All relationships thus tend toward instrumental ones, secondary to career interests (Habermas, 1983; see also Rasmussen, 1982:25f).

Habermas is indebted to Freud for help in uncovering meanings of indirect or distorted communication. Socially engendered power, internalized, suppresses and distorts self-understanding. An unreflective self mirrors these distortions outward. Lack of reflection facilitates pseudocommunication, which further limits reflectivity. The trouble with Freud, according to Habermas, is that his conceptual framework, which was medical/physical, was too narrow to allow for an appropriate understanding of his own practice (1972:245f). The healing truths that emerge from psychoanalysis do so always *in dialogue*, in which all assumptions—cultural, historical, as well as those grounded in unique childhood experiences—can be questioned. To be upheld, statements must be defensible within the discourse—"discursively redeemable."

"Communicative competency," or the "ideal speech situation" in Habermas rests on certain social conditions and bears recognizable characteristics. The four characteristics of communicative competency are truth (the statements adequately portray realities), truthfulness (the speaker is forthrightly trying to express the way things are—not hiding or obscuring), comprehensibility (the speaker possesses adequate linguistic skills to be understood) and understandability (the statement is made in a normatively appropriate situation so that it can be assimilated by the listener) (Habermas, 1979:29). These characteristics of the "ideal speech situation" are part of the ontological structure of all human societies. Habermas contends that without making the assumption that speech acts are so characterized, social interaction will tend to disintegrate. The irony of existence in post-modern, post-capitalist societies is that most of the time one or more of these assumptions are violated in actual communication. At the same time, for talk to continue and tasks to be completed, we must all speak "as if" the assumptions are fulfilled.

Habermas outlines the social dimensions which allow for "ideal speech" situations to be approximated. These include "institutional unboundedness" and the absence of strategic motivations and power-based distortions. Within an institution or organization there will be pressures to continue discourse that maintains the existing power relationships. Private, voluntary interaction alleviates such effects. With institutional constraints diminished, only those internalized remain to be considered. Since adults were socialized within a given institutional order, private interaction will tend to reflect institutional norms. Critical reflection can reveal these processes and expose them to change.

Communicative competency, or discourse, is an unrealizable ideal in current social situations. However, one can treat the "ideal speech situation" as a Weberian ideal type, a model which never actually exists in its full manifestations. The ideal speech situation is what the clinician attempts to realize. It becomes an exemplar which enables those participating to attempt to realize such communication in other spheres of their lives. In practice, such communicative situations will exhibit the following characteristics: 1) speakers will have symmetrical chances to speak; 2) assumptions and conceptual frameworks which govern the situation may be called into question by any speaker; and 3) attempts to dominate, or strategic motivations on the part of actors, must be cast aside (see McCarthy, 1978:310f).

The data presented here are illustrative of Habermas' diagnosis of the detrimental effects of "power-saturated" situations in modern life. In addition, data are presented which shed light on how relatively successful we were in establishing the "ideal speech situation" in the groups.

DATA: QUALITATIVE

The time schedules, daily journals, and transcripts of tape-recorded conversations in the home indicated that Habermas' concepts of "power-distorted communication" and "colonization of the lifeworld" were in evidence in these women's lives. In the process of trying to expand their horizons and to earn requisite income, women must meet the demands of the university and corporate worlds. Women who previously spent full time maintaining a household and caring for children had to make changes in their schedules accordingly. The data from the time schedules (see Malhotra, 1984) indicate that household activities did not decrease when the women who were married and/or had children entered school. Rather, they reported spending less time in sleep, in leisure activities, and with children.

Nancy's experience of frustration and lack of satisfaction was typical of mothers in the study. Nancy is a divorced mother, age 47, with a daughter 16 and a son 12. Her daily life as reflected in her diary and time schedules is a whirlwind of carpools, cooking, working at a dull, low-paying job, filling out health insurance claims, balancing her checkbook, household chores, yard work, shopping, homework, dealing with dental bills and psychologist's bills for her children, keeping the car running, and feeding and clothing her family. She expresses frustration at the hassles and lack of satisfactions in daily life, and at seemingly never getting anything done to her satisfaction. The little time she has for social life she has found to be disappointing due to a shortage of single men in her age bracket. She was working 30 hours a week, taking 12 hours of class work, and driving both children to and from school and to all of their activities. She seemed to blame herself for her failures, saying that perhaps if she were better organized she could get more done. Her time schedules actually reflect an extremely intense organization which allowed her to keep up with the multiple demands on her time and energy. With her schedule, a necessary car repair turned out to have a traumatic impact on her family's life for the week.

Some success in alleviating the effects of what Habermas calls "institutional boundedness" and "power distortions" in communication was evident in the groups. For each aspect of the data provided, some women decided they did not wish to provide it or they provided it only in limited form. Interestingly, in their evaluation of the effect of each aspect of the research on their self-understandings and/or behavior, the home taping, transcript and analysis had an effect on the largest percentage of those who complied (see Malhotra, 1984). About one-fourth of the women chose not to submit this aspect of the data, however. In discussion they said that they could not get their family members to participate, or that they could not get them to exhibit "normal" conversation on the tape. Two participants refused because they felt it invaded their privacy. The strongest negative response was to the home taping.

Another indication of a feeling of lack of pressure in regard to data provided was the varying length, frankness and intensity of the diaries. Some diaries are soliloquies about deeply personal and important conflicts. Although she said little in the group discussions, one woman used her diary to explore her feelings about her disintegrating marriage. Other diaries were written at a superficial level. This indicates that pressures upon participants in regard to level of disclosure were minimal. The depth of self-reflection was at each woman's discretion.

Participants were encouraged to be involved at all levels of the process, including involvement in data analysis and writing and presenting results. This was actualized by several of the participants who wrote and presented papers at a professional meeting based on aspects of the research (see Owens, 1981; Stabel, 1981; Stem, 1981). The norms surrounding the functioning of the small groups also facilitated communicative competency in Habermas' sense. Each group independently decided to maintain the norm of confidentiality, that is, not to reveal the content of group discussions outside of the group. Participants did directly effect the data-gathering process in other ways. For example, the suggested format for keeping the four weekly time schedules was found to be too cumbersome by the women. One of them suggested a revised format which was supported by the others and implemented.

The discussions were about everyday life experiences, but took place out of their usual context. This would serve to inhibit what Habermas calls "institutional boundedness" which tends to distort communication (1979: 40f). The discussions also involved self-reflection and dialogue bearing some similarity to a psychoanalytic hermeneutical process. The small groups provided an occasion for a critical eye to be cast upon childhood and cultural influences upon the self. The effect of early primary relationships on current patterns of activities was a focus of the autobiographies and of the phenomenologically based time studies as well as the discussions surrounding them.

Communication in the groups was characteristically "constraint free." With few exceptions, the women did contribute to the ongoing discussions. An emphasis on concepts that elucidated the nature and the effect of power on one's own experiences facilitated this. For example, the group members read Marilyn French's *The Women's Room*, which is a devastating critique of the effect of male domination. In one part of the novel, Myra, the main character, uses the imagery of "diapers and green beans" to express the central foci of her life while she was the wife of a medical student. Later, she had become an efficient physician's wife, faithfully administering the consumption and maintenance of the upper-middle-class life. These experiences of Myra's served as a springboard for recounting and sharing understandings of similar experiences. One woman recalled her struggles to take care of two babies and her husband's needs while attending school. Another, who had been a homemaker for many years, spoke of her similar feeling of boredom and powerlessness during the time she raised the four children (now young adults) while her husband's career blossomed. He traveled to conferences in Hawaii and other exotic places while she stayed home with the children. In addition, she was required to make all the management decisions regarding the children and to carry them out including moving the family and getting them settled in new schools ten times. A third participant recounted her feeling of bitterness. At the beginning of the term she had helped her three children prepare for school and packed her husband's clothing for a business trip. Since these kinds of services were not reciprocated, she found herself starting the semester in college with her own wardrobe in disarray.

Two participants said little in the group discussions. It was evident through reading the narrative documents that their silence did not signify lack of involvement. They found that the disclosures in the group were distinctly related to the reflective processes. One woman informed the researcher that her silence was due to being in the process of divorce. She did not feel comfortable talking about it openly. However, she said that the readings and discussions were helping her to understand and to cope with her own experience.

Direct observation of the groups indicated that Habermas' four criteria of the ideal speech situation, or communicative competency, were fulfilled to a considerable extent. Comprehensibility was shown in the patience with which the women questioned a Nigerian woman, until they learned to decipher her broken English. Similarly, understandability, or speaking within appropriate norms, seemed to be high, which in part attests to the time spent in each group at the beginning to reach operative norms for the discussions. Little or no pressure was brought to bear by a group member or leader for anyone to disclose information. One negative instance was observed when a woman brought up a sensitive subject of importance to her but was ignored by the group. This large, physically unattractive woman spoke of her difficulty in finding suitable male companions and resorting to masturbation. No one, not even the group leader, responded to the comment. Apparently, this topic at this time was not within the normative boundaries to be dealt with adequately by the group.

That the truth content was high in the groups was evident in the consistency between the content of the discussions and that found in the narrative documents. Consistent expression of deviant viewpoints took place and was encouraged. The group members seemed to feel comfortable in openly challenging the statements of each other which they did not agree with or find plausible. One woman's truth content was challenged by the group to the point that she took action to support her contention that her husband was ideally equalitarian in his relationship with her. To face the challenge, she brought her husband to the group for them to meet!

The sensitivity to "power" ironically caused the researcher to fail to curtail the exertion of power by a group member. In reviewing the videotapes, the researcher noted that her own hesitancy to influence the discussions caused her to allow one group member to take up an inordinate amount of group time in speaking of her own problems and concerns. This was corroborated by the diaries of several of the other group members who expressed boredom and anger with this participant's domination of the group.

The group process also in some ways exceeded the boundaries of Habermas' "ideal speech situation," for the Habermasian model stresses truth-seeking and the development of a rational process of decision-making. The communicative process as described by Habermas neither includes nor precludes the embodied expression of pains and joys, desires and wonders. Dallmayr (1981) refers to such experiences as "other voices." Intense emotions are evident in communicative acts which create meaning and coherency for the self and thus make possible an adequate expression of political interests (see Denzin, 1984). Such authentic self-formative speech acts relate desires to contexts and uncover the sources and transmissions of power in everyday life. Interests otherwise expressed may be only transmissions of unrecognized authorities or even of repressive desublimations" (Marcuse, 1964).

Such expressions may, perhaps even necessarily, be metaphors (McFague, 1975). They may mirror repressions and frames of which we are yet unaware as our needs search for linguistic form. They always have emotional content. They are always expressive of desires. Such kinds of motivations, which Habermas would label "strategic," cannot be eliminated; they can only be censored (Kristeva, 1980).

QUANTITATIVE FINDINGS: A SUMMARY

Attempts were made to systematize and verify the qualitative results. Several instruments were constructed by groups of research assistants. The first of these was an assessment of each participant's "communicative competency" based on Habermasian criteria as observed on the videotapes of group interaction early and late in the process. Secondly, transcripts and analyses were completed of the audiotapes of family dinner-time conversations. The communicative competency and level of dominance of participants at home were based on these transcripts.

These data were factor analyzed. The first factor indicated that the judgments associated with communicative competency tended to be coherent and were positively associated with being supportive and stimulating. The items from the assessment of communicative competency in the home setting consistently loaded on a different factor from those in the group settings. This suggests that the group and home settings involved different sets of capabilities on the part of the participants. More tendency to be domineering was exhibited in the home setting. While this was to be expected in interactions with children in contrast with peer interaction, only a third of the conversations included children. This finding does confirm that the group processes were relatively domination free. Comprehensibility, normative appropriateness, and sincerity were judged to be higher in the group settings while objective truth content was judged to be slightly higher in the home.

In summary, there was a distinct difference between the communicative competency ratings demonstrated in the home and in the group setting. The participants, for the most part, demonstrated an ability to share and to communicate on a different level in the group setting, perhaps due to the approach taken in the setting which encouraged open discourse. The home setting is institutionally bounded. Also, pragmatically necessary tasks must be accomplished. Discourse oriented toward increased understanding is not an everyday dinner-time objective.

A detailed analysis of the interaction shown on the videotapes was also done by a team of research assistants who were unaware of Habermas' theories. They recorded such elements as open and closed body patterns, hesitant or confident speech, frequency of supportive comments and of origination of topics. What is of pertinence here is the changes that were evident in the patternings of these behaviors between the early and late tapings. These data seem to support the contention that Habermas' principles were in practice in the groups and that therapeutic results obtained from the processes. Minimal discomfort, as exhibited by closed body language and hesitant speech patterns, was in evidence.

Effect of Research on Participants

Elsewhere, analysis has been presented of the effects of being involved in the research on the lives of the participants (Malhotra, 1984). Based on evaluations of their own involvement and on their diaries kept throughout the process, group involvement in the research had changed the understandings or behaviors of participants. Eighteen (34%) of the participants reported both changed behaviors and understandings; 24 (45%) reported changed understanding only. Those remaining reported no effect from some aspects of the research, and five did not complete the evaluation.

CONCLUSION: HABERMAS' PERSPECTIVE IN RELATION TO CLINICAL PRACTICE IN SOCIOLOGY

Habermas has provided a basis not only for understanding, but also for alleviating the conditions of contemporary mass society. The clinical sociologist, both in the role of researcher and clinician, must transform these concepts into practice. The role of "clinical sociologist" already implies power—the power of the expert. To practice Habermasian clinical sociology thus requires that the clinician be aware of this and make efforts to alleviate these effects. In order to accomplish this, it is important that the clinician take the attitude of solicitous watchfulness. To borrow from Heidegger: the therapist would be seen as a cultivator, providing the soil and conditions for growth.

The Habermasian clinician must come to the situation with sufficient self-understanding to be aware of how his or her own past experiences may effect perceptions and emotional reactions. The capacity for constant self-reflection may be the product of having been psychoanalyzed or having experienced other sensitizing therapeutic or educational processes.

Ongoing supervision is one way this may occur, however that supervision itself should be Habermasian. The institutional constraints existing in the situations which bring the clinical sociologist and client into contact must be ameliorated to every extent possible. For example, clients must be free from reprisal for opinions, attitudes or feelings expressed. Codes of ethics that emphasize meeting the needs of the client as opposed to those of the sociologist in the clinical situation are important social reinforcements, as are professional associations.

Traditionally, therapy is divided into assessment or diagnosis and treatment. In the Habermasian framework, these are not really separable processes. However, it may be valuable to assess the extent of power-distorted communication (see Malhotra and Deneen, 1982) in the interaction of consultees. Also the extent to which the everyday life of clients has been fragmented and colonized by media, commercial and governmental powers would be important to note. A

Habermasian clinical sociologist would also assess tendencies for communication to be strategically oriented or oriented toward reaching meaningful understanding.

Applied to group practice, groups would be structured to allow for all assumptions to be questioned. The clinical sociologist would seek to facilitate self-reflection and provide support for the discovery of the effects of domination on interaction.

A major shortcoming of Habermas' "ideal speech situation" as a model for clinical sociological practice with groups is its cognitive-rational emphasis. Groups of persons engaged in in-depth reflection and mutual truth seeking speak in many voices and with vivid emotions. They speak as beings existing with bodies and the realities inflicted by bodies. These aspects were an evident part of the group processes discussed in this paper. Aspects of these processes were covered in the study through the use of the Meadian framework and Schutzian phenomenology. A discussion of the usefulness of these sociological theories for clinical practice as studied in this research must remain for a future paper.

This study has attempted to demonstrate that effective clinical sociology with small groups can be conducted from a Habermasian perspective. As such it is an example of the uniqueness, richness and conceptual independence of the field of clinical sociology.

If clinical sociology is to serve the interests of human emancipation, it must draw more intently upon the work of its great theorists in its charting of workable, nonexploitative practice. Habermas is one such theorist. As Habermas successfully points out in *Theory and Practice* (1974), a theory that allows for the constitution of a discourse that unmasks power-distorted relationships cannot itself change those relationships. Those changes can only be brought about by those whose consciousness is thereby changed. Manipulative techniques must be discarded by clinical sociologists interested in human emancipation. In Habermas' words:

> The vindicating superiority of those who do the enlightening over those who are to be enlightened is theoretically unavoidable, but at the same time it is fictive and requires self-correction. In a process of enlightenment there can only be participants. (1974:40)

NOTES

1. Thanks to Jeffrey LaMar Deneen, Shirley Rombough, Peggy Maher and Carol Stabel, who served as group leaders. Deneen, Maher, Stabel, as well as Jerrian Stem, Ann Tidball, Tamera Bryant, Dai-Na Sun, Beth Germscheid, and Cathy Pruit also served as research assistants. Azzi Abderahmahne, Ann Shea, Ashwin Nyas, Steven Kurtz, Timothy Nissen, and Bobby Moodley coded the videotapes. This research was funded by several grants from the Texas Woman's University Office of Research and Grants Administration.

REFERENCES

Dallmayr, Fred
    1981   Twilight of Subjectivity. Amherst: University of Massachusetts Press.
Denzin, Norman K.
    1977   Childhood Socialization. San Francisco: Jossey-Bass.
    1978   The Research Act. New York: McGraw-Hill.
    1984   On Understanding Emotion. San Francisco: Jossey-Bass.
Farris, Buford and James Marsh
    1982   "Habermas' communicative ethics and social work practice." Paper presented at
            the Midwest Sociological Association Annual Meeting, Kansas City.
Goffman, Erving
    1961   Asylums. New York: Doubleday.
Habermas, Jurgen
    1970   Toward A Rational Society, trans. by Jeremy J. Shapiro London: Heinemann.
    1972   Knowledge and Human Interests. Boston: Beacon.
    1974   Theory and Practice, trans. by John Viertel, London: Heinemann.
    1979   Communication and the Evolution of Society. Boston: Beacon.
    1983   Theory of Communicative Action, vol. I. Boston: Beacon.
Kristeva, Julia
    1980   Desire in Language. New York: Columbia University Press.
Malhotra, Valerie
    1984   "Research as critical reflection: a study of self, time, and communicative compe-
            tency," Humanity and Society 8, no. 4:468–477.
Malhotra, Valerie and Jeffrey LaMar Deneen
    1982   "Power-saturated vs. appreciative conversations among children and between chil-
            dren and adults." Paper presented at the Xth World Congress of Sociology, Mexico
            City.
Marcuse, Herbert
    1964   One Dimensional Man. Boston: Beacon Press.
McCarthy, Thomas
    1978   The Critical Theory of Jurgen Habermas. Cambridge, MA: MIT Press.
McFague, Sally
    1975   Speaking in Parables. Philadelphia: Fortran.
Owens, Lorrie
    1981   "Doing nothing: the effects of keeping time schedules on research participants."
            Paper presented at the East Texas State University Fall Sociological Research Sym-
            posium.
Rasmussen, David
    1982   "Communicative action and philosophy: reflections on Habermas' Theorie Des
            Kommunikativen Handelns," Philosophy and Social Criticism 9, no. 1:1–29.
Stabel, Carol
    1981   "An analysis of the effects of writing daily journals." Paper presented at the East
            Texas State University Fall Sociological Research Symposium.
Stem, Jerrian
    1981   "The effect of writing a Meadian autobiography." Paper presented at the East Texas
            State University Fall Sociological Research Symposium.
Stivers, Richard A.
    1982   Evil in Modern Myth and Ritual. Athens: University of Georgia Press.
Suransky, Valerie Polokow
    1982   Erosion of Childhood. Chicago: University of Chicago Press.

Book Reviews

Counseling in Marital and Sexual Problems: A Clinician's Handbook, 3rd ed., edited by Robert F. Stahmann and William J. Heibert. Lexington, MA: D.C. Health and Company, 1984, 263 pp., $18.00

Lance W. Roberts
University of Manitoba

Marriage and family therapy is one area in which numerous clinical sociologists display their abilities. The volume under review promises to be of relevance to these practitioners as it is billed as a "clinician's handbook" to marriage and sexual counseling. The book's goals are to pass along "information, ideas, and guidelines" to students and practitioners of family therapy.

Academic insight confirms what everyday experience suggests, namely, that real marriages and families are dense causal systems consisting of a multiplicity of interacting forces. Moreover, the roster of concerns that such social systems encounter is similarly complicated. In an attempt to be a useful reference to this complex subject matter, the editors of this volume have assembled 16 contributors and 17 chapters to accomplish the task. The result is what might be anticipated—an athematic and uneven presentation.

Briefly, the book's contents include the following. A coeditor begins the volume with a chapter containing a complicated typology of counseling approaches, as well as a discussion of the limited data on therapeutic outcomes and a useful summary of several concerns all counselors need to keep in mind. This chapter is followed by one that describes a comprehensive instrument for use in initial interviews. The application of this structured initial interview instrument is advocated in a later chapter dealing with couples whose relationships are affected by changing definitions of sex roles. Robert Beavers provides an excellent review of what pure and applied research shows are the cognitive and behavioral attributes of "healthy couples." Vincent Foley also makes a clear, concise contribution by outlining and evaluating alternative paradigms for alcohol counseling.

The book contains two chapters on sexual issues. One is a straightforward piece on talking with couples about sexual concerns, which reminds us that the counselor's orientation is especially important to defining the atmosphere in which such sessions are conducted. In addition there is a well-crafted chapter by Corydon Hammond, which reviews the multiple causes of sexual dysfunction and methods of medical and interview assessment.

Two chapters focus on premarital counseling. In one, the editors present their views on the content and form such prewedding sessions ought to take. This is followed by a well-organized chapter which calls our attention to several religious and value dimensions deserving consideration in premarital counseling.

The editors also wrote an insightful chapter that identifies seven modal types of marriages and goes on to provide descriptions, cameos, and treatment suggestions for each. Other contributions in this volume include: James Harper's provocative ideas on how ordinal position data can be used in systemic marital therapy; approaches and concerns for counseling childless couples and those of middle age; the place of hypnotic techniques in marital and sexual therapy; reconceptualizing the status of extramarital involvements; elaborating the utility of employing an intergenerational orientation to couple conflict; and outlining an approach to divorce counseling.

From this content summary one of the volume's strengths is apparent; namely, it covers a wide variety of topics relevant to marriage counselors. It is unfortunate that a more comprehensive index was not provided. Moreover, although some of the chapters are stodgy, commendably, all have been kept to a length of 20 pages or so. Additionally, most chapters close with useful summaries.

Few practitioners of marriage and family therapy can claim mastery over the broad and interacting web of concerns that comprise troubled and failing marriages and families. Consequently, most who practice the craft are bound to encounter problems that test their own limits. This volume is valuable for these occasions, for it contains adequate reviews of the topics it covers. Overall, it is fair to say that most chapters contain enough sensitizing concepts and ideas to get a therapist oriented to a presenting problem and make an informed referral when required.

Reviewing the roll of authors in this volume reveals that clinical sociologists are underrepresented as contributors. It is apparent that although many of us practice marriage and family therapy, too few of us write about it. This substantive clinical area is in serious need of the kind of unifying theoretical perspective and empirical underpinning that sociology could supply. Although interventions in real families require an idiographic approach, few things are more useful to such an exercise than nomothetic understanding. The theory and practice of marriage and family therapy could both profit from a broader dissemination and application of sociology's resources, with a spin-off benefit being added credibility to the clinical sociological enterprise.

Working with the Elderly: Group Process and Techniques, 2nd ed., by Irene Burnside, Monterey, CA: Wadsworth Health Sciences Division, 1984, 700 pp., $17.25 paper.

Rae B. Adams
Abilene Christian University

The second edition of *Working with the Elderly: Group Process and Techniques* is written primarily for persons skilled in the techniques of group dynamics and for group facilitators and leaders who work with the elderly, either in an institutional or other structured group setting. Titles of the sections are: Overview; Theoretical Frameworks; Basics of Group Work; Practice of Group Work; Reminiscing Therapy; Multidiscipline Perspectives on Group Work with the Elderly; and Instruction for Group Workers and Epilogue. The second edition has been expanded over the first by 19 new chapters for a total of 38. Burnside (Department of Nursing at San Jose State University) has written approximately 40% of the book's content with the remainder of the material by contributors from a variety of disciplines.

As with most texts on aging, the book begins with a profile of the contemporary elderly population, with demographic studies to support the fact that the elderly as a group are increasing in number. The author then presents four theoretical frameworks which are recommended for group work with the elderly: Maurice Linden's Dual Leadership Approach; Life-Review Therapy, which is associated with Robert Butler and Myrna Lewis; extrapolations of Irvin Yalom's psychiatric theory related to the maintenance of groups; and William Schutz's Fundamental Interpersonal Orientation. Part Three is a collection of topics related to group work in general and presents a rationale for leaders or therapists to utilize the group setting when working with the elderly. In the author's words, Part Four is the "how to" section of the book, with most of the remaining sections addressing the application of theories and processes. There is, however, a concentration on reminiscing and life-review therapy, with the justification that reminiscing therapy is so popular among therapists who work with older clients.

The text is designed with learning aids such as learning objectives and key works which preface each chapter. At the end of chapters are several exercises which can be used to reinforce and test the knowledge and skills presented in the material. Also, each chapter is supplemented by a list of resources available on the topics covered. These include films, audiovisuals, tapes and organizations. The large number of references cited, especially by Burnside, lend credibility to the work as well as furnish excellent additional resource materials for the student.

The Theoretical Frameworks. Principles of Maurice Linden, a 1950s pioneer in group work with the elderly, are presented. A study utilizing Linden's principles and techniques was conducted by Burnside. With the exception of the use of the term "senile," Linden's model was found to be as appropriate in today's setting as it was when first introduced.

Life-review therapy is explained in an article by Myrna Lewis and Robert Butler. Life-review is a technique frequently used to improve reality orientation for the elderly client. Whether it is more effective than other techniques is debatable in many cases. That the elderly client is responsive may be due simply to the fact that recalling the past is a pleasant experience. Long-range effectiveness may also be questioned. The technique's popularity and wide use may be due to the ease with which it can be learned and applied.

Yalom did not formulate his principles of group work with the elderly specifically in mind. However, Burnside believes that "students, health care workers and administrators, and instructors can profitably adapt his ideas for group work with older people" (p. 61). The major problem with presenting Yalom's theory and practice, especially in a book designed for "beginner group leaders" (p. iii) is that Yalom's work is extremely technical and, as pointed out by Burnside, uses psychiatric jargon freely (p. 61). Unless the leader or therapist is familiar with Yalom's work and comfortable with the application of the techniques, he or she may have no effective measurement of change related to the use of the therapy. For example, 12 general categories of "curative factors" are presented, but application would be extremely difficult unless the group leader were familiar with Yalom's model.

William Schutz's theory of fundamental interpersonal orientation is also presented. However, since Schutz's theory and techniques are not tied to medical jargon they are more easily understood. Although the material is presented in a brief six pages, it would appear that the beginning group leader could easily grasp the concepts and adequately resolve the theory-application dilemma.

The Group. While the author states that it is not her intention to teach group dynamics, when viewed collectively, Chapters 7–13 are filled with excellent "how-to" material in a group dynamics setting. The chapters are especially beneficial since the applications are specific to the elderly. Wise beginning leaders will incorporate the concepts discussed into their own styles to the extent that they become adept in the facilitator's approach to groups. Bravo to Burnside, Baumler, Weaverdyck, and Szafranski, the chapters' authors, for a compilation of excellent, easily understood material. The material is "down-to-earth," leaving no doubt that the authors are writing from hard-earned experience.

Other chapters which are practical and easily adaptable for beginning leaders not having specific training in psychotherapeutic techniques and jargon are those dealing with reality orientation and remotivation therapy. While the student should become more familiar with these frameworks or theories, the concepts related to applications covered in the text could certainly be more easily mastered than others that could have been selected by Burnside.

Music and dance therapy are also discussed. Leaders who are not technically trained in either area are assured that, with limited skills or interest, they can become effective in their applications.

Self-help groups are also addressed and recommended, but while the purpose of such groups are clearly identified, the "how-to" is somewhat weak. However, the references given at the end of the chapter are extensive so the inspired reader could be guided toward excellent sources for further study.

The section on multidisciplinary perspectives on group work with the elderly should provide a sense of support for potential group leaders from among the fields of nursing, clinical sociology, social work, psychology, psychiatry, and counselors from other general areas. Each discipline has a somewhat different but common focus in working with the aged. Even bibliotherapy, in which literature is used as a tool in the therapeutic process, is explored.

The use of volunteers is addressed. While Burnside points out that the use of nonprofessionals as facilitators needs to be researched, their use is very necessary and important in specific areas of psychosocial care (p. 262). Excellent suggestions for selection and training are given.

Reviewer's Notes.   If there is a fault with the text it is its ultra-comprehensive approach to dealing with the elderly in groups. Yet, with the increasing demand being placed on all types of counselors and therapists to address the physical and emotional needs of the elderly, it is doubtful that too much information and encouragement can be given. It would appear that this sentiment is shared by Burnside; the last section of the book, "Instruction for Group Workers and Epilogue," is one more, final effort to furnish yet a few more guidelines which could be useful. The material is worthwhile, even if somewhat repetitious. Although the organization of the massive amount of material presented in the book is cumbersome, the content is well worth the effort on the part of the reader. Burnside's text is a valuable contribution to those who do group work with the elderly.

The Disabled State, by Deborah A. Stone, in the Health, Society and Policy Series edited by Sheryl Ruzek and Irving K. Zola. Philadelphia: Temple University Press. 1984, 241 pp., $24.95 cloth.

S. Randi Randolph
United Health Services, Binghamton, NY

In *The Disabled State*, Deborah A. Stone, a political scientist, offers a theory of how the state uses medical certification to reconcile two seemingly incompatible distributive systems: work and need. It includes an analysis of government and intellectual justifications that give coherence to activities related to the concept of disability. Stone then shows how medical certification emerged as an administrative mechanism for redistributive policies such as social insurance and social welfare.

The Introduction identifies cross-national patterns in disability pension programs and reviews standard explanations of the "crises" of these programs in contemporary welfare states. While these explanations may provide answers about short-term fluctuations in program statistics, Stone believes that the notion of disability, a keystone, allows supporting structures of the welfare state and the economy at large to remain in place. Yet the concept of disability is problematic for the resolution of what Stone terms the "critical distributive problem for all societies," the conflict between work and need as the basis for claims on resources.

In Chapter 2, Stone traces the origins of disability as an administrative category in three countries in three historical periods: English Poor Law, German Social Insurance, and American Social Security Disability Insurance. In each, disability has been an administrative device to place boundaries around need-based distribution of resources. The German program in the 1880s was a model for subsequent social insurance programs; it based disability on inability to earn a certain amount. Bismarck's strategy was to unify the country and to strengthen the economy; social insurance was part of that larger strategy.

The United States was the last industrial state to introduce social insurance beginning in 1935. In the 1950s disability was added to the Social Security program. Controversy about the American program centered on definition of disability and method of disability certification. During early hearings physicians tried to persuade Congress that clinical judgment could not provide the objective determination desired by program advocates. Private insurance representatives testified that courts had consistently liberalized the definition of disability. Despite these warnings, Congress supported a disability insurance program. To soothe fears of conservatives and the American Medical Association that a federal disability program would represent a step toward nationalization of medical care, policymakers assigned the task of disability determination to state agencies rather than to the Federal Security Administration.

In the third chapter, "Disability as a Clinical Concept," Stone describes how clinical medicine, in the last half of the nineteenth century, offered a model of illness that legitimized claims for social aid and offered a method of validation that allegedly rendered administration of the category feasible. A major change in the concept of disease absolved individuals from responsibility for and control over their condition. Diagnostic techniques for visualizing the interior of the body and measuring physiological processes gave medicine a new kind of vision, literally and metaphorically. Assessment of eligibility for the American disability benefit program was dominated by the concept of impairment. The medical profession claimed impairment was a purely medical phenomenon, whereas disability was viewed as a value-laden medical/administrative/legal concept. The disability guides created by the AMA were based on an erroneous, but "pervading faith that a phenomenon of functional impairment, totally independent of context, can be precisely measured" (p. 113). According to Stone, this faith did not take into account the fact that evaluation of impairment is full of errors of reification and false claims of measurement precision.

The mechanisms for restricting access to the disability category are examined in Chapter 4. The Social Security Administration's medical consultation staff had separated clinical data into categories that supposedly could and could not be manipulated. Nevertheless, Social Security executives apparently had an underlying distrust of physicians. Their medical listings were not published for many years because they thought both patients and physicians would use them to their advantage. To further restrict access to benefits, "consultative exams" were established. Nevertheless, policymakers soon realized that clinical criteria were not restrictive enough. They could not protect eligibility decisions from manipulation because judgments of impairment rest on diagnostic decisions which are subject to an enormous degree of uncertainty.

Chapter 5 covers three major sources of pressure for expansion of disability programs: individuals seeking aid, gatekeepers of the programs, and high-level policymakers. As applicants move from the primary, work-based system to the secondary, need-based system, they have opportunities to manipulate the presentation of their case. However, stronger pressures for expansion come from other sources. The clinical concept of impairment was supposed to provide a tight boundary around need-based distribution. But, the system of determination, in which administrative agencies became dependent on patients' personal physicians for information, promoted lenient clinical decisions. The courts have traditionally been even more liberal than clinicians and administrators. The economic context also exerts pressure for expansion, particularly during recessionary periods with high unemployment. Disability programs can transfer older workers from the labor force to the need-based system when the number of jobs decreases. As Stone points out, disability pension programs have expanded in a number of welfare states with widespread and relatively long-lasting recessions.

The concluding chapter focuses on the political dynamics of disability expansion. In times of welfare "crisis," the mythology holds that the program user is the culprit and administrators are accomplices. Stone suggests a different interpretation of program expansion, which can be found in the dynamic concept of disability which incorporates larger social tensions. Three dimensions of the concept are subject to definitional expansion: moral worthiness, incapacity, and clinical methods. When new phenomena outside the realm of individual responsibility can be shown to cause incapacity, a consensus forms that individuals should be compensated from collective resources. The incapacity dimension was originally defined as physical capacity but has been extended to social, emotional, and intellectual performance. Clinical methods of definition allow expansion as measurement of physiological processes becomes more sophisticated. Subjective factors such as pain are given clinical specification and epidemiological research creates pressure for expansion through discovery of statistical patterns.

Stone identifies the beneficiaries of a flexible disability category. Employers benefit in competitive markets when they are under pressure to make their workforce more productive. Legislators have a strong interest in flexibility, which allows them to satisfy individual requests and resistance from their constituency at large. Agencies responsible for determining eligibility have a stake in keeping the concept flexible so they can respond to legislative changes of mood. Service agencies benefit in that they are rewarded in the political and budgetary world by demonstrating that large numbers of problem cases exist. Lastly, interest groups use standard pressure-group tactics to obtain statutory recognition of new categories of disability.

Finally, Stone examines the breakdown theories that have been predicting a collapse of the American Social Security system. She asserts that these theories make erroneous assumptions about the state and society. The existence of internal conflict or contradictory tendencies does not mean that the state will become incapacitated even though it has become disabled. She states that the expansion of disability programs is not the source of panic for policymakers and administrators. Their sense of crisis comes from a loss of flexibility in the concept of disability itself. She suggests that the most important option of the state may be to abandon the no-fault insurance model of compensation in order to raise questions of responsibility and prevention.

Reviewing *The Disabled State* turned out to be more challenging than I had anticipated. A wealth of information is contained in this relatively short volume. Also, Stone's political science perspective, which sheds new light on the notion of a "crisis" in disability insurance programs, is not one that I had previously encountered in the medical sociology literature. Her attempt to weave the concept of disability in and out of the professional norms and organizational behaviors of three major social institutions in a cross-national and historical perspective is an ambitious undertaking, but one to which justice has been done. I was convinced by Stone's argument that the concept of disability is problematic for contemporary welfare societies. I am less sure that she answered all the questions she posed for herself throughout the book. I was somewhat disappointed that her concluding suggestion about the state's option seemed to overlook the economic pressures she described earlier.

The *Disabled State* does not offer clinical sociologists practical solutions, but it does provide the basis for understanding the political intricacies of the disability insurance programs that affect many of us in our personal and/or professional lives. Stone's scholarship is impressive, and although her writing style and vocabulary are strictly academic, the book is not pedantic. The time and effort spent reading and thinking about her analysis were enjoyable and worthwhile. I recommend the book to my colleagues.

Group Workers at Work: Theory and Practice in the Eighties, edited by Paul H. Glasser and Nazneen S. Mayadas. Totowa, NJ: Rowman and Littlefield, 1986, 296 pp., $39.50.

Howard Rebach
University of Maryland, Eastern Shore

Few sociologists are trained in group work even though we are often exposed to small group theory and research in our graduate programs. However, a strong theoretical foundation is not adequate preparation for practice with groups. Hence, borrowing useful information from other fields can advance our own work.

Group Workers at Work is an interesting collection of symposium papers written by and for social workers. The Introduction and second section (Chapters 2–5) trace the evolution of group work from a broadly applicable technique for education and social change to narrow use as individual psychotherapy conducted in groups. The small group has been "rediscovered" as a technique in social planning and administration, community organization and development, and organizational development in large formal organizations. This reemergence of small group process in other than psychotherapeutic settings calls for the attention of clinical sociologists.

Ephross notes the ubiquity of task groups on the job and in communities: "Task groups occupy a great deal of time in the lives of a broad spectrum of people . . . what goes on in such groups makes a great deal of difference both to the inner lives of participants and to various institutions and processes in society at large." In these task groups planning occurs, decisions are made, and courses of action adopted. This fact of social life should command the attention of clinical sociologists or any social change agent. Group work is critical whether a small group is itself the target of change and program development or a base for achieving wider social change.

The historical course of group work in social work practice in Section 2 may seem of little value to clinical sociologists. But, the first three chapters are worthwhile because they sensitize us to the variety of contexts for small group interventions. Group work can be a means for change and for growth and development of individuals and of small groups such as families and work units, or for broader change in communities and society.

Overall, the first section of the book is too long and often redundant. The first five chapters could be reduced to one longer, tighter chapter. And the chapters in Part III could have been given more space. These essays introduce useful topics for beginners, but not enough to proceed on; they are rather a guide to some things to learn more about. For those who have training and experience in group work, Chapters 6–10 provide valuable material.

Maier examines "play" and "playfulness" as part of group sessions. Group leaders should be aware that members may be least able to play when it is most needed. Maier provides a conceptual framework and examples for integrating playfulness into a working group rather than using isolated behavioral sequences out of context. "Play encourages people to stretch beyond their usual capacity, beyond their usual concepts of themselves." It gives group members an added ability to deal with events. Play in a group is an interactive process that stimulates members' involvement and cohesion. Play is also a resource for creativity or freeing a group that gets stuck—as in playing with ideas as a way of creative problem solving. Play can also teach members new modes of expression. In play, members are often relieved of constraints, may look at themselves or the situation in novel ways, explore actions and ideas with low cost for failure, yet learn to risk. Given that play itself is part of life and that playfulness is often forgotten, people with problems need to relearn to play.

Garland examines loneliness in the life cycle of a small group. Garland argues that the context of modern urban society alienates humans from each other as well as from themselves, though we try to escape from loneliness. The context heightens the anxiety as people feel manipulated by forces beyond their control yet somehow responsible for their own fate. But needs for loneliness exist and compete, throughout the life cycle, with needs for affiliation. Loneliness becomes problematic for individuals when the steps taken to relieve loneliness perpetuate outsider status. Group leaders must understand the developmental stages of small groups and the dominant themes and issues at each stage which contribute to the dialectic process of loneliness and affiliation. The group facilitator's own orientation to issues of loneliness and affiliation are also of major importance to the group process.

Gentry reviews consensus as a form of group decision making. Though majority rule techniques reach decisions more rapidly, consensus is more effective if members must be rallied to act on the decision. Research reviewed showed that groups could be trained in consensus decision making. Such groups produced better decisions, produced more creative ideas, handled conflict better, and got more information and ideas from members when compared to untrained groups that used majority-rule decision making. The article includes guidelines for instructing groups in the consensus process and case examples. This is a good article which directs the reader toward understanding and use of consensus and the value of it.

In Chapter 9, Garvin discusses assessing and changing group conditions—group structure, group process, and the shared meanings—to aid the group in goal attainment. The first step in changing group conditions is assessing them. The article provides some simple assessment devices that can be used to measure each of the group conditions to be fed back to the group as resources for change.

In Chapter 10, Etcheverry, Siporin, and Toseland provide a useful discussion of role-playing as a technique used in groups. They review the ways role-playing can be used. They also draw attention to common mistakes in the use of role-playing and describe ten techniques that can be used.

Parts IV and V include papers on applications of group work for specific purposes. These chapters are the best part of the book. Hartford and McCoy discuss support groups for caretakers of older relatives. The paper takes us step by step through the various decisions and rationales of the group leaders—the authors—as they develop their approach. It covers the set of things group facilitators must consider and how the set was applied for this particular purpose. Schoenfelder and Cobb, in Chapter 12, do the same in describing a group intervention for children of divorce. In Chapter 13, Peirce describes group work with alcoholics as an alternative to the model of Alcoholics Anonymous. Peirce's comparison of the two approaches should be especially interesting to persons who work in alcoholic treatment settings. Sundel and Sundel describe assertiveness training groups, presenting their session-by-session program in some detail as well as data from their evaluation of their approach.

The chapters in Part V are on work with minority groups. Colca (Chapter 15) describes a small group intervention to facilitate school desegregation in Buffalo, New York. The paper gives a natural history of the experience, the group process, and problems and recommendations. Hirayama and Vaughn (Chapter 16) describe group work with alienated, chronically ill, elderly blacks that succeeded as an outreach program and provided strong help for participants in managing tasks of health care and daily functioning. Another good paper describes an intervention with Chicano youth in school (Brown and Arevelo, Chapter 18) which includes theoretical development, a model for doing the group, and a description of it. The group was seen to mediate tension and potential culture clash between the youth and the Anglo school system.

In the final section, Chapter 20 is a very good article on a method for training group workers using "video stimulus-modeling methodology," a method developed by the authors of the paper (Mayadas and Duehn) which combined modeling with video feedback and behavioral rehearsal. The article and technique should be studied and considered carefully by anyone training people to work with groups.

Overall, this book provides many useful ideas for clinical sociologists who work with small groups. The historical materials are somewhat long, but other chapters offer helpful material for work with small groups.

Child Maltreatment and Paternal Deprivation: A Manifesto for Research, Prevention, and Treatment, by Henry B. Biller and Richard S. Solomon. Lexington, MA: D.C. Health, 1986, 320 pp., $26.00.

Katherine Williams
Fairfax County Juvenile and Domestic Relations District Court, Virginia.

When I was asked to review this book, I looked forward to the task. Child maltreatment is an important subject, and the role of fathers in child development has only recently received the attention it deserves. The title was exciting, alluding to a cohesive plan for research, prevention and treatment. On cursory examination the work appeared well suited to clinical sociologists, promising a multidisciplinary approach, research and clinical experience coming together around child maltreatment.

Both authors are psychologists but do not confine themselves to a psychological perspective. Henry Biller's numerous publications on paternal deprivation make him one of the leading experts. He has also been involved in a number of practice settings. Richard Solomon is codirector of a multidisciplinary group practice specializing in child abuse.

The beginning is direct, but the initially clear focus waivers. The proposed connection between child maltreatment and paternal deprivation becomes tenuous. Two books uneasily coexist under the same title. One offers an overview of child maltreatment; the other reviews effects of paternal deprivation on child development. The book is not divided into sections, but the chapters fall into three areas: child maltreatment, effects of paternal deprivation on child development, and a short final section on research and treatment. Though often informative, overall the book promises more than it delivers.

The thesis of this book is the existence of a complex connection between paternal deprivation and child maltreatment: Paternal deprivation contributes directly and indirectly to most child maltreatment. Child maltreatment, as defined, includes severe cases of abuse and neglect as well as inappropriate and inadequate parenting. But this definition creates some problems integrating the two halves of the book.

Chapters 2–4 cover the historical and cultural context and current problems of defining child maltreatment, its incidence and epidemiology, and current theoretical models. Chapter 5 on sexual maltreatment is a puzzle. The authors do not deal in detail with the types of abuse on the continuum of maltreatment they developed. Why they have a chapter on sexual maltreatment and not on physical abuse or severe neglect is never explained. The chapter seems adrift, as if the authors had material on sexual abuses lying about and thought this would be a good place for it.

The research review in Chapters 6–10 shows effects of paternal deprivation on cognitive functioning, self-esteem, personal adjustment, moral development, antisocial behavior, family interaction patterns, and sex role development. These chapters and the bibliography provide a concise and informative introduction to the effects of paternal deprivation on child development, valuable to clinical sociologists working with children and families.

Though central to the thesis of the book, the authors assert, without support, that children in single-parent families are at greater risk of maltreatment because of stress on single parents (read "mothers"). That is, single-parent mothers are more likely to be abusive because they lack the emotional support of a husband. This could be a valid point that would have made the connection between paternal deprivation and child maltreatment much clearer and more compelling. Unfortunately, the authors never pick up this thread. They chose, instead, to attend to the consequences of paternal deprivation for personality development.

One of the problems I had writing this review was in integrating the two parts of the book using the bridge supplied by the authors. They attempt to link child maltreatment and paternal deprivation by using a definition of child maltreatment so broad it includes relatively benign situations as well as severe abuse and neglect. The authors apparently consider all children who are experiencing paternal deprivation as maltreated. Unfortunately, they do not make a strong case that the effects they discuss are severe enough to be labeled "maltreatment." They do not convince me that paternal deprivation, per se, is maltreatment.

But the linkage bothers me: Though the authors give the disclaimer that some children may be better off separated from abusive fathers, it seems unfair to label single mothers "abusive." Single mothers bear a hard burden raising children; it is not useful to imply their children are maltreated because fathers are not present. It is especially harsh to call "maltreated" a child who has lost a father through death.

As a practical matter, I'm not sure how often intervention for "maltreatment," defined this broadly, would be implemented given the limited resources of most social service agencies and the extent of physical abuse and neglect. This is not to imply that there are no negative consequences for children without a father figure. The evidence presented shows developmental differences between children with positive father relationships and those without. What has not been shown is that these differences constitute abuse.

Chapter 9 concerns sex role development. Several studies cited report that boys raised in female-headed households are less aggressive in play. The implication is that this is bad for the child, but the tie to maltreatment is tenuous. It assumes that socialization into traditional male roles is the best outcome for a male child; any other outcome is maltreatment.

As another example, "an inhibiting sexist attitude toward a daughter can be viewed as maltreatment by the father." An inhibiting sexist attitude may have negative consequences for a daughter's personality development, but this statement referred to the fact that fathers typically engage in less rough-and-tumble play with their daughters. Again, it is hard to see this as maltreatment. Much less space is given to the effects of father absence for sex role development in girls. In fairness, this may be more a reflection of that fact that less research exists on girls, rather than an oversight of the authors.

The first section has several good features. The second section has many good features. The problem is integrating the two sections into the promise of the book's title. Clinical sociologists and other readers will learn a lot about the consequences of paternal deprivation for child development but not much about child maltreatment as it is usually understood.

The subtitle of the book promises a "manifesto" for research, prevention and treatment. The proportion of the book devoted to these areas is not as great as the title implies. The text runs for 232 pages; 3 pages are devoted to research implications. The authors correctly call for longitudinal, multidisciplinary studies to assess the long-term effects of child maltreatment and paternal deprivation. Longitudinal research of the type called for is extremely expensive and funding for such studies is becoming scarce. Some speculation on innovative ways to overcome this problem would have been useful.

The value of the chapter on intervention requires the understanding that the authors are referring only to the "child maltreatment" of father absence. Setting aside the "maltreatment" label, the authors offer interesting suggestions for avoiding the negative effects of father absence. The more innovative suggestions are structural rather than individual: Educational systems and the mass media should give more attention to educating fathers and potential fathers on their role in child development. Welfare systems should be encouraged to support, not undermine, father-present families. Workplaces should support paternity leave so that fathers will have time to spend with newborns. Schools should provide incentives to male teachers, especially in the lower grades, who could serve as male role models for father-absent children. Schools should also encourage males from the community to come into the schools to share their work with the children.

Despite the promise of the title, the authors do not succeed in linking paternal deprivation and child maltreatment. The broad definition of maltreatment isn't strong enough by itself to unify the parts of this book. This does not mean that clinical sociologists and others who work with families and children will not find the book useful. The summary of the effects of father absence is excellent and helpful to those working with families of divorce. The suggestions for structural changes are excellent, although perhaps not realizable in the near future. The book does not provide all the solutions but does sensitize us to some of the problems.

SOCIOLOGICAL PRACTICE ASSOCIATION:

A Professional Organization of Clinical and Applied Sociologists

The SOCIOLOGICAL PRACTICE ASSOCIATION, founded in 1978 as the Clinical Sociology Association is a Professional Organization of Clinical and Applied Sociologists. Members include organizational developers, program planners, community organizers, sociotherapists, counselors, gerontologists, conflict interventionists, applied social science researchers, policy planners on all levels including international practice, and many others who practice, study, teach or do research by applying sociological knowledge for positive social change. The Association's value orientation is humanistic and multidisciplinary.

Benefits of Membership in the Sociological Practice Association

- Receive *Clinical Sociology Review,* the annual journal of the Association
- Receive the *Practicing Sociologist* newsletter four times each year
- Take part in association sponsored training conferences and workshops at reduced rates
- Work on a committee and be eligible for membership on the SPA Executive Board
- Participate in the SPA annual business meeting
- Work on any of a variety of issues that may interest you such as credentials, curriculum, training, ethics, membership or the annual program
- Be listed in the SPA Membership Directory
- Be eligible to apply for certification as a Clinical Sociologist
- Be part of a dynamic and significant movement in the social sciences
- Work with others toward a relevant sociology for the 1980s

For more information and a membership application, please contact Dr. Elizabeth Clark, President, SPA, RD 2, Box 141 A, Chester, NY 10918.

DATE DUE